MW01087751

Before *Bostock*

Before *Bostock*

THE ACCIDENTAL LGBTQ PRECEDENT
OF *PRICE WATERHOUSE V. HOPKINS*

Jason Pierceson

University Press of Kansas

© 2022 by the University Press of Kansas
All rights reserved

Published by the University Press of Kansas (Lawrence, Kansas 66045), which
was organized by the Kansas Board of Regents and is operated and funded by
Emporia State University, Fort Hays State University, Kansas State University,
Pittsburg State University, the University of Kansas, and Wichita State
University.

Library of Congress Cataloging-in-Publication Data

Names: Pierceson, Jason, 1972– author.
Title: Before Bostock : the accidental LGBTQ precedent of Price Waterhouse
     v. Hopkins / Jason Pierceson.
Description: Lawrence : University Press of Kansas, 2022. | Includes index.
Identifiers: LCCN 2021038313
     ISBN 9780700633142 (cloth)
     ISBN 9780700633159 (ebook)
Subjects: LCSH: Discrimination in employment—Law and legislation—United
     States—Cases. | Sexual minorities—Legal status, laws, etc.—United
     States—Cases.
Classification: LCC KF3467.5 .P54 2022 | DDC 344.7301/53—dc23
LC record available at https://lccn.loc.gov/2021038313.

British Library Cataloguing-in-Publication Data is available.

Printed in the United States of America

10 9 8 7 6 5 4 3 2 1

The paper used in this publication is recycled and contains 30 percent
postconsumer waste. It is acid free and meets the minimum requirements of
the American National Standard for Permanence of Paper for Printed Library
Materials Z39.48-1992.

For Dylan

Contents

Acknowledgments

This book is an extension of my work on transgender rights litigation, which followed a previous focus on marriage equality litigation. This transition was greatly facilitated by an invitation from a group of remarkable scholars—Jami Taylor, Daniel Lewis, and Donald Haider-Markel—to join their excellent project on transgender rights. Working with and learning from them provided the foundation for this project. I cannot thank them enough for the invitation.

The College of Public Affairs and Administration at the University of Illinois–Springfield also provided support for this book. It is not always easy to write extensively at a teaching institution, but the college staff made it much easier.

I have worked with some excellent editors, but David Congdon at the University Press of Kansas is one of the very best and deserves special thanks for his support of this project from the moment we first discussed the idea. I would also like to thank the anonymous reviewers of the book proposal and book manuscript for their excellent feedback and suggestions. The book is much stronger because of them.

Finally, my husband, Dylan White, deserves enormous credit for supporting me through the writing process. His patience and encouragement have been invaluable. I could not have done it without him.

1. LGBTQ Rights, Statutory Interpretation, and Judicial Policymaking

Title VII of the Civil Rights Act of 1964 states:

> It shall be an unlawful employment practice for an employer—(1) to fail or refuse to hire or to discharge any individual, or otherwise to discriminate against any individual with respect to his compensation, terms, conditions, or privileges of employment, because of such individual's race, color, religion, sex, or national origin; or (2) to limit, segregate, or classify his employees or applicants for employment in any way which would deprive or tend to deprive any individual of employment opportunities or otherwise adversely affect his status as an employee, because of such individual's race, color, religion, sex, or national origin.

On April 22, 2019, the US Supreme Court agreed to hear three cases with significant implications for the future of LGBTQ (lesbian, gay, bisexual, transgender, and queer) rights: *Altitude Express v. Zarda, Bostock v. Clayton County,* and *R. G. & G. R. Harris Funeral Homes v. EEOC.* On June 15, 2020, the Supreme Court ruled in *Bostock*—in a 6-to-3 decision, with a majority opinion authored by conservative justice Neil Gorsuch—that Title VII of the Civil Rights Act of 1964 prohibits employment discrimination on the basis of gender identity and sexual orientation. More specifically, the Supreme Court held that the word "sex" in the statute includes gender identity and sexual orientation.[1] The decision was a surprise to many if not most observers; however, in some ways, it was not completely unanticipated. It was grounded in a recent but well-developed shift in jurisprudence on the question of LGBTQ rights in federal law, it was the result of a carefully crafted and executed strategy in the federal courts, and it was strongly supported by public opinion. In particular, in the years immediately preceding the decision, the Equal Employment Opportunity Commission (EEOC) and most federal judges—even those appointed by Republican presidents—had concluded that gender identity–based discrimination is prohibited by law; this was followed by a less well developed jurisprudence embracing the notion that discrimination of the basis of sexual orientation is also forbidden. Thus, ruling against transgender plaintiff Aimee

Stephens in *Harris Funeral Homes* would have been a repudiation of this legal trend, in addition to being contrary to public opinion.

Remarkably, in its internal deliberations, the Supreme Court struggled more with the issue of gender identity–based discrimination than sexual orientation, despite the more robust jurisprudence related to the former. This appeared to be the result of real or perceived potential policy issues, such as restroom use in the workplace, or the "massive social upheaval" Justice Gorsuch referenced during oral arguments. As later chapters demonstrate, after decades of exhibiting equal skepticism of both gender identity– and sexual orientation–based discrimination, federal judges' attitudes started to change sometime around 2000, with gender identity claims faring better in federal courts. Indeed, by the time the Supreme Court took up the issue directly, a robust jurisprudence had developed in support of gender identity claims. Even so, the Supreme Court was more conflicted about gender identity and Title VII, and for the justices, this was more of a policy issue than an issue of pure jurisprudence or legal analysis.[2]

The most important precedent for *Zarda, Bostock,* and *Harris Funeral Homes* is a 1989 Supreme Court case that did not deal directly with LGBTQ rights: *Price Waterhouse v. Hopkins.* Interestingly, these three cases did not present the court with the constitutional questions contained in the leading LGBTQ rights cases: *Romer v. Evans* (1996), *Lawrence v. Texas* (2003), *Obergefell v. Hodges* (2015), and *Masterpiece Cakeshop v. Colorado Civil Rights Commission* (2018). Rather, these cases involved the question of whether gender identity and sexual orientation should be covered by the provision in Title VII of the Civil Rights Act of 1964 outlawing discrimination in employment "because of . . . sex," among other factors such as race and religion. This involved statutory rather than constitutional interpretation. Of course, in 1964, members of Congress did not explicitly intend for either category (gender identity or sexual orientation) to be included in the Civil Rights Act. The US movement for the rights of sexual minorities had been active for only a decade, and the movement for transgender rights was still in its infancy. Both sexual and gender minorities faced overwhelming social stigma and opprobrium, and all levels of government actively discriminated against and persecuted LGBTQ individuals. However, when interpreting statutes, judges do not always rely on legislative intent as a method of determining their meaning.

Attempts to enact federal protections for sexual and gender minorities stalled for decades, making litigation a preferred path for activists and individual LGBTQ plaintiffs seeking a legal remedy for employment discrimination. Transgender plaintiffs enjoyed significant success, as federal judges below the Supreme Court ruled quite consistently that, based on *Price Waterhouse v. Hopkins*, discrimination on the basis of gender identity is prohibited under Title VII as a form of "sex stereotyping" or "per se" discrimination on the basis of sex. Less consistently, federal courts found that sexual orientation is also prohibited by Title VII.

PRICE WATERHOUSE V. HOPKINS

Ann Hopkins was denied a promotion to partner at the accounting firm Price Waterhouse because she was too masculine. Although the case was primarily about a technical legal issue related to federal antidiscrimination law (the parties' burden of proof), an opinion by justice William Brennan asserted that Hopkins had been discriminated against because of her sex—not because she was a woman but because she contravened traditional gender norms about acceptable behavior in the workplace. Hopkins, he found, had been subjected to illegal "sex stereotyping." As Brennan stated: "An employer who objects to aggressiveness in women but whose positions require this trait places women in an intolerable and impermissible Catch-22: out of a job if they behave aggressively and out of a job if they do not. Title VII lifts women out of this bind."[3] Brennan's opinion on sex stereotyping was a plurality, not a majority, opinion, and as noted, the primary consensus among the justices concerned burden of proof. Thus, scholars such as R. Shep Melnick assert that the decision is used improperly as a binding precedent on the question of sex stereotyping, while others argue that the concurring justices likely found the sex stereotyping analysis uncontroversial (see chapter 3).

The case was an "accidental" precedent for LGBTQ rights for several reasons. Ann Hopkins was a straight, cisgender woman who did not see herself or her case as part of the LGBTQ rights movement. Neither did LGBTQ rights activists, who were still reeling from an unexpected and demoralizing defeat three years earlier in *Bowers v. Hardwick*. In that case, the Supreme Court ruled that the Constitution did not prevent states from enacting laws prohibiting private, consensual same-sex intimacy (i.e., sodomy laws). The Supreme Court thus signaled that it would not be an ally of the LGBTQ movement. The federal judiciary had become quite conservative through a succession of

Republican presidential appointments, just when the rising movement could have used its support.

Yet *Price Waterhouse* became foundational for activists, bureaucrats, and judges in expanding Title VII to protect gender and sexual minorities—not immediately, but gradually and powerfully. This book explores why this happened and how this accidental precedent has played a decisive role in LGBTQ rights litigation. More generally, it examines how law and litigation strategies can be successfully mobilized by marginalized groups, as well as the limits of such strategies. As Gordon Silverstein notes, litigation can be an effective and relatively efficient way to enact policy change, especially for groups stymied by the political process.[4] While there is no guarantee of success, the pull of litigation is strong in this context, and the LGBTQ rights movement has relied extensively on this strategy to achieve success, despite the setback in *Bowers*.

The first federal court citation of *Price Waterhouse* in the context of transgender rights occurred in 2000. By later in the 2000s, federal courts were consistently applying the case to protect transgender individuals. Reflecting this trend, the EEOC held in 2012 that Title VII prohibits discrimination on the basis of gender identity, and in 2015 it ruled that Title VII also applies to sexual orientation. The federal courts were slower to extend Title VII protection to sexual orientation, but in a groundbreaking decision, the Seventh Circuit Court of Appeals did so in 2017, followed by the Second Circuit in 2018. The more conservative Eleventh Circuit ruled against such a claim in 2017. This "circuit split" on sexual orientation likely led the Supreme Court to take up the issue.

Few books explore the LGBTQ rights movement in the context of statutory interpretation; most focus on constitutional issues or on the lack of explicit statutory protections. Opponents of LGBTQ rights argue that legislators never intended to protect those rights and that enacting legislation is the only way to do so. There are two major problems with that claim. First, even before *Bostock*, numerous lower federal courts rejected this view, arguing that the statutory text requires expanded protections or that evolving standards require new interpretations. Second, a unanimous Supreme Court ruled in 1998 in *Oncale v. Sundowner Offshore Services* that same-sex sexual harassment is prohibited by Title VII. The opinion was authored by justice Antonin Scalia, a strong critic of attempts to ascertain legislative intent. Scalia argued that the plain language of Title VII, along with the Supreme Court's previous acknowledgment of sexual harassment as an actionable Title VII claim, led to the outcome in this case, even though the authors of the Civil Rights Act of 1964 never considered such a scenario. In fact, *Oncale* looms large in this area of legal policy. Combined with *Price Waterhouse*, it has led scores of federal judges appointed by presidents of both parties, as well as the EEOC, to find that Title VII protects LGBTQ rights. These two cases have proved to be a potent legal combination. Scalia's decision was highly consequential, in that it severed the analysis of Title VII from the issue of legislative intent, which had sharply limited efforts to view discrimination of the basis of "sex" as including protections for LGBTQ employees. *Oncale* did not end debates over textualism, especially among conservatives, but it narrowed the scope of judicial inquiry and ultimately set the stage for Gorsuch's approach in *Bostock*.

The issue can be seen primarily as a debate among legal conservatives. Most liberal judges agree that Title VII covers gender identity and sexual orientation, while conservative judges remain divided. For instance, one of the most conservative judges on the federal bench, William Pryor, agreed that Title VII prohibits discrimination on the basis of gender identity in a 2011 decision. Before retiring from the bench, Reagan appointee Richard Posner argued that sexual orientation is included in Title VII's protections as part of the Seventh Circuit's groundbreaking 2017 decision. The three 2020 cases were decided in the context of this debate among judicial conservatives, with Gorsuch and chief justice John Roberts joining the Supreme Court's liberals. In recent years, federal judges appointed by Democrats have been more comfortable with broad applications of Title VII to discrimination based on gender identity and sexual orientation.[5] Had Hillary Clinton won the presidency in 2016, this trend likely would have continued, and there would have been little question how the Supreme Court would apply *Price Waterhouse* in this context. However, the hostility to LGBTQ rights expressed by the Republican Party and Donald Trump, along with the appointment of many conservative federal judges, including three Supreme Court justices, has made this legal question more uncertain.

JUDICIAL POLICYMAKING

Critics of using litigation to expand statutory protections for LGBTQ rights argue that it is undemocratic to do so. They claim that advocates for LGBTQ rights have only one legitimate path to protection: persuading lawmakers to enact new legislation. This is an overly simplistic understanding of the politics of LGBTQ rights. First, it has been extensively demonstrated that majoritarian institutions are not favorable vehicles for LGBTQ-supportive policies, for several reasons: the uncompromising nature of morality politics or highly conflictual politics (in contrast to economic policy, for instance); the relatively small size of the LGBTQ community, combined with the historical opprobrium it has faced; the outsized role of the religious right in the Republican Party and its powerful role in policymaking; legislators' tendency to overestimate the conservatism of their constituents; and the poor track record of LGBTQ rights in popular initiatives and referenda.[6]

Second, legislative institutions are not always responsive to public opinion. Arguably, if the United States had a more majoritarian electoral system, the courts would not be called on to make policy to the same degree. In this alternative scenario, the Equality Act—the proposed bill that would add sexual orientation and gender identity to Title VII and other federal civil rights statutes—would have been signed into law by president Hillary Clinton after the 2018 midterm elections in which the Democrats won the majority in both houses of Congress due to their large margin of victory in the nationwide vote. Although there is strong public support for adding sexual orientation and gender identity to federal antidiscrimination law (and many Americans think such protections already exist), this is unlikely to become policy as long as Republicans hold the White House or part of Congress and can block it through the filibuster.

As Silverstein notes, "law's allure," or the impulse to legalize political conflicts, can be quite compelling when the political system is blocked. The legalization of political debates—what Silverstein calls "juridification"—"seems to be most defensible and least costly in those cases where courts offer the only viable path to get around fundamental institutional barriers posed by federalism, the separation of powers, or institutional rules like the filibuster."[7] While Silverstein fears the democracy-weakening element of an overreliance on litigation and legalization, he notes that this form of politics is entrenched in the United States, and many other scholars agree with him.[8] The independent power of the courts, the potency of claiming rights in a rights-imbued political culture, and the lack of policy uniformity and consistency that results from federalism and the separation of powers create an environment conducive to litigation-based political and social movements. For instance, because power is dispersed in the US political system, particularly through federalism, activists often use federal litigation to achieve their goals and create policy uniformity, a tactic that Thomas Burke describes as the "control incentive."[9]

Federalism has been a double-edged sword for LGBTQ activists. For decades, with a few exceptions, the only progress in the LGBTQ rights movement came at the state and local levels. The election of openly LGBTQ public officials, the enactment of LGBTQ-supportive and -protective policies (such as antidiscrimination and relationship equality laws), and protective court decisions took place at the subnational level starting in the 1970s. The Republican Party's blocking of LGBTQ policies at the state and federal levels explains why a litigation strategy is needed to achieve basic civil rights protections for LGBTQ individuals. As Jeremiah Garretson notes, Republican policymakers "remain recalcitrant on gay rights." This opposition is just as strong, or stronger, when it comes to transgender rights.[10]

While the Democratic Party has evolved into a strongly pro-LGBTQ party after decades of ambivalence, the Republican Party has maintained strong opposition to LGBTQ rights and equality. As discussed in later chapters, a significant part of the conservative movement denies that transgender individuals and those with nonconforming gender identities actually exist, asserts that sexual diversity should be punished (not legally protected), is skeptical of antidiscrimination laws in general, and sees religious freedom as the vehicle to undo rights and protections for sexual and gender minorities. For instance, a Republican-appointed federal judge ruled that, under the Religious Freedom Restoration Act, Aimee Stephens's employer, Harris Funeral Homes, was exempt from Title VII mandates.[11] Even moderate scholars like Melnick describe laws and policy innovations for transgender individuals as an "experiment" that should not be in the hands of bureaucrats and judges. Indeed, Melnick views the Trump administration's rollback of and opposition to LGBTQ rights as a necessary corrective to bureaucratic and judicial policy changes, especially the "unusually aggressive" actions of the Obama administration.[12]

Much of the recent literature that is critical of judicialized politics contains a strong normative objection to using courts to achieve policy change. At the most basic level, it is argued that this approach is undemocratic. Robert Kagan critiques litigation as adding muddled "adversarial legalism" to the policy process, a position to which Melnick largely subscribes, and Gerald Rosenberg describes the Supreme Court as the "hollow hope" of progressive activists.[13] These authors and others have offered strong critiques of the effectiveness of litigation, with a concurrent normative stance against court involvement in policymaking. In describing the scholarly approach of separating law and politics, of distinguishing legislative policymaking from judicial policymaking, Michael McCann and William Haltom critique Kagan's method, noting that it is "less attentive to the dynamic interactions among institutional, instrumental, and ideological factors, more inclined to view litigation and lawyers as insular than as interdependent and contingent forces, and less open to viewing legal action as a desirable, much less noble, form of participation. It veers closer to the type of highly critical, positivist account of judicial impact studies offered by Gerald Rosenberg."[14] Scholars have also challenged the empirical foundations of such an approach. In particular, Rosenberg's notion of an inevitable backlash to progressive litigation has been strongly questioned and undermined.[15]

Interestingly, a key difference between activist conservatives and conservatives on the bench is the presence of powerful precedents and the dynamics of legal interpretation, especially statutory interpretation. Whereas conservatives are quite critical of federal antidiscrimination laws related to sex and gender, including sexual harassment and transgender rights, conservative federal judges have expanded or affirmed these laws through their interpretations of Title VII, just as Justice Scalia did in *Oncale*. LGBTQ legal activists have built on this approach.

One of the major paradoxes of the LGBTQ rights movement is that, during the years when statutory civil rights were being expanded for racial minorities, persons with disabilities, and women, the LGBTQ community did not receive the benefits of that expansion. In fact, opponents of civil rights expansion used the specter of protecting LGBTQ rights as a reason to oppose the civil rights policy regime. There was indeed a "minority rights revolution," but sexual and gender minorities were excluded, corresponding to decades of hostility from society and government.[16] Now that these rights have become more popular, it seems strange to oppose their protection by the courts. Essentially, opponents tell the LGBTQ community: only if you create supermajority politics and wrench the religious right from the Republican Party can you obtain federal protection against discrimination. This seems misguided and inconsistent with the trajectories of other rights movements. For instance, even though the Equal Rights Amendment (ERA) failed (largely due to conservative gender politics), the Supreme Court created a jurisprudence that does much of what feminists hoped the ERA would do.

The reality is that courts have been open to LGBTQ litigants, and they have gone to court on a variety of issues since the rise of the modern LGBTQ rights movement. Most of the early litigants were not part of a national coordinated strategy but were motivated by what sociolegal scholars call "legal consciousness." More recently, LGBTQ activists have engaged in sophisticated, gradualist litigation strategies utilizing the power of legal reasoning and the role of precedents to change and expand policies.[17] These strategies are not unusual. Scholars have documented highly successful litigation strategies by conservative groups aimed at achieving policy change. In fact, judicial conservatism has increasingly advocated for an active judiciary focused on protecting conservative rights, such as the Supreme Court's creation of an individual's right to bear arms for the first time in 2008, more than two hundred years after ratification of the Second Amendment.[18] Courts are significant policymakers in the US political system, spurred by activists intending to change policy through litigation. This book furthers an understanding of how that process works, especially in the context of statutory rights.

Law and doctrine are important to judges; they are not simply politicians in robes. However, in the federal courts, ideology also matters. Robert Howard and Amy Steigerwalt describe the reality of judicial policymaking nicely when they assert: "Judges have beliefs, ideologies, and attitudes, and, within constraints of law and politics, judges will try to craft an opinion or ruling in accordance with those principles."[19] Judicial innovation in the realm of LGBTQ rights comes primarily from Democratic appointees in the federal courts or from progressive state judicial systems, often in states where judges are not directly elected by voters. When judges are first asked to change a law, Democratic and Republican appointees usually join together to protect the legal status quo, but Democratic appointees eventually become innovators. As the law evolves, some conservatives buy into it, while others attempt to preserve the status quo. In the case of marriage equality, activists targeted progressive state judiciaries to establish supportive case law and policy change, starting in the 1990s. Given the relative conservatism of the federal judiciary at the time, activists avoided the federal courts, and federal litigation was strongly discouraged by national and regional litigation groups. The federal courts were initially engaged in around 2010, but only after a new judicial framework for the issue had been developed in state courts and the federal judiciary had become less conservative. Many conservative judges, as well as most liberal judges, recognized the constitutional infirmities of state and federal bans on same-sex marriage and similar arrangements, especially after 2013, when the

US Supreme Court declared that part of the Defense of Marriage Act (DOMA) was unconstitutional. From 2013 to 2015 the legal consensus was that the US Constitution protected the right of same-sex couples to marry, but many judicial conservatives resisted and argued against this approach, including the dissenting justices in *Windsor v. U.S.* (the DOMA case) and *Obergefell v. Hodges*: Antonin Scalia, John Roberts, Clarence Thomas, and Samuel Alito.[20]

Legal actors with a shared ideology often create an interpretative community, with the goal of shaping legal opinion. Amanda Hollis-Brusky calls this a "political epistemic network (PEN)" through which members "share a common policy project to which they can apply their shared beliefs and interpretative understandings of politically contested meanings or texts." She focuses on the conservative Federalist Society, but progressive legal actors engage in similar activities. For instance, LGBTQ activists drew from the innovative interpretations of legal scholars and worked with them to create a litigation strategy intended to change how Title VII was interpreted. Hollis-Brusky argues that these networks are most important when legal innovation is the goal of activism. She states, "By working to legitimize a set of ideas in the legal profession, PENs make it easier for judicial decision-makers who share these beliefs to articulate them in their opinions without the fear of being perceived as illegitimate."[21] As she notes, this fits with and draws from Lawrence Baum's concept of "judicial audience," or the notion that judges anticipate how their decisions will be received by other legal and political elites.[22] They desire approval and fear rejection, not necessarily by the public or distant political actors but by their peers and associates. This allows for legal innovation, but it also supports boundary maintenance through real or anticipated disapproval, particularly in an era of ideological polarization.

Ideology also matters in the realm of LGBTQ workplace discrimination. As noted earlier, judges appointed by Democrats tend to be legal innovators, whereas Republican appointees in the lower courts may not be innovators themselves, but they sometimes go along with established legal innovations, especially those related to discrimination based on gender or gender identity. Other Republican appointees strongly resist innovation in this arena, even if that innovation becomes well established. This fits with an important 2006 study of circuit court judges and ideology. The authors found that ideology, as measured by the appointing president's political party, significantly affected judicial outcomes in a wide range of legal areas, including sex discrimination and sexual harassment. They wrote: "In sex discrimination cases from 1995 to

2004, Republican appointees voted in favor of plaintiffs 35 percent of the time, whereas Democratic appointees voted for plaintiffs 52 percent of the time. Hence, we find strong evidence of ideological voting in this context." They go on to state: "When Republican appointees and Democratic appointees differ, it is often because their own commitments lead them to read the law in different ways—and sometimes radically different ways."[23] For instance, in the context of LGBTQ rights, some judges read *Price Waterhouse* as a watershed case, while others try to sharply limit its relevance. This is largely connected to ideology.

STATUTORY INTERPRETATION

With the federal legislative process blocked, LGBTQ activists have demanded an expanded interpretation of Title VII, one that extends beyond the view that it applies only to cisgender women and men. Commonly invoked against this expansive view is the legislative intent approach to statutory interpretation: the law must be interpreted in a manner consistent with the intent of the legislators who wrote and approved it. Given that the LGBTQ rights movement was quite small and highly marginalized in 1964 when the Civil Rights Act was passed, this approach effectively undermines any attempt to use Title VII to protect LGBTQ individuals from discrimination on the basis of gender identity or sexual orientation. Narrow textualism is another method of potentially excluding LGBTQ individuals. Under this approach, judges consider not the intent of the legislators but the meaning of the words themselves at the time of the law's adoption. This often involves consulting dictionaries, and central to this context is the meaning of "sex." A narrow textualist might assert that in 1964, "sex" referred to sex assigned at birth, certainly not to sexual orientation. Arguably, the judicial path would be foreclosed in this case, leaving advocates to focus on the political arena. These narrow approaches reflect a normative concern about judicial power. Specifically, if judges go beyond a rudimentary understanding of the text or ignore legislative intent, they can be accused of inserting their own policy preferences in an antimajoritarian fashion. Thus, debates about statutory interpretation echo debates about constitutional interpretation and the normative fear of or discomfort with an active judiciary.

Textualist approaches were developed in the latter decades of the twentieth century mostly by conservative academics and jurists who criticized other prominent approaches such as legislative intent and purposivism. Like originalism in constitutional interpretation, textualism was intended to limit judges' discretion and lessen their ability to substitute their own policy preferences for the policies of other, arguably more politically accountable, branches of government. From the New Deal onward (until the textualist backlash), the trend in statutory interpretation was to empower judges to ascertain the larger policy purpose of legislation. This purpose could evolve over time as society changed in various ways. However, some conservative jurists, such as Scalia, thought this gave judges far too much discretion, and they proposed restricting judges to the text as a way to constrain judicial power. But conservatives were not the only ones who saw flaws in the purposive approach. Scholars in the critical traditions that arose in the 1970s (e.g., critical theory, critical race theory, feminism, queer theory) began to argue that the legislative process contained class, race, gender, and sexuality biases, undermining the notion that legislatures operate in the interest of broad sections of society or anything approaching the public good. Further, scholarship emphasized the heavy influence of interest groups, usually those with financial clout and insider access, in the legislative process. Thus, modern statutory interpretation operates in the context of reduced trust in both legislatures and judges. As historian William Popkin notes, "Contemporary statutory interpretation attempts to grapple with the collapse of optimism about legislation on which modern purposivism relied, without a corresponding revival of faith in judging."[24]

Narrow textualist and legislative intent approaches present problems beyond the fact that judges seldom adhere to them consistently. For instance, based on these approaches, sexual harassment would not be actionable under Title VII. However, feminist scholars and activists convinced judges and the EEOC that creating a hostile, highly sexualized work environment or firing someone for rebuffing a sexual advance is actionable under Title VII. In addition, statutory text is often vague and contradictory, the product of a highly decentralized and fragmented legislative process. Sometimes this vagueness is deliberate, as legislators hope to pass along difficult policy decisions to administrators and judges. Legislative history is notoriously contradictory and difficult to ascertain; anticipating a judicial search for legislative intent, legislators and their staffs often stack the deck with committee statements, reports, and floor speeches. As Leif Carter and Thomas Burke note, "Given the realities of the legislative process, judges should be wary of concluding that legislators ever collectively intend anything."[25] In the context of Title VII, legislative intent is not a prominent factor, as the legislative record surrounding the pro-vision is limited. However, legislative intent should not be conflated with the motives of those legislators who pushed for its inclusion and approved it. Nar-ratives that Title VII was simply a poison pill used by racists to kill the Civil Rights Act and that little thought or planning went into its enactment have been debunked by scholars, as discussed in chapter 2.

Purposivism, in contrast, requires judges to ascertain the broad purpose of a statute or the policy problem the legislature was trying to address. This approach takes into account that the purpose of the statute may evolve with changing social circumstances, and it allows interpreters to understand the larger purpose in an evolving context. It may be seen as a reaction to the lim-itations of the narrow textualism and legislative intent approaches. Critics as-sert that it gives too much independence to judges, permitting them to insert their own policy preferences into their interpretations. William Eskridge Jr. describes an even more robust form of this approach called "dynamic statu-tory interpretation," which accepts that interpretations will evolve with socie-tal changes and is less concerned about the implications for judicial power. As Eskridge states, "Statutory interpretation is multifaceted and evolutive rather than single-faceted and static, involves policy choices and discretion by the interpreter over time as she applies the statute to specific problems, and is re-sponsive to current as well as the historical political culture."[26] Obviously, this approach allows gender identity and sexual orientation to be read more easily into Title VII. A similar approach, referred to as pragmatism, de-emphasizes textualism and legislative intent in favor of a focus on outcomes and a recog-nition that judges may need to update legislation to satisfy an evolving society. Posner is often connected with pragmatism, and his approach to Title VII is discussed later in this chapter.

A final approach to statutory interpretation is for judges to utilize canons or rules of construction that have evolved over time. The challenge is that there are scores of rules, and some of them are contradictory. Their applica-tion often invokes the same charge of judicial freelancing as other approaches, yet lawyers and judges assert that these are neutral rules that restrict judicial discretion. Often they are utilized in conjunction with other approaches. Tex-tualists like Scalia, for instance, are willing to use canons related to linguistic issues but reject broader policy-related canons.[27]

In reality, judges seldom adopt one approach exclusively and consistently. "The rise of textualism may have been exaggerated," Frank Cross notes.[28]

Rather than take a stance on a preferred method, this book assumes that all these approaches will be used by activists and judges in the context of interpreting Title VII, with some approaches (purposivism, dynamic statutory interpretation, pragmatism) facilitating the inclusion of sexual orientation and gender identity and others (narrow textualism, legislative intent) restricting their inclusion.

However, the story is a bit more complicated in the real world of active interpretation. As noted earlier, the decision in *Oncale* was pivotal in connecting *Price Waterhouse* to issues of sexual orientation. The unanimous decision was authored by Justice Scalia, a noted textualist. Throughout his academic and judicial career, Scalia maintained a normative stance, though imperfectly applied, against judicial activism. This led him to take an originalist approach to constitutional interpretation as a way to constrain judicial discretion by locking constitutional meaning at a given historical moment and applying textualism in statutory interpretation. Interestingly, he was also a strong critic of the legislative intent approach, for the reasons articulated by the critics cited earlier. He thought it was easier to discover constitutional meaning through "original public meaning" rather than through the intentions of a statute's authors.

In *Oncale*, lower courts ruled that same-sex sexual harassment was not actionable under Title VII, relying on the reasoning of judge Ann Williams in a similar case from Illinois (involving a male-dominated work environment). In that case, Judge Williams took a purposive approach, asserting that Title VII was intended primarily to protect women from discrimination in the workplace; therefore, an all-male workplace could not be a place of discrimination against men, even if men were harassed there. She wrote that had the plaintiff been a woman, the employer "would have taken action to stop the harassment." Judge Williams found that "the harassment was pervasive and continuous from the time [plaintiff] Goluszek began until he was fired." However, she wrote: "The discrimination Congress was concerned about when it enacted Title VII is one stemming from an imbalance of power and an abuse of that imbalance by the powerful which results in discrimination against a discrete and vulnerable group. Title VII does not make all forms of harassment actionable, nor does it even make all forms of verbal harassment with sexual overtones actionable."[29] Williams could not conceive that discrimination on the basis of real or perceived sexual orientation constituted an actual and illegal power imbalance, or more likely, she could not conceive that Congress had intended to address same-sex sexual harassment. In hindsight, it might have been too soon for a district court judge to make that leap only two years after the Supreme Court found sexual harassment to be actionable under Title VII. Williams had been appointed to the bench by Republican Ronald Reagan, but she was eventually elevated to the Seventh Circuit by Democrat Bill Clinton. Interestingly, she was in the majority when the Seventh Circuit ruled in 2017 that sexual orientation was protected by Title VII, the first federal appellate court to do so.[30]

A unanimous Supreme Court rejected this type of reasoning in *Oncale*. Notably, Justice Scalia wrote that a search for statutory purpose was misguided:

> We see no justification in the statutory language or our precedents for a categorical rule excluding same-sex harassment claims from the coverage of Title VII. As some courts have observed, male-on-male sexual harassment in the workplace was assuredly not the principal evil Congress was concerned with when it enacted Title VII. *But statutory prohibitions often go beyond the principal evil to cover reasonably comparable evils, and it is ultimately the provisions of our laws rather than the principal concerns of our legislators by which we are governed.*[31]

Thus Scalia was the author of a major LGBTQ rights case that dealt only with statutory interpretation, even though he was a vigorous dissenter in the Supreme Court's expansion of constitutional protections for sexual minorities. In *Oncale*, Scalia may have been caught between his hostility for legislative intent–based statutory interpretation and the court's precedents that expanded Title VII to include sexual harassment. "The statute made me do it" approach was also evident in his 1993 concurrence in *Harris v. Forklift Systems*, a decision unanimously affirming the court's inclusion of sexual harassment in Title VII. In that case, he declared that nothing in the statute precluded the court's approach to sexual harassment, especially given "the inherently vague statutory language."[32]

Various approaches to statutory interpretation were present in the opinions of the judges of the Seventh Circuit in *Hively v. Ivy Tech Community College*, the groundbreaking federal decision in which the court, sitting en banc, found that sexual orientation should be included in Title VII, thus overruling its own decision in *Ulane v. Eastern Airlines* (1984). Of the eleven judges, eight had been appointed by Republican presidents and three by Democrats. All three Democratic appointees were in the majority, along with five of the Republican appointees. Directly citing *Price Waterhouse* and *Oncale*, judge Diane Wood wrote for the eight-member majority and rejected textualist and legislative intent approaches, utilizing purposivism instead. As she stated, "It is . . . neither here nor there that the Congress that enacted the Civil Rights Act in 1964 and chose to include sex as a prohibited basis for employment discrimination (no matter why it did so) may not have realized or understood the full scope of the words it chose." Thus, she continued, "the logic of the Supreme Court's decisions, as well as the common-sense reality that it is actually impossible to discriminate on the basis of sexual orientation without discriminating on the basis of sex, persuade us that the time has come to overrule our previous cases that have endeavored to find and observe that line."[33] Wood and the other judges determined that the broader purpose of the statute should be fulfilled, rather than prioritizing an attachment to the text or to legislative intent. This decision created new policy in the Seventh Circuit, as Indiana did not possess an antidiscrimination law inclusive of sexual orientation.

Judge Posner wrote separately to emphasize his pragmatic approach and its open acknowledgment that judges need to "update" statutes, especially if a significant amount of time has elapsed since their original enactment. "A broader understanding of the word 'sex' in Title VII than the original understanding is thus required in order to be able to classify the discrimination of which Hively complains as a form of sex discrimination. That broader understanding is essential." Rather than focus on *Price Waterhouse* and *Oncale* (in fact, he was critical of Scalia's opinion, which he called "rather evasive"), Posner referenced the decisions by the Seventh Circuit and the Supreme Court embracing marriage equality as an indication of social evolution on the question of sexual orientation.[34] This evolution was also a personal one for Posner, who had strongly opposed lesbian and gay rights in his 1992 book *Sex and Reason*.[35]

Judge Diane Sykes argued for the three dissenters that the majority's approach amounted to "the circumvention of the legislative process by which the people govern themselves." Instead, she took an originalist-textualist approach (discussed more fully later) that involved applying "the statutory language as a reasonable person would have understood it at the time of enactment."[36] This, of course, would not allow sexual orientation, sexual harassment, or gender identity to be covered by Title VII. This is an even narrower position than Scalia's in *Oncale*. However, as Richard Hasen notes, many followers of Scalia-inspired textualism take a narrower view than he did, including current Supreme Court justice Brett Kavanaugh.[37] A noted textualist and Reagan appointee on the Seventh Circuit, Frank Easterbrook, did not join the textualist dissenters but voted with the majority. He posed a question during oral arguments that pointed in the direction of viewing sexual orientation–based discrimination as sex-based discrimination because it demands that women be in relationships only with men. This form of discrimination, emphasized by Wood in the majority opinion, is often referred to as associational discrimination.[38] Thus, for Easterbrook, the understanding of the text at the time of adoption was not sufficient to fully understand the dynamics of discrimination in the *Hively* case.

The approach taken by Sykes reflects a recent development in conservative and libertarian jurisprudence—the application of constitutional originalist techniques to statutes, an approach not advocated by Scalia. Law professor Katie Eyer has documented "a new counterargument" to LGBTQ rights claims under Title VII, "couched in the language of 'statutory originalism.'" The idea is to ascertain how the public would have interpreted the language and purpose of Congress, as some originalists do when interpreting the Constitution. In the past several decades, constitutional originalists have shifted from "original intent" to "original public meaning," or a shift from the Constitution's drafters to citizens. Eyer correctly notes that this approach is closely related to the search for legislative intent: it is a "new modality of statutory interpretation, which resembles, if anything, the discredited 'Congressional expectations' approach." Of course, this is precisely the opposite of Scalia's approach, most prominently reflected in his decision in *Oncale*. Eyer calls statutory originalism an attempt to "sidestep" Scalia's decision.[39]

One final consideration is worth exploring. When judges interpret a statute in a way that is inconsistent with the views of legislators, those legislators can overturn that decision by amending the statute or enacting a new one. This remedy is a majoritarian one, unlike in cases involving constitutional interpretation, where a supermajoritarian constitutional amendment is required, at least at the federal level. Put differently, the costs associated with statutory interpretation are lower for judges. While they may be accused of being antidemocratic, there is a fairly routine democratic remedy for opponents of any particular judicial interpretation of a statute. In fact, the canon of constitutional avoidance requires judges to engage in statutory interpretation as a way to resolve a dispute without turning the case into a constitutional matter, when possible. In reality, legislative overrides are infrequent, but the notion of being less undemocratic may make judges more likely to engage in aggressive interpretation rather than a deferential formalism such as narrow textualism.

An important case from LGBTQ rights history is illustrative. In 1989 the New York Court of Appeals (the state's highest court) ruled that same-sex partners should be considered "family" under the state's 1946 rent-control statute. The law prevented landlords from substantially increasing rents for existing tenants and their survivors. A state agency interpreted the law as covering surviving spouses "or some other member of the deceased tenant's family who has been living with the tenant."[40] The law also protected tenants and their survivors from eviction, as long as the rent was paid. Miguel Braschi sued to prevent his eviction from the Manhattan apartment he had shared with his partner Leslie Blanchard, who died in 1986 of complications from AIDS. Only Blanchard's name was on the lease, so American Civil Liberties Union (ACLU) attorney William Rubenstein had a decision to make about litigation tactics. Should he argue that Braschi and Blanchard were spouses, as many in the emerging marriage equality movement urged (which would implicate the constitutional right to equal protection or due process), or should he try to convince the judges that Braschi and Blanchard were family under the rent-control statute and its administrative interpretation? As Carlos Ball explains, Rubenstein chose the latter approach, which was ultimately successful:

> The objective was to make the court comfortable with the notion of providing legal recognition to a same-sex relationship in a relatively narrow and safe context. The context was relatively narrow because the case arose from the interpretation of a somewhat obscure provision of New York's Rent Control Law. . . . If the gay rights movement, in the late 1980s, had tried to achieve something more ambitious through the courts than what it attempted in *Braschi*, the effort would have likely ended in failure.[41]

Adding a group or groups to an already existing statutory framework is arguably less judicially radical than creating a new constitutional right or applying an old one in a new fashion.

In addition, narrow statutory interpretations by the courts do not enshrine those interpretations in the Constitution, thus allowing the political process to address the question, at least in theory. For instance, an adverse statutory ruling for advocates of LGBTQ rights would not be as devastating as

Constitution-based decisions such as *Bowers v. Hardwick* (1986) and *Baker v. Nelson* (1972), which declared that the right to privacy does not apply to sexual minorities and that no part of the Constitution compels state or federal recognition of same-sex marriage. As Sean Farhang points out, a narrow reading of Title VII protections in several Supreme Court cases in 1989 (including *Price Waterhouse* on the question of burden of proof, not sex stereotyping) led to those decisions being overturned by the Civil Rights Act of 1991.[42] However, as noted earlier, increased partisan polarization and the connection between the religious right and the Republican Party make the contemporary setting less hospitable to civil rights expansion than were the late 1980s and early 1990s. Congress is not likely to expand civil rights in the foreseeable future.

THE CONNECTION TO CONSTITUTIONAL ISSUES

Although this book deals primarily with statutory interpretation, constitutional issues are in the background because legal and political advocates often draw from constitutional concepts to frame or bolster their statutory arguments. For instance, in the 1979 case *DeSantis v. Pacific Telephone & Telegraph Company*, the Ninth Circuit Court of Appeals reinforced its finding that Title VII does not protect against employment discrimination on the basis of sexual orientation by citing the Constitution's lack of protection for sexual minorities at that time.[43] Even today, most federal judicial circuits employ a lower level of review under the federal equal protection clause for sexual orientation–based discrimination than for discrimination based on race or gender. Of course, how courts have interpreted the equal protection clause and which groups are better protected are different from the question of either explicit or implicit (through interpretation) statutory protection. Opponents of LGBTQ rights often argue that sexual and gender minorities are not "protected classes" under the US Constitution (some state constitutions may be more inclusive) and thus should not be added to antidiscrimination statutes. But this confuses how statutes and constitutions operate. Even if a right or a protection against discrimination is not included in a constitution by either clear text or judicial interpretation, legislators can create rights and protections. For instance, persons with disabilities have roughly the same federal constitutional status as sexual minorities, but Congress enacted the Americans with Disabilities Act in 1990. The constitutional status of transgender rights is a bit more complicated (and transgender rights are better protected), given the heightened protection for gender based on Supreme Court precedents.

Relying on the foundation it had laid in the context of racial discrimination, the Supreme Court increased safeguards related to sex and gender under the equal protection clause in the early 1970s. The court had ruled that classifications based on race were "inherently suspect" and that these suspect classifications should be subjected to strict scrutiny, or the most searching and least deferential form of judicial review. The court created a test for ascertaining which classifications were suspect: the trait in question should be irrelevant to the issue at hand and immutable, and the group must have encountered a history of discrimination and be politically powerless. Due to concerns about the perceived biological essentialism of sex, and to preserve some policies that made distinctions on the basis of gender, the court created the category of heightened or intermediate scrutiny. In most cases, the rational basis test, which is generally deferential to governmental policies that discriminate, had been used to evaluate discrimination. This change in the court's view of gender-based discrimination was the result of an ACLU litigation strategy led by Ruth Bader Ginsburg, and it was part of the expansion of constitutional and statutory protections against gender-based discrimination represented by the Civil Rights Act of 1964, congressional passage of the ERA, and the Educational Amendments of 1972 (Title IX), among other policies at the state and federal levels.[44] The connection between these developments and LGBTQ rights is explored in chapter 2.

The landmark decision in *Loving v. Virginia* (1967) offers another important form of analysis under the equal protection clause that is relevant to a discussion of discrimination under Title VII. Supporters of Virginia's ban on interracial marriage argued that the ban was racially neutral—it applied to all races and prevented all forms of interracial marriage. The Supreme Court, however, rejected this argument and held that the law upheld a system of racial supremacy and was unconstitutional, despite its "neutrality." Judge Wood later made this point in defending the *Hively* majority's approach to Title VII, writing that "these laws were long defended and understood as non-discriminatory because the legal obstacle affected *both* partners. The Court in *Loving* recognized that equal application of a law that prohibited conduce only between members of different races did not save it." She also referenced the Supreme Court's protection of sexual minority rights in *Romer v. Evans*, *Lawrence v. Texas*, and *Obergefell v. Hodges*. As Wood noted, the majority's approach "must be understood against the backdrop of the Supreme Court's decisions, not only in the field of employment discrimination, but also in the area of broader discrimination on the basis of sexual orientation."[45] Thus, there is a direct relationship between constitutional interpretation and statutory interpretation. The changes in constitutional interpretation represented by *Romer*, *Lawrence*, and *Obergefell* facilitated changes in statutory interpretation relating to LGBTQ rights for many federal judges.

INTRODUCTION TO THE THREE CASES

Aimee Stephens transitioned while working at a Michigan funeral home in 2013. After writing a letter informing her employer that she would be presenting as a woman, she was fired, ostensibly for violating the company dress code. Her employer explicitly stated that religious beliefs were the reason for Stephens's termination. She filed a complaint with the EEOC, and the agency sued under Title VII on her behalf. A federal judge, emphasizing the religious motivation for the termination of employment, found in favor of the funeral home; however, the Sixth Circuit Court of Appeals, an innovator on the question of transgender rights, overturned that decision. The funeral home appealed to the Supreme Court. Tragically, Stephens died only weeks before the Supreme Court decision. Her wife continued the litigation on her behalf.

Donald Zarda was fired in 2010 as a skydiving instructor after disclosing his sexual orientation to a client, who, through her boyfriend, informed Zarda's employer. According to Zarda, the disclosure was intended to reassure the female client while they were strapped together in a tandem dive, but she claimed that he touched her inappropriately, which Zarda denied. In addition to suing his employer under New York's antidiscrimination law, which included protections for sexual orientation, Zarda filed a federal claim under Title VII. He died in 2014 in a BASE-jumping accident, but his estate continued the litigation. The estate was not successful until 2018, when the Second Circuit Court of Appeals, sitting en banc, overturned a three-judge panel and found in Zarda's favor. His former employer appealed to the Supreme Court.

Gerald Bostock's participation in a gay softball league, and his supervisor's knowledge of this fact, led to Bostock's firing in 2013 from his position as child welfare services coordinator for Clayton County, Georgia, despite a meritorious job record. A few months later, he filed a complaint under Title VII with the EEOC. Both a federal district court and the Eleventh Circuit Court of Appeals ruled that Bostock had no claim under Title VII, as litigants could not attempt to "bootstrap" sexual orientation onto the law's sex-based provision.[46] Bostock appealed to the Supreme Court.

For all three plaintiffs, the legal foundation created by *Price Waterhouse* would lead, gradually and with great planning and strategy, to an outcome no one envisioned in 1989 but one that is consistent with the connections among race, gender, and sexual orientation that activists had been making for decades.

TERMINOLOGY

This book uses several terms in the context of LGBTQ rights. Although "lesbian," "gay," and "bisexual" are commonly understood, the terms "transgender" and "queer" may need to be defined. "Queer" is used to describe a nonnormative sexual orientation; it has become more common as individuals have reclaimed the former slur. "Transgender" dates from the 1990s and encompasses a range of gender variations. It has replaced the term "transsexual," which was very common before the 1990s but is now considered outdated, given its narrow focus on biological sex as opposed to gender. Individuals can transition in a variety of ways, not only the medical transitioning implied by the term "transsexual." In court cases from the 1970s and 1980s, this term was commonly used by plaintiffs, defendants, lawyers, and judges. This continued into the 1990s and 2000s, but in the past decade or so, it has been largely replaced by the more inclusive term "transgender." Terms such as "gender variant," "gender nonconforming," "gender nonbinary," and "genderqueer" are also used to describe individuals who transgress traditional gender norms and the traditional gender binary in some way. "Cisgender" refers to a gender identity that corresponds with one's sex assigned at birth. The terms "gender minorities" (including transgender and gender nonconforming individuals) and "sexual minorities" (including lesbian, gay, and bisexual individuals) are often used in this book. I sometimes use "LGB" to refer specifically to lesbian, gay, and bisexual individuals and movements based on sexual orientation to distinguish them from activism surrounding gender identity.

Having established the main themes and issues of the book here, the following chapters explore LGBTQ rights before *Price Waterhouse* and examine its effects. Chapter 2 examines discrimination against LGBTQ individuals in the 1960s and 1970s and the enactment of Title VII of the Civil Rights Act of 1964. In particular, it highlights the connections between the movement for gender equality and LGBTQ rights. Chapter 3 discusses *Price Waterhouse* and *Oncale* and demonstrates how those cases shifted the legal foundation for Title VII interpretation, destabilizing the blanket denial of LGBTQ protections. Chapter 4 examines the legal movement for transgender rights and examines how legal activists deployed the new approach to Title VII in a gradualist strategy to protect transgender workers from discrimination. It also examines the crucial role played by the EEOC. Chapter 5 explores these dynamics in the context of discrimination on the basis of sexual orientation. Chapter 6 examines the cases of Gerald Bostock, Aimee Stephens, and Donald Zarda in the lower courts, and chapter 7 explores developments in the Supreme Court and the aftermath of the court's significant decision. It concludes by pulling together the main themes of the book and establishing what has been learned about the decades-long effort to achieve federal antidiscrimination protections for the LGBTQ community through the courts.

2. The History of LGBTQ Rights, Sex, and Title VII

As reflected by the opinions in *Hively v. Ivy Tech Community College*, the connection between Title VII and discrimination based on gender identity and sexual orientation is disputed both politically and legally. Opponents of an inclusive interpretation emphasize that inclusion is supported by neither a textual connection nor an intent or purpose behind Title VII. Their argument is that only cisgender individuals—or at best, individuals who are subjected to sex stereotyping—are covered under the law and that sexual minorities certainly are not. Only an explicit political process resulting in legislative inclusion of these categories would be legitimate. Underlying this approach is the notion that, both historically and analytically, gender identity and sexual orientation are separate concepts from sex. Further, Title VII has not evolved over time to include legal concepts, such as sexual harassment, that were not explicitly intended to be the target of Title VII. However, this is an ahistorical and overly simplified assessment.

This chapter emphasizes two important correctives to this approach. First, gender and sexual minorities faced overwhelming social, political, and legal marginalization in 1964, so it makes little sense to argue that Congress explicitly rejected their inclusion in Title VII. Second, by the 1970s, activists and policymakers across the ideological spectrum were making connections between sex-based discrimination and discrimination on the basis of sexual orientation and gender identity; this occurred as the LGBTQ rights movement accelerated and in the context of the debate over the Equal Rights Amendment (ERA). This chapter examines these elements and traces the history of the discussion of sex discrimination at the time of the enactment of Title VII and in the decades afterward, setting the stage for the Supreme Court's 1989 decision in *Price Waterhouse* and its expansion of the interpretation of Title VII. This chapter looks at legal and political developments related to race, sex, gender identity, and sexual orientation in the 1960s and 1970s in an integrated manner, exploring connections through ideas, events, and activists.

This approach is a corrective to many contemporary scholars, such as R. Shep Melnick, who view sex, gender identity, and sexual orientation as quite distinct from one another because sex is solely biological, and Title VII prohibits discrimination only on that basis. Moving beyond this understanding, according to Melnick, has only "added to the divisions within our already polarized nation."[1] This represents a cramped understanding of the evolution of Title VII and the development of the LGBTQ rights movement. Arguably, the sex discrimination part of Title VII was more immediately consequential for cisgender women, given their entry into the workforce and the shifts in family norms and gender roles. Further, the provision was not the result of a grassroots movement; it was advocated by some women's rights activists and legislators, most of them elite insiders. The broad-based, grassroots women's movement did not fully develop until *after* the enactment of Title VII. The provision was not simply a "poison pill" that failed to have its intended deadly effects, but neither was it the type of explicit and widely accepted provision demanded by critics of broad interpretations of Title VII. And an expansion to include sexual harassment was certainly not anticipated by those who approved the law. Critics like Melnick fail to understand the connections among sex, gender identity, and sexual orientation. They make the mistake of erecting a historical and analytical wall between sex and gender on one side and gender identity and sexual orientation on the other. They also ignore the role played by activists such as Pauli Murray, who saw Title VII through a dynamic and intersectional lens.

LGBTQ RIGHTS: 1950S–1970S

Three years before Congress passed the Civil Rights Act of 1964, the US Supreme Court received its first case involving discrimination on the basis of sexual orientation. In *Kameny v. Brucker* (1961), the court found that the firing of Franklin "Frank" Kameny from the Army Map Service was legally valid. This ruling reflected the lack of protection against discrimination and harassment for gender and sexual minorities at the time, with the exception of First Amendment rights related to the publication and dissemination of some LGBTQ periodicals. Although this chapter addresses primarily employment discrimination, it is important to note the significant public oppression faced by gender and sexual minorities. Scholars have noted the civil rights revolution, especially in the context of race and ethnicity, but there was no such revolution for sexual and gender minorities. In fact, quite the opposite was true: the state and society were at war against them. Kameny's dismissal reflected the dynamics of the so-called Lavender Scare (similar to the anticommunist Red Scare), whereby federal employees suspected of homosexuality were dismissed from their jobs.[2] The government did not consider including sexual and gender minorities under the Title VII umbrella and reject the notion; rather, from the perspective of governing elites, the idea was politically and legally inconceivable.

The policy under which Kameny was dismissed was promulgated in 1953 by President Dwight Eisenhower through Executive Order 10450. The order stated that federal employment could be denied on the basis of "any criminal, infamous, dishonest, immoral, or notoriously disgraceful conduct, habitual use of intoxicants to excess, drug addiction, [or] sexual perversion."[3] This policy remained in place, especially with regard to sexual minorities, until 1975. Eisenhower's executive order was based on the US Senate's Hoey Committee Report of 1950, which focused on the "threats" posed by sexual minorities employed in the federal government. The report declared: "Sex perverts, like all other persons who by their overt acts violate moral codes and laws and the accepted standards of conduct, must be treated as transgressors and dealt with accordingly."[4] The policy was enforced by the Civil Service Commission.

In the 1950s all states had sodomy laws on the books, and many jurisdictions outlawed cross-dressing. Sexual and gender minorities also faced police harassment for violating these laws and others, such as alcohol-related regulations (allowing bars to be raided and patrons to be harassed and arrested) and sexual solicitation laws. At all levels of government, gender and sexual minorities faced overwhelming criminalization and state-sanctioned discrimination.[5]

This negative legal terrain led Kameny's attorney, former congressman Byron Scott, to quit the case. This left Kameny on his own to petition the Supreme Court after losing in the DC Court of Appeals. Kameny's self-authored petition was a remarkable document, but the Supreme Court was unpersuaded and dismissed his appeal without comment. A court clerk described Kameny's certiorari petition in a manner that effectively summarized the Supreme Court's approach in particular and the government's approach more broadly: "[Petitioner] would have us strike down the whole idea that homosexuals can be discriminated against, but I doubt if that presents a substantial issue."[6]

Thus, as of the early 1960s, there were no legal principles, such as due process and equal protection, and no administrative law doctrines, such as arbitrary and capricious decision making, that allowed individuals to challenge their firing from the federal government for their actual or perceived sexual orientation, and this was confirmed by the Supreme Court. Far from being protected against discrimination, sexual and gender minorities were treated as criminals and threats to national security. This began to change after enactment of the Civil Rights Act of 1964 and favorable interpretations by the DC Court of Appeals, which commonly handled cases involving the federal bureaucracy. This change was also the result of a more militant homophile advocacy movement centered around the Mattachine Society of Washington, DC, cofounded by Kameny in 1961, soon after his Supreme Court rejection. As Rick Valelly notes, the Mattachine Society, along with the local chapter of the American Civil Liberties Union (ACLU), "developed a litigation strategy for challenging the commission's discriminatory policy." In addition, as Marc Stein has demonstrated, litigation campaigns were contemplated and organized in the 1960s, with homophile activists viewing courts as potential allies. Employment discrimination cases were a significant aspect of this litigation strategy.[7]

Although much of this litigation was unsuccessful, some limited victories chipped away at the federal prohibition of sexual minorities' employment in civilian positions in the government. One of the cases taken up by the Mattachine Society involved founding member Bruce Scott, who had previously been fired from a position in the Department of Labor due to this sexuality. He and Kameny strategized a test case, including a media campaign, in which Scott would reapply for a federal job, be denied due to "immoral conduct," and sue, arguing that sexuality was irrelevant.[8] They lost in federal district court but won in the DC Circuit. Although this case dealt with only applicants for federal jobs, it provided leverage for activists to challenge the employment prohibition as well. Combined with another case challenging the dismissal of a gay employee (decided in 1969 by the same judge), this litigation, along with other lawsuits and activism, led to a policy change in the Civil Service Commission in 1973 that was formalized in 1975.

Activists of this era viewed antidiscrimination laws as central to their efforts, and they were directly inspired by the tactics of the civil rights movement and the legal and philosophical arguments against racial discrimination. For instance, a resolution from a national lesbian and gay rights conference in 1966 called for "social and economic equality of opportunity" for sexual minorities.[9] In a 1964 speech Kameny, widely regarded as one of the intellectual leaders of the 1960s homophile movement, repeatedly emphasized the importance of a "civil rights philosophy" modeled on the approaches of the NAACP and the Congress for Racial Equality.[10] Employment discrimination, especially by the federal government, was central to demonstrations in 1965 in Washington, DC, and Philadelphia by activists led by Kameny. These protests were inspired by the 1963 March on Washington. A contingent of the DC Mattachine Society, including Kameny and Jack Nichols, had attended that march, and Nichols envisioned similar protests on behalf of the rights of sexual minorities. Messages on picket signs included: "Homosexual Americans Demand Their Civil Rights" and "Sexual Preference Is Irrelevant to Federal Employment." Ernestine Eckstein, the only African American participant, made connections between the civil rights movement and the nascent homophile movement. For instance, Eckstein stated in a 1966 interview that she thought the homophile movement was not litigating enough. Her sign at the 1965 demonstration outside the White House read: "Denial of Equality of Opportunity Is Immoral." She would eventually become involved in feminist aspects of the movement for racial equality through the organization Black Women Organized for Political Action.[11]

The federal employment litigation strategy achieved initial success in 1965 in Bruce Scott's case. That decision was authored by noted liberal judge David Bazelon, who advocated marginalized groups' use of the courts to assert their rights. As he wrote in 1983:

> For nearly 200 years of this nation's history, few blacks, Hispanics or Asian-Americans, to name only a few of the victims of oppression, would have thought of taking their claims to court. If the so-called litigation crisis is due in any significant part to the increase in social expectations of the disadvantaged and to society's growing sensitivity to these issues, then in my opinion the increase in litigation is a healthy one.[12]

Kameny and Scott had found a good judge for their test case.

Future chief justice Warren Burger was the dissenting judge in *Scott v. Macy*, previewing the homophobic judicial conservatism reflected in his infamous concurring opinion in *Bowers v. Hardwick* (1986). In *Bowers*, Burger quoted Blackstone's position that consensual same-sex sexual intimacy was a "malignity worse than rape," and he lobbied Justice Lewis Powell Jr. to change his initial vote in favor of declaring sodomy laws unconstitutional.[13] In Scott's case, Bazelon found the government's decision arbitrary and the charge of immoral conduct too vague. He also considered the decision stigmatizing. Reflecting the larger political and legal approach to the topic, Burger declared: "Whether it is sound legislative policy to attempt to deal with sex deviates under the criminal law is not open to judges but one can hardly doubt that such conduct is regarded as immoral under contemporaneous standards of our society."[14] Thus, he had no difficulty deferring to the executive branch.

Bazelon again questioned the government's policy in 1969 in *Norton v. Macy*, this time in the context of firing a federal employee, not simply denying a job applicant. Clifford Norton was fired by NASA after being detained by the morals squad of the DC police department for allegedly asking another man for sex—one of the ways the police in this era routinely harassed sexual and gender minorities. He was turned over to NASA security authorities after his arrest. Bazelon argued that there was no connection between real or perceived nonnormative sexual orientation and job performance. He found Norton's firing to be a violation of due process for its arbitrary nature and, potentially, a violation of the right to privacy. Indeed, he cited *Griswold v. Connecticut* and the emerging jurisprudence surrounding privacy rights. Bazelon was one of the few judges who connected the dots between sexual diversity and privacy.[15] Though not completely foreclosing the possibility that sexual orientation could be grounds for dismissal, Bazelon found that a general claim of immorality was too broad and not legally sustainable in this instance; a negative connection to federal employment must be proved. He thus established what came to be known as the "rational nexus" test in the context of federal employment, but this test was inconsistently applied.[16] More significantly, he pushed back against the elite consensus of this era and its nearly universal condemnation of sexual and gender diversity. As he noted, "A pronouncement of 'immorality' tends to discourage careful analysis because it unavoidably connotes a violate of divine, Olympian, or otherwise universal standards of rectitude."[17]

Bazelon created a legal foundation on which future judges would rely. However, as Gregory Lewis notes, in the short term, "the *Norton* decision had little apparent impact on the Civil Service Commission or the courts."[18] The system of federal discrimination was too deeply embedded, and outside of the very small homophile activist community, there was no political will to change the status quo. Kameny and other activists had been lobbying the Civil Service Commission since 1965, but the commission consistently dismissed their arguments and continued to fire federal employees for immorality. More directly consequential was a class-action case from the West Coast organized by the San Francisco–based Society for Individual Rights. A federal district court judge found in the group's favor in 1973, relying heavily on *Norton* and noting that the Civil Service Commission was ignoring that decision.[19] The commission finally responded to this political and legal pressure, eliminating the policy later that year.

However, the issue was not fully resolved. The case of John Singer illustrates the interrelated nature of sex-based and sexual orientation–based discrimination. Singer and his partner, Paul Barwick, lived in a Seattle commune of LGBTQ rights activists and were part of the more radical post-Stonewall movement, which was also active in other cities and college towns. They had met at the local chapter of the Gay Liberation Front. As part of the couple's activism, they filed a lawsuit over the denial of a marriage license. Their lawsuit was inspired by a gender-neutral definition of marriage in state law, thus allowing the possibility (at least in theory) of same-sex couples marrying, combined with a new equal rights amendment in the state constitution, approved by voters in 1972. The Washington Court of Appeals ruled against them, joining the overwhelming rejection of legal arguments for same-sex marriage at the time.[20]

Singer was gender nonbinary, as reflected by the clothing he wore to his job as a clerk in the Seattle office of the Equal Employment Opportunity Commission (EEOC). He was not secretive about his sexual orientation—in fact, he informed his employer about it—but he was eventually investigated by the Civil Service Commission and fired for his openly gay appearance, the notoriety surrounding the marriage lawsuit, and his LGBTQ rights activism. Singer eventually started using a new name, Faygele ben Miriam: *faygele*, a Yiddish word sometimes used as an antigay slur; and *ben Miriam*, or son of Miriam, to honor his mother, a feminist and radical.[21] As Rhonda Rivera notes, "The Singer case can be seen as representative of the new wave of cases in federal employment brought by openly gay persons," rather than by individuals outed by government authorities.[22] In the letter informing Singer of his dismissal, the Civil Service Commission wrote: "The information developed by the investigation, taken with your reply, indicate that you have flaunted and broadcast your homosexual activities. . . . Your activities in these matters are those of an advocate for a socially repugnant concept."[23] The Ninth Circuit used the "flaunting" argument to distinguish the case from *Norton*, ruling that the commission's decision was justified because of the EEOC's potential embarrassment. The court acknowledged that the policy had changed while the case was being argued, but it did not apply the new rule.[24] Given the change in policy, the Supreme Court reversed and remanded the decision, and Singer was awarded back pay after years of foot-dragging by the commission.[25] The war on LGBTQ federal employees was coming to an end, but discrimination was still a problem in the military and in the issuance of security clearances.

EARLY ANTIDISCRIMINATION ACTIVISM AND OPPOSITION

Challenging discrimination in court continued in the 1970s, but activists also engaged legislative bodies to add protections, with mixed success. Contesting federal employment discrimination was a significant element of the pre-Stonewall homophile movement, but the focus shifted in the 1970s to the inclusion of sexual orientation in local, state, and federal antidiscrimination laws and legal frameworks. Calls for gender identity–based protections would come later. Success was achieved at the local level when East Lansing, Michigan, enacted a sexual orientation–based antidiscrimination law in 1972. Minneapolis created the first gender identity–based law in 1975. Cities and college towns were the sites of many early policy innovations. However, the religious right soon took action to repeal these local laws. The first repeal occurred in Boulder, Colorado, in 1974, but the most famous repeal was in Miami-Dade County, Florida, in 1977, spearheaded by Anita Bryant's "Save Our Children" campaign. Indeed, the religious right's primary focus has consistently been to oppose and repeal antidiscrimination laws.[26] Thus, concerns about religious freedom did not spring up as a counterbalance to these laws out of a sense of compromise; they were part of a line of more direct opposition. In 1974 feminist and Democratic congresswoman Bella Abzug, representing a significant LGBTQ constituency in New York City, proposed a bill that would add sexual orientation to the Civil Rights Act of 1964, the first such federal proposal. Activists and advocates were following the civil rights model, relying on legislation to enshrine antidiscrimination protection. Beyond eliminating sodomy laws and protesting police harassment, enacting these policies was a focus of activism in the 1970s and beyond.[27]

An exhaustive examination of these developments is beyond the scope of this book (more contemporary developments are explored in chapters 4 and 5), but highlighting federal, state, and local efforts in the 1970s and 1980s illustrates the ongoing centrality of antidiscrimination policies in the emerging LGBTQ rights movement. It also illustrates the political barriers faced by these activists. After getting little support in Congress in the 1970s, activists refocused on Congress in the 1980s, and the first hearings on bills to address legal protections for sexual orientation took place. However, this did not lead to any serious legislative activity. By the 1990s, activists were concentrating on the Employment Nondiscrimination Act (ENDA), but given the difficult political terrain faced by advocates in Congress, the act was limited to employment discrimination, covered only sexual orientation, and contained significant religious exemptions.

Local laws faced constant opposition by religious right activists and the possibility of repeal. This backlash led to the Supreme Court's decision in *Romer v. Evans* (1996), a challenge to the religious right–driven Amendment 2 in Colorado (a ban on local antidiscrimination protections for sexual orientation), but the prospect of repeal persisted for decades. As Amy Stone notes, "The Religious Right is far more successful at the ballot box, where it can rely on voters' homophobia, than in the legislative and judicial arenas." Wisconsin was the first to enact statewide protections for sexual orientation–based discrimination in 1982, and other states followed. To date, however, only twenty-two states have enacted such protections, and they vary in terms of coverage for public accommodations. Minnesota was the first state to include protections based on gender identity in 1993. As I have written elsewhere, there are regional and partisan dynamics at play in the states: "Protections are lacking in all of the South and the Great Plains, as well as more conservative Midwestern states (Indiana, Michigan, Missouri, and Ohio). Activist mobilization, combined with Democratic Party control of state government, explains most of the positive outcomes." Religious right and Republican opposition is a significant barrier to LGBTQ rights protection at the legislative level, thus encouraging a focus on the bureaucracy and the courts.[28]

THE CIVIL RIGHTS ACT AND THE INCLUSION OF SEX

The inclusion of the word "sex" in Title VII was not the result of years of direct mass mobilization and legislative engagement with a clear purpose, the standard often applied to LGBTQ antidiscrimination protections. Nor was it a trick or a mistake, an attempt to create a "poison pill" to hinder the effort to outlaw racial discrimination. It was grounded in the general activism of the women's movement and the particular context of wage inequality, brought to the forefront by women's increased entry into the workforce during World War II. Many feminist activists and women in Congress supported the measure, although there was some opposition from other women and women's groups. However, there is not an extensive legislative record behind the provision, and certainly not one that would justify a legislative intent approach to statutory interpretation. Jo Freeman describes the addition of "sex" to Title VII: "In only a few hours, Congress initiated a major innovation in public policy, one which rippled through the country for several years."[29] With the questions surrounding gender identity and sexual orientation, this ripple has been felt for decades.

The sex-based provision of Title VII is also part of a decades-long conversation about the Equal Rights Amendment, first proposed in 1921 by Alice Paul and first introduced in Congress in 1923. From the 1920s to the 1970s, constitutional (both textual and interpretive), statutory, and executive order–based protections against sex discrimination were woven into debates about the legal status of women, with organizations and activists differing on which approach was best. The debates over the ERA and statutory protections were not distinct conversations; however, activists were divided by philosophy, class, race, education, and party. For instance, the National Woman's Party (NWP), led by Paul, took a more gender-neutral approach to the issue of discrimination against women, favoring the ERA as the primary vehicle for achieving equality. These activists tended to be middle- to upper-middle-class educated professionals, many of whom were Republicans. Other activists were concerned that this approach would jeopardize the protective legislation from previous decades—that is, legislation "protecting" women from workplace dangers by imposing different standards for men and women. These activists were often associated with the Democratic Party (Eleanor Roosevelt was opposed to the ERA, for instance) and labor unions and were more concerned about the interests of working-class women. Indeed, fear of undermining these laws, and the gender role assumptions underlying them, was a significant constraint on women's legal progress until the 1960s. This concern led to a gradualist approach for most activists and government officials through agencies such as the Labor Department's Women's Bureau.[30]

The original version of the ERA read: "Men and women shall have equal rights throughout the United States and in every place subject to its jurisdiction." It was changed in the 1940s to read: "Equality of rights under the law shall not be denied or abridged by the United States, or by any State, on account of sex."[31] The amendment gained traction in Congress in the aftermath of World War II. It was approved by a majority of the Senate (38 to 35), but not the necessary supermajority, in 1946.[32] However, a return to gender traditionalism in the postwar years undermined this progress. As Cynthia Harrison notes, "The ERA stood little chance of passage because it represented an affirmation of absolute equality for women at a moment when heightened recognition of sex roles served a number of national functions, most important of which was the re-creation of a stable and familiar society in the wake of the social chaos of wartime."[33] Women's groups and activists outside of the NWP actively worked to oppose and undermine the ERA, as they had since its initial introduction in Congress. As Hugh Davis Graham describes the dynamic: "In the ensuing four decades of intramural feminist conflict, the anti-ERA protectionist wing held dominance."[34]

The Equal Pay Act of 1963 and John F. Kennedy's creation of the President's Commission on the Status of Women represented a reengagement of the issue and the more gradualist approach of most activists. This momentum was soon translated into Title VII. Although the Civil Rights Act of 1964 was unquestionably driven by the civil rights movement and concerns over racial discrimination, feminist activists saw an opportunity to more robustly secure women's employment equality. Thus, the enactment of Title VII was not an attempt at sabotage but the culmination of decades of activism and debate on the question of sex discrimination. However, it was not the product of a mass-based social movement; that would appear later in the decade, after the enactment of Title VII.[35]

Howard W. Smith of Virginia, a segregationist Democrat and opponent of the Civil Rights Act, proposed adding sex to Title VII. Smith was a longtime advocate of protecting women from discrimination, and feminists had worked with him on the issue for about a decade. He had offered a similar amendment in 1956 and had sponsored the ERA since 1943.[36] Smith was not alone in his support for the amendment in the House of Representatives. Of the eleven women in the chamber, all but one either favored the amendment or did not oppose it. Democrat Edith Green of Oregon was the sole female voice of opposition during the debate. The leader of the small caucus of women in the

House supporting the amendment was Martha Griffiths, a Michigan Democrat. Griffiths had recruited Smith to offer the amendment, as he was influential among southern Democrats. The amendment was approved after some debate and remained in the bill throughout the legislative process—a rather unimpressive history for such a highly consequential part of the law.

The debate on February 8, 1964, began with a colloquy between Smith and Emanuel Cellar, the Democratic chair of the Judiciary Committee, a strong advocate for the Civil Rights Act, and an opponent of the amendment. In response to Smith's contention that women were a minority worthy of protecting from workplace discrimination, Cellar noted that he was powerless at home against his wife. He emphasized biological essentialism and distinguished sex-based discrimination from that based on race.[37] The conversation improved somewhat when women joined the debate. Congresswoman Griffiths pointed out the sexism among the House members, as evidenced by the laughter from the men in the chamber during the early phase of the discussion. She then emphasized one of the primary concerns of the NWP and Smith: that white women would be solely unprotected if the act were passed without reference to sex. In her words, "white women will be last at the hiring gate."[38] This, of course, represented a complete lack of understanding of the position of women of color in society, and it reflected the racist attitudes of the white NWP membership, Smith, and other southern Democrats. As Pauli Murray, a black, queer, and gender nonbinary civil rights attorney and activist, noted: "If 'sex' had not been added to the equal employment opportunity provisions of the Civil Rights Act of 1964, Negro women would have shared with white women the common fate of discrimination since it is exceedingly difficult to determine whether a Negro woman is being discriminated against because of race or sex."[39] But this was at the heart of Griffiths's argument for the amendment as she declared, "A vote against this amendment today by a white man is a vote against his wife, or his widow, or his daughter, or his sister."[40] Katherine St. George, a New York Republican, declared: "We are entitled to this little crumb of equality. The addition of that little, terrifying word 's-e-x' will not hurt this legislation in any way. In fact, it will improve it. It will make it comprehensive. It will make it logical. It will make it right."[41]

The arguments of Representative Green reflected the conventional view in the Democratic Party that the amendment would jeopardize protective legislation (emphasizing biological differences), would derail passage of the act, and failed to account for the much greater problem of race-based discrimination.

Green realized that she was increasingly out of step with the trajectory of the women's movement, acknowledging that she would likely be referred to as an "aunt Jane," but the act's original purpose was too important to jeopardize. She also contested the argument that the amendment offered black women better protection under the law. Green declared, "She [a black woman] has a double discrimination. . . . She has suffered 10 times as much discrimination as I have. If I have to wait for a few years to end this discrimination against me, and my women friends—then as far as I am concerned I am willing to do that if the rank discrimination against Negroes will be finally ended under the so-called protection of the law."[42]

The amendment passed with significant support from southern Democrats, but the bill itself passed the House with a different coalition, lending support to the claim that some members had tried to torpedo the bill. The amendment passed by an anonymous vote of 168 to 133, but Griffiths (who served as a teller) later disclosed that most of the "yes" votes came from southern Democrats and Republicans.[43] It is likely that those Republicans joined northern Democrats to pass the final version of the bill. Freeman notes that Texas Democrat John Dowdy, an opponent of the Civil Rights Act, made another attempt to add sex to other provisions of the bill and to add age to Title VII—a broader poison pill—but that attempt failed. She writes, "The overall voting pattern [on a series of amendments] implies that there was a large group of congressmen (in addition to the congresswomen) who were serious about adding 'sex' to Title VII, but only to Title VII. It is not consistent with an interpretation that the addition of 'sex' was part of a plot to scuttle the bill."[44] In fact, the outcome was driven by a number of factors, many of them tied to the ongoing conversation about the legal status of women—a conversation that would continue with the ERA and the interpretations of Title VII. But if a judge is searching for a clear record to bolster legislative intent, the evidence is limited.

Although many of the actors who considered adding sex to Title VII were limited by their political agendas and biases, others understood the dynamics in a more intersectional manner. Pauli Murray was one of the latter. They (Murray) had been active for decades in the movement for racial justice and were a member, at the invitation of Eleanor Roosevelt, of the Civil and Political Rights Committee of the Commission on the Status of Women established by President Kennedy. They were a leading legal thinker on questions of race and gender and saw strong connections between the two forms of discrimination.

According to Serena Mayeri, "No one did more than Murray to make race-sex analogies the legal currency of feminism."[45] For instance, they were instrumental in getting the commission to recommend a legal strategy that convinced the Supreme Court to apply the equal protection clause of the Constitution to sex-based discrimination.[46] They referred to discrimination against women as "Jane Crow," starting in the 1940s. Their arguments were foundational for the ACLU litigation undertaken by Ruth Bader Ginsburg. Murray also influenced the shape of Title VII. As the bill was pending in the Senate, they wrote a memo supporting the addition of "sex" by emphasizing, contrary to many of its congressional advocates, that it would mostly benefit African American women. Murray's memo also emphasized the Jane Crow arguments they had been making for decades:

> That manifestations of racial prejudice have been more brutal than the more subtle manifestations of prejudice by reason of sex, in no way diminishes the force of the equally obvious fact that the rights of women and the rights of Negroes are only different phases of the fundamental and indivisible issue of human rights. It is against the background of their parallel development that the "sex" amendment to Title VII must be viewed.[47]

This widely circulated memo was crucial to the Senate's retention of the "sex" amendment.[48]

Murray's intersectional thinking likely derived from several personal sources, and they viewed identity as an important factor in understanding intersectionality. They were denied admission to the University of North Carolina because of their race and to Harvard because of their sex. Although Murray never publicly disclosed their gender identity and sexual orientation, they were attracted to women and explored the idea of hormone therapy in the 1930s and 1940s, embracing a more masculine personal identity despite being assigned female at birth. As Rosalind Rosenberg notes, Murray's various identities and struggles with identity "gave her an unusually broad sense of the arbitrariness of classification and the psychological burdens of discrimination."[49] Indeed, identity was a powerful analytical tool in Murray's legal and political work. They believed that a lack of appreciation for the discrimination faced by women stemmed from a dearth of women on the bench. In a 1962 report to the Commission on the Status of Women they wrote: "One of the greatest obstacles to achieving insights into the issue of discrimination against women is that the courts which pass upon this issue are overwhelmingly male and have little understanding of the problem. Many judges appear to recoil from the concept that discrimination because of sex is the equivalent of discrimination because of race, yet women who suffer the effects have little difficulty in recognizing the parallel."[50] Thus, they called for the appointment of more women to the federal courts, including the Supreme Court.

The discussion of Murray's role in the enactment of Title VII and in theorizing about the legal status of women is not designed to "prove" that Title VII should be broadly interpreted. Rather, like the discussion of other activists in this chapter, it is intended to illustrate the dynamic interactions between forms of discrimination in the minds of activists and to caution against the tendency to legally separate different forms of discrimination from one another, as opponents of a dynamic interpretation of Title VII would like to do. It also demonstrates that Title VII's history is complex and not accidental. It became a vehicle for legal change that was unanticipated by most but is largely recognized today, and it became a setting for an exploration of the links between discrimination and marginalization, especially that based on race, sex, gender identity, and sexual orientation.

It also demonstrates that the inclusion of "sex" in Title VII was aspirational rather than the result of decades of mass mobilization and a clear consensus about its purpose. As Nancy MacLean points out, for activists like Murray, "Title VII provided them a wedge with which to open up the whole gender system to question. It served as the mechanism with which once-private grievances could be turned into classically political issues, the subjects of public debate and policy."[51] Thus, from the start, Title VII was largely an empty vessel, and its trajectory would be filled in by the theories, movements, and litigation of activists.

SEX AND SEXUAL ORIENTATION IN THE MARRIAGE EQUALITY MOVEMENT

The product of an accelerating women's movement, the Equal Rights Amendment was passed by Congress in 1972 and sent to the states for ratification. This increased the connections between sexual orientation–based discrimination and the ERA and similar state-level provisions, in addition to the Supreme Court's inclusion of sex-based discrimination under the equal protection clause. For instance, in these measures, activists saw constitutional support for same-sex marriage, as did opponents of LGBTQ rights. Part of this connection related to the overlap between sex and sexual orientation and related forms of oppression and the formal interpretation of such provisions: if a man and a woman could get married but two women could not, the latter was the case because one of them was the "wrong" gender. The other element of the connection was grounded in path dependency, or the notion that policy change can be difficult and is often facilitated by adhering to certain trajectories, or paths, in policy. For instance, it would be easier to include sexual orientation–based discrimination in sex-based constitutional policies as they were proposed and enacted. This latter approach would persist into the contemporary marriage equality movement. The Hawaii Supreme Court's groundbreaking marriage equality decision in *Baehr v. Lewin* (1993) was the first time a court accepted an argument in favor of marriage equality. That decision was grounded in gender-based constitutional analysis, given that the state constitution explicitly prohibits discrimination on the basis of sex. In making their potential policy innovation, the judges saw that this was an easier path rather than trying to create a new jurisprudence grounded in sexual orientation–based constitutional analysis.

Peggy Pascoe noted the connections made between sex and sexual orientation in the 1970s:

> A small but determined group of lesbian and gay couples saw in these developments reason to hope that they might win the right to same-sex marriage. They used feminist insistence on the use of nonsexist language to support their claim that laws that defined marriage as a contract between "parties" could be interpreted to include same-sex couples. They thought it logical that a Supreme Court that found "race" an "unsupportable" basis on which to deny entrance to the civil right of marriage could be persuaded to say the same about "sex." And they believed that, as they put it, allow[ing] George to marry Sally, but forbidding Linda to do the same thing, was sex discrimination, and so a violation of both the constitutional guarantee of equal protection and the proposed Equal Rights Amendment.[52]

This type of analysis played a role in the Washington State case brought by the activists from Seattle (discussed earlier). That case involved two men, but women also applied for marriage licenses around the country throughout the

1970s, such as the plaintiffs in a case from Kentucky. In 1975 a lesbian couple engaged in a sit-in at the Cook County clerk's office in Chicago to protest the denial of same-sex marriage licenses.[53] So many same-sex couples applied for licenses that states made their gender-neutral marriage laws more explicit. Shaped by women's rights activism, county clerk Clela Rorex began granting marriage licenses to same-sex couples in Boulder, Colorado, in 1975.[54] The previous year, Boulder had been the site of the enactment and repeal of a sexual orientation–inclusive antidiscrimination ordinance.

In 1974 the Boston PBS station WBGH televised a debate on same-sex marriage featuring Frank Kameny and Elaine Noble. Later that year, Noble would become the first openly LGBTQ state-level elected official in the nation. She had strong connections to the emerging feminist and lesbian-feminist movements, exemplified by her relationship with noted lesbian-feminist activist and author Rita Mae Brown. Noble was active with the Boston-area chapters of the Daughters of Bilitis and the National Organization for Women (NOW), but she left both organization because of their exclusionary policies—the Daughters for not allowing trans women to be members, and NOW for its infamous fear of lesbians and the "lavender menace."[55] When asked by an opponent in the debate whether same-sex marriages would have a "head of household," Noble responded that one of the goals of the women's movement was to create more equality within mixed-sex marriages.[56] The prospect of same-sex marriage was so threatening in the 1970s that conservative opponents of the ERA used it in their "parade of horribles." Same-sex marriage threatened to destabilize gender roles, but it was also the product of already changing roles and expectations resulting from feminist arguments.

A doomed but notable attempt to legalize same-sex marriage in Washington, DC, in 1975 also demonstrates the extent to which some activists connected the legal language and concepts surrounding sex and the issue of same-sex marriage. A family law revision aimed primarily at allowing no-fault divorce included gender-neutral language, and its sponsor, Arrington Dixon, intended to use his bill to facilitate debate about the potential legalization of same-sex marriage. The city had enacted a sexual orientation–inclusive antidiscrimination law in 1973, one of the first large cities to do so. Although the bill's gender-neutral language was ultimately withdrawn, significant lobbying and discussion occurred, including testimony by Kameny before the city council in favor of the legalization of same-sex marriage. Kameny worked with activist Eva Freund and leveraged her connections with and standing in the local chapter of NOW. Freund had created the Sexuality Task Force in the DC chapter, and she and NOW had been instrumental in enacting the 1973 law. In her testimony, she emphasized the discrimination faced by women in DC, including lesbians.[57]

Of course, the early movement for same-sex marriage was not central to the post-Stonewall movement, and it should not be overemphasized. The most common stance, derived from feminist critiques of marriage, was that marriage is an inherently conservative and patriarchal institution and is not worth pursuing. But for many activists, it was a natural extension of legal and political developments of the 1960s and 1970s surrounding gender, sexual orientation, and marriage. By the late 1970s, however, the first wave of marriage equality activism receded, undermined by other priorities (e.g., a continued focus on antidiscrimination laws) and by the rise of the religious right. Indeed, as Pascoe notes, Florida in 1977 was noteworthy not only for the repeal of the Miami-Dade antidiscrimination law but also for state lawmakers' refusal to ratify the federal ERA, banning of adoption by LGB individuals, and creation of a sex-specific marriage law.[58]

Opposition to same-sex marriage within the LGBTQ movement led to the discouragement of new litigation as the issue was reengaged in the 1980s. However, opposition also came from those who thought same-sex marriage was not legally possible because there was no realistic legal path to the equal treatment of same-sex couples. Fundamental rights analysis required courts to find that an important unenumerated right was long-standing. In addition, the Supreme Court's baldly heterosexist ruling in *Bowers* strongly signaled that sexual orientation had no elevated constitutional standing. To get beyond the rational basis test under the equal protection clause, litigants needed to establish trait immutability, a history of discrimination, and political powerlessness. Although Evan Wolfson and others had theorized how this might be possible, the legal barriers were virtually insurmountable—unless, perhaps, a sex- or gender-based frame was used. This frame had fallen out of favor in lesbian and gay rights activism by the 1980s, but it underwent a revitalization among some legal academics by the end of the decade.[59]

Some saw sex-based arguments as a viable path to the judicial legalization of same-sex marriage. It was the approach taken by Hawaii's high court in the case cited earlier, but contemporaneous federal litigation also reflected a sex- or gender-based path-dependent strategy. A recent Georgetown Law School graduate filed a lawsuit with the support of professor William

Eskridge, a prominent scholar of statutory interpretation and LGBTQ rights (see chapter 1). Craig Dean and his partner, Patrick Gill, sued in DC court over the denial of a marriage license. Because of the lack of a sexual orientation–based path, they relied on statutory arguments, particularly the argument that the DC law was gender neutral. Part of the original law referred to "persons" and "parties" (the Dixon bill would have expanded this gender-neutral language). They asked the DC court to disregard the failure of the Dixon bill and to focus on the fact that activists and Dixon clearly thought the bill would have legalized same-sex marriage. The lawyers' argument (Dean represented himself, along with Eskridge) was a rejection of legislative history and intent; they asked the court to apply the statute's gender-neutral language, reverting to the approach taken in 1970s litigation. But in emphasizing the role of activists, one can see Eskridge's dynamic approach to statutory interpretation. In essence, he argued that the meaning of marriage in the District of Columbia was now broader because of the social changes reflected in the activists' arguments and demands. Relying on legislative intent was not a good path because the DC Council had clearly rejected the legalization of same-sex marriage. A focus on text and purpose, or on text alone, was the only plausible approach to statutory interpretation that might convince the court. As a document submitted during the litigation noted, "Statutory interpretation focuses on the language actually adopted by the legislature, and not upon the legislature's failure to act."[60] This argument eventually played a significant role in the legal debate on the applicability of Title VII to LGBTQ protections. And it figured prominently in justice Neil Gorsuch's analysis in *Bostock v. Clayton County.*

Eskridge also agreed with the new approach taken by legal academics such as Andrew Koppelman, who made the more substantive argument that denying same-sex marriage was a form of sex discrimination. As Koppelman argued in a 1994 law review article: "A deeper form of the sex-discrimination argument, developed by Sylvia Law, is that any effort by the state to hardwire sex differences into the concept of marriage perpetuates traditional sex-based stereotypes of man-as-breadwinner and woman-as-housekeeper. Same-sex marriage is required by a genderless Constitution precisely because it unlinks functional roles from sex stereotypes."[61] Although sexual orientation–based arguments were also made (as well as a free-exercise claim argued before the trial court), sex-based analysis was a significant part of the legal foundation of the case.

Notably, Frank Kameny thought sexual orientation was playing too large a role in the arguments of Dean and Eskridge. In a letter to Dean he wrote:

> I am concerned that in pursuing your case, you are making it a matter of *sexual orientation* discrimination. . . . You are not being discriminated because you are Gay. You are being discriminated against because of your sex, and this is a case of *gender* discrimination. . . . It would seem to me that as a matter of fact, logic, law and cultural prejudices, you would do much better to frame your case and your arguments in terms of *sexual discrimination*, rather than in terms of *sexual orientation discrimination.*[62]

He wrote a letter to Eskridge citing similar concerns.[63] Kameny's views were framed by his 1970s marriage equality activism and its connection to issues of sex or gender discrimination, as well as his decades of experience fighting social, political, and legal hostility to sexual orientation–based claims. He identified both the legally more open path of sex- or gender-based claims and the still-blocked path of sexual orientation–based claims.

In the long run, the sexual orientation–based path would be taken by most state courts and eventually the federal courts. This was reflected by the willingness of one DC judge to make a sexual orientation argument for same-sex marriage. Although the trial court judge and the appellate court judges in the majority dismissed both the statutory and the constitutional arguments in *Dean*, judge John Ferren found that sexual orientation could be subjected to heightened scrutiny.[64] However, this approach took some time to catch on in state courts; not until 2008 did a state high court take a similar approach (earlier decisions used a rational basis analysis). The US Supreme Court still has not done so, even though it has ruled in favor of same-sex marriage. Analyzing sexual orientation–based discrimination claims under the lower standard of rational basis review has persisted, supporting the notion that this would have been a difficult path to create.

Consequently, when the Hawaii Supreme Court faced this issue in 1993, a majority of the court invoked a sex-based analysis to find that the state's ban on same-sex marriage was likely unconstitutional. This argument was not formally presented to the court; it appeared only in a footnote in an appellate brief on behalf of the same-sex couples suing the state. Analyzed through a path-dependency lens, this makes sense for judges engaging in a potentially groundbreaking decision. The state constitution contained an equal rights amendment, enacted in 1978, and sex-based classifications triggered strict scrutiny. At the time, however, there was some confusion about which level of review was required by sex-based classifications: heightened or strict scrutiny. In *Baehr v. Lewin*, the supreme court made it clear that strict scrutiny was the appropriate level of review—an established path and a powerful remedy. Eventually, on remand, a trial court found that the state did not meet this test, but the legal process was cut short by a voter-approved amendment eliminating the judiciary's power to define marriage.[65]

Although it was not a dominant approach, the application of sex-based legal provisions to sexual orientation persisted. For instance, a few years later in Vermont, the notion that denying same-sex marriage licenses was sex discrimination was presented in oral arguments before the state supreme court. The majority invoked a robust rational basis test under a sexual orientation–based analysis and found that the state had no rational basis for the discrimination. One of the five judges, Denise Johnson, wrote a concurrence stating that the denial of same-sex marriage licenses was indeed a form of sex discrimination, triggering a higher level of review. Arguments were also presented that Vermont's marriage statute did not require different genders. Although the majority rejected the gender-neutral and sex-based approaches, they continued to be invoked and applied in the 1990s and beyond. A Maryland trial court judge found in 2006 that the state's ban on same-sex marriage was unconstitutional under a sex discrimination analysis. In particular, the judge noted the politics surrounding the federal ERA, as well as a state version enacted in 1973, and marriage equality activism in Maryland in the early 1970s. That judge, M. Brooke Murdock, had been involved in women's legal activism before becoming a judge.[66]

From the start of the marriage equality movement, and with the women's movement in the background, the sex or gender argument was prominent in the minds of activists and some judges, because of both the logical connections to discrimination on the basis of sexual orientation and the difficulty of creating a new path to elevate the status of sexual orientation in the law. This dynamic alone does not establish a definitive interpretation of Title VII, but it is illustrative of the imagined (in activists' legal consciousness) and real (in judges' rulings) connections between sex and sexuality. At the very least, it undermines the argument that the two have little to do with each other and that Title VII ought to be interpreted narrowly because connections among sex, gender identity, and sexual orientation are novel creations.

SEXUAL HARASSMENT

Sexual harassment law developed over time through the expanded interpretation of Title VII. It was significantly driven by feminist legal analysis and was neither connected to the legislative intent behind Title VII nor explicitly affirmed by federal statutes. The idea of sexual harassment as a form of sex discrimination began to develop a decade after the enactment of Title VII. As many scholars have noted, it is almost a purely judicially created policy, with assistance from the bureaucracy.[67] Title VII is the statutory provision undergirding current sexual harassment law; Congress has not enacted a separate statute, and court rulings serve as the basis for the law. Although it has its critics, sexual harassment is a well-developed area of the law, and there is little possibility of a return to the pre-1970s approach. The legal pathway for sexual harassment was similar to that leading to the inclusion of sexual orientation and gender identity. First, individuals went to court stating a statutory claim under Title VII. Next, this legal activism was supported by feminist activists and litigation organizations. After some initial failures in the federal courts, victories were achieved, and this supportive jurisprudence spread. This trend was then recognized and validated by the EEOC.

To use Melnick's term, the creation of sexual harassment policy involved considerable "leapfrogging," which he defines as "courts and agencies each taking a step beyond the other, expanding regulation without seeming to innovate."[68] Melnick objects to this approach, arguing that it lacks the clarity, accountability, and consistency of the legislative process. He understands that this is a deeply embedded aspect of the US policymaking process, but Melnick is highly critical of civil rights policy innovations that involve leapfrogging, including sexual harassment policy.

Initially, LGBTQ individuals who went to court claiming discrimination under Title VII (discussed later) had no support from civil rights organizations. The same was true of women who felt they were the victims of sexual harassment. The attorneys involved in the early litigation were not part of an organized movement, but they were significantly influenced by the Civil Rights Act of 1964 and the general climate of civil rights thinking and activism. As Anna-Maria Marshall notes:

> The evolution of sexual harassment law owes a great deal to the initiative and creativity of private practitioners who were vigorously representing their clients.

Although they did not have any particular political commitments, they were young attorneys whose relative inexperience may made them naïve about their chances of success and whose fledgling practices made them willing to take on almost any case. Yet they also attended law school soon after the civil rights laws were passed. Familiar with [the] structure of antidiscrimination law, influenced by the ideas of the rights movement, and willing to take risks, they wrote briefs and made arguments to judges that resulted in judicial opinions that helped establish cause of action for sexual harassment.[69]

Litigation involving LGBTQ plaintiffs started at the same time but would take longer to gain a foothold in the federal courts. The women's movement was larger and more developed, and the LGBTQ community faced stronger social, political, and legal marginalization. But Title VII inspired both women facing sexual harassment and LGBTQ individuals facing discrimination in the workplace to turn to the courts.

When women and their attorneys began to conceive of sexual harassment as a form of discrimination, Title VII was a logical and powerful legal avenue. However, it required theorizing and activism to convince judges and policymakers that sexual harassment was a prohibited form of employment discrimination. According to Abigail Saguy, "to win their case American feminists and lawyers have had to make a legal case in U.S. courtrooms that sexual harassment violates an existing statute. For strategic and intellectual reasons, they chose to build sexual harassment jurisprudence on Title VII."[70] Initially, federal courts did not accept this new interpretation of Title VII, but by the late 1970s, they began to embrace the approach, creating legal momentum. In 1986 the Supreme Court unanimously endorsed the notion that Title VII prohibits sexual harassment in the workplace in *Meritor Savings Bank v. Vinson.* The court did not engage in an extended analysis of legislative intent; it simply applied the new feminist interpretation of Title VII.[71] The Supreme Court also relied extensively on the EEOC's approach. Similar to the agency's later aggressive stance on gender identity and sexual orientation, "between 1977 and 1981," the EEOC under Eleanor Holmes Norton "took an active role in sexual harassment as a legal and policy issue."[72] The EEOC joined sexual harassment suits on an amicus basis, and in 1980 it issued important guidelines defining sexual harassment under Title VII. As chief justice William Rehnquist wrote for the unanimous court in *Meritor,* "Since the Guidelines were issued, courts have uniformly held, and we agree, that a plaintiff may establish a violation of Title VII by proving that discrimination based on sex has created a hostile or abusive work environment."[73] In 1998 another unanimous court applied this legal framework to same-sex sexual harassment in *Oncale*, this time under Antonin Scalia's pen, again refusing to invoke or apply a legislative intent analysis.

Thus, sexual harassment provides a remarkable parallel to the connection between Title VII and gender identity and sexual orientation. It was a judicially created policy in response to individuals who felt discriminated against, even though such an interpretation of Title VII had not been discussed or envisioned at the time of its enactment in 1964. The creation of sexual harassment policy demonstrates that policymaking in the United States does not always result from an explicit legislative process. Judicial and bureaucratic policymaking has been an integral part of civil rights in particular. Critics of this approach in the context of LGBTQ rights need to grapple with this reality and explain why this path is acceptable for some civil rights policy innovations but not others.

TITLE VII AND LGBTQ RIGHTS

The first LGBTQ rights cases connected to Title VII were decided in 1975. Over the course of several decades, federal judges would consistently rule against claims that Title VII offered protections based on gender identity or sexual orientation. They also consistently ruled that sex was biological and that Congress intended to protect only cisgender persons from employment discrimination. They took a very formalistic approach to the concept of sex discrimination, rejecting theories such as sex stereotyping. In contrast to its support for victims of sexual harassment, the EEOC was not an ally for LGBTQ claimants during this period and would not assist federal judges by engaging in leapfrogging. Thus, the 1989 decision in *Price Waterhouse* was a significant departure from established jurisprudence and provided the foundation for a reconceptualization of the applicability of Title VII to LGBTQ discrimination. In the fifteen years before *Price Waterhouse*, federal judges relied heavily on legislative intent and legislative history to exclude anything beyond this formalism. Judges took note of attempts to add sexual orientation to federal antidiscrimination law and used these failed efforts as further evidence of a lack of legislative intent to protect gender and sexual minorities. Some also viewed gender identity and sexual orientation as the same thing, often conflating the two.

Only a few judges challenged this consensus, but they pointed to future shifts in jurisprudence, especially on the issue of gender identity–based discrimination. Despite the reluctance and hostility of judges and bureaucrats, victims of gender identity– and sexual orientation–based discrimination and their private attorneys saw potential in Title VII, as LGBTQ activism grew in the 1970s. A broader understanding of "sex" triggered federal legal claims, but few of the cases discussed here were test cases brought by national or regional LGBTQ rights organizations. Lambda Legal was founded in 1973, but as a new organization, it had limited resources and reach. As Ellen Andersen describes the situation, "Litigators bringing gay rights cases worked in virtual isolation from each other, because mechanisms for communication and coordination were largely absent."[74] The ACLU's Lesbian and Gay Rights Project would not be established until 1985. Although local ACLU chapters supported various LGBTQ rights litigation from the 1950s through the 1970s, a nationally coordinated campaign came later. In fact, for a time, the national ACLU declined to support the LGBTQ rights movement.[75] For the most part, these cases involved local litigants and their attorneys who saw some promise in Title VII's language and general purpose; they also saw some connections to feminist legal strategies. As historian Katherine Turk notes, "attempts to analogize sexual orientation discrimination to sex discrimination borrowed some of feminists' most innovative legal strategies."[76] As demonstrated below, the litigation strategy for sexual minorities was somewhat more intentional, while the more marginalized movement for transgender rights led to a much more local and random approach to litigation.

Three 1975 cases set the stage for the pre–*Price Waterhouse* approach: *Smith v. Liberty Mutual Insurance, Voyles v. Ralph K. Davies Medical Center,* and *Grossman v. Bernards Township Board of Education.* In *Smith,* Bennie Smith applied to work in the mailroom of the Liberty Mutual office in Atlanta, but he was not hired because he was deemed to be effeminate. He sued, arguing that Title VII prohibited discrimination on the basis of sex. Interestingly, Smith did not identify as a gay man, but he expressed an interest in activities that were not considered masculine, including dancing and sewing.[77] Judge James Clinkscales Hill, a Nixon appointee, dismissed the suit on the grounds that Title VII did not offer protection on the basis of "sexual preference," and he saw no problem with employers making decisions based on gender stereotypes. The judge found that Liberty Mutual had appropriately "concluded that the plaintiff, a male, displayed characteristics inappropriate to his sex, the counterpart being a female applicant displaying masculine attributes."[78] Overall, Hill's opinion was a bit grandiose, citing the English monarchy during the American Revolution and the German Third Reich as regimes that were not sufficiently supportive of freedom, such as the freedom to discriminate in employment decisions. However, his holding was not grandiose, as it was based on only a cursory finding of a lack of legislative intent for Title VII to challenge gender norms. On appeal, the Fifth Circuit upheld the decision in 1978.[79]

Both *Smith* courts relied on *Willingham v. Macon Telegraph Publishing*, a Fifth Circuit decision from 1974 involving a plaintiff who had not been hired as a layout artist due to the length of his hair. In the wake of a large local music festival, the *Macon Telegraph* did not want to lose advertising revenue by being linked to "counter-culture types."[80] After an initial loss, Willingham won on appeal, but that decision was eventually overturned by the Fifth Circuit sitting en banc. Remarkably, the first appellate panel offered an expansive interpretation of Title VII in the context of gender norms, one that anticipated the more dynamic approach of *Price Waterhouse*. It ruled that an employer's dress and grooming code that differentiated on the basis of sex violated the law: "Such a code treats applicants differently because of a sex stereotype: only males are prohibited from wearing their hair long."[81] However, the full panel nullified this approach and applied a narrow, legislative intent–based approach: "We perceive the intent of Congress to have been the guarantee of equal job opportunity for males and females. . . . [A] hiring policy that distinguishes on some other ground, such as grooming codes or length of hair, is related more closely to the employer's choice of how to run his business than to equality of employment opportunity."[82] Federal courts would continue to struggle with the issue of dress codes for decades, but the dominant early approach was to allow employers to enforce gender norms in the workplace through these codes. Furthermore, this approach was used to prevent any attempts by LGBTQ individuals to rely on Title VII for protection when they were fired or not hired.

The EEOC also relied on *Willingham* when it ruled in 1975 and 1976 that sexual orientation was not covered by Title VII. This was consistent with a 1974 ruling that gender identity was not covered by Title VII (discussed later). As early as 1966, a nonbinding general counsel opinion concerning sexual orientation–based discrimination was issued taking the same stance. Also invoking legislative intent and narrow textualism, the EEOC found that employment decisions based on "sexual practices" did not violate Title VII.[83] Indeed, it embraced gender essentialism in declaring, "The Commission is of the opinion that when Congress used the word 'sex' in Title VII it was referring to a person's gender, an immutable characteristic with which a person is born."[84] Thus, the courts and the bureaucracy were united on this question, and in fact, the Fifth Circuit's *Smith* opinion cited the EEOC decisions.[85] It was a closed legal loop.

Transgender plaintiffs did not fare any better in the 1970s, despite a closer potential connection to the text through the word "sex." In *Voyles v. Ralph K. Davies Medical Center*, hemodialysis technician Carol Lynn Voyles informed her employer that she planned to undergo gender affirmation surgery. She was fired because the medical center feared that coworkers and patients would not approve and that the transition would have a "potentially adverse effect" on them.[86] Judge Spencer Williams, a Nixon appointee, adopted the dominant legislative intent approach in finding that Title VII did not apply across the board to LGBTQ plaintiffs. As he stated, "Situations involving transsexuals, homosexuals, or bi-sexuals were simply not considered [by Congress], and from the void the Court is not permitted to fashion its own judicial interpretation."[87] Williams also noted that Congresswoman Abzug's proposed bill would not apply to transgender discrimination. He was arguing that even as Congress was starting to address discrimination on the basis of sexual orientation, it was rejecting protections on the basis of gender identity, despite the presence of the word "sex" in the statute. Hence, according to Williams, only Congress could expand civil rights protections, not the federal courts.

Paula Grossman was the first transgender person to use Title VII to challenge a dismissal after she was fired in 1972 from her teaching job in Bernards Township, New Jersey, for transitioning during the 1971–1972 school year. The commissioner of education and the state board of education affirmed the decision of the local school board, which was affirmed by a New Jersey appellate court.[88] Grossman had worked as a teacher in the district since 1957. The school board cited her "deviant" behavior and "abnormality," in addition to "conduct unbecoming a teacher."[89] In defense of the teacher's dismissal, the commissioner stated that "Grossman knowingly and voluntarily underwent a sex-reassignment from male to female. By doing so, he [*sic*] underwent a fundamental and complete change in his [*sic*] role and identification to society, thereby rendering himself [*sic*] incapable to teach . . . because of the potential her (Grossman's) presence in the classroom presented for psychological harm to the students of Bernards Township." This statement reflects the profound societal and official stigma attached to transgender individuals in the 1970s. Grossman's legal action also resulted in the first EEOC statement on Title VII and gender identity in 1974, as noted earlier. The agency took the same approach it had taken in the sexual orientation cases, asserting a lack of legislative intent to extend the statute beyond binary genders. Relying on this ruling, judge George Barlow, a Nixon appointee, declared: "In the absence of any legislative history indicating a congressional intent to include transsexuals within the language of Title VII, the Court is reluctant [to] ascribe any import to the term 'sex' other than its plain meaning."[90]

These early losses did not stop LGBTQ litigants. However, neither the EEOC nor the federal judiciary were open to their arguments, with some notable exceptions in dissenting and overturned opinions that began to chart a new path forward. As Andersen notes, there was limited media coverage of these cases and little coordination among attorneys. By the 1980s, the futility of this litigation was apparent as the decisions piled up (and cited one another) and as national organizations' litigation efforts became more sophisticated. More jurisprudential support existed for sodomy law challenges and family law cases. The AIDS crisis also sidelined federal legal and political efforts aimed at fighting discrimination.[91]

The Ninth Circuit Court of Appeals issued the first appellate opinion on Title VII protection based on gender identity in 1977 in *Holloway v. Arthur Andersen & Co.* Reflecting the dominant approach outlined in the cases cited earlier, the majority (in a 2-to-1 decision) asserted that "this court will not expand Title VII's application in the absence of Congressional mandate." The majority also dismissed the idea of interpreting "sex" as anything more than biological and binary, noting in a footnote that Ramona Holloway was terminated not because of her transition but because her feminine appearance was disruptive. Other footnotes addressed attempts to add sexual orientation to the Civil Rights Act and cited *Smith, Voyles,* and *Grossman.*[92] The most notable element of the case was the dissent by judge Alfred Goodwin, a Nixon appointee, who imagined a different legal avenue from the well-worn path taken by his colleagues and other judges of the era. It was an all-Republican panel consisting of Goodwin, Leland Nielsen (also a Nixon appointee), and J. Blaine Anderson (a Ford appointee). Unusual for a judge in these cases, Goodwin made a distinction between discrimination on the basis of sexual orientation and discrimination on the basis of gender identity, or as he called it, "sexual identity." He also rejected a dependence on the legislative history or legislative intent approach, arguing that the discrimination at issue was a form of sex discrimination covered by the text. Goodwin accepted that individuals may transition from their sex assigned at birth, and he described Ramona Holloway and her transition with a compassion and understanding that were lacking in most legal analyses of the time. As he argued, "This is a case of a person completing surgically that part of nature's handiwork which apparently was left incomplete somewhere along the line."[93]

Judge John Grady, a Ford appointee, echoed this approach in *Ulane v. Eastern Airlines,* but his decision was overturned by the Seventh Circuit in perhaps the most powerful and consequential pre–*Price Waterhouse* gender identity ruling. It became the federal gold standard until 2000. In departing from the dominant legal consensus enshrined by the Seventh Circuit, Grady declared: "I was unimpressed by the reasoning of the majority of the Court in *Holloway* . . . , and was very comfortable with the analysis of Judge Goodwin, who dissented in that case." Grady, like Goodwin, distinguished sexual orientation and gender identity, rejected a legislative intent approach, and embraced a dynamic textualism, asserting that "the discharge need only have some causal connection to a sexual consideration in order to be prohibited by statute."[94] Moving beyond the gender binary, he argued that "sex is not a cut-and-dried matter of chromosomes."[95] In doing so, he ruled against Eastern Airlines and its decision to fire pilot Karen Ulane for transitioning, finding that all the reasons presented by the airline were pretextual. For instance, Eastern had argued that Ulane imposed a safety risk and would be a distraction for other pilots and staff.

A unanimous panel of the Seventh Circuit overruled this approach, asserting that Congress did not intend such protection and that if it desired to expand the law's meaning, it could have amended the statute. Further, the appellate court erased Ulane's gender identity through the prism of biological essentialism: "It is clear from the evidence that if Eastern did discriminate against Ulane, it was not because she is female, but because Ulane is a transsexual—a biological male who takes female hormones, cross-dresses, and has surgically altered parts of her body to make it appear female."[96] This is more akin to the "deviant" understanding of transgender people espoused by the school board in *Grossman* than the sympathetic approach taken by Judges Goodwin and Grady. At least the *Ulane* court used the correct pronouns—"she" and "her"—but it was legally obliged to do so, as Illinois had allowed Ulane to amend her birth certificate to reflect her gender identity. However, this state recognition was not enough to offer federal legal protection. Two of the judges on the panel, Edward Dumbauld and Walter Cummings, were Democratic appointees (Kennedy and Johnson, respectively), and the third, Harlington Wood Jr., was elevated to the Seventh Circuit by Ford after initially being appointed a federal district judge by Nixon. The dominant approach thus transcended partisan appointment dynamics in the pre–*Price Waterhouse* era.

Although this book is not a judicial biography, it is useful to note the background of judges who departed from the dominant approaches of their eras in ways that supported LGBTQ rights. Like Judge Bazelon, Judge Grady was a legal innovator and was not constrained by the reasoning of other judges, even those who sat above him. As a former law clerk noted, "He was completely unafraid of whether a higher court might disagree with him. He used to say of court decisions: 'That's why they call them opinions.'" He had been inspired to become an attorney after reading Irving Stone's biography of Clarence Darrow.[97] Only a few years before the *Ulane* litigation, Grady had ruled against the constitutionality of the Hyde Amendment, a law limiting federal funding of abortion, and a similar Illinois law.[98] Though appointed by Ford, Grady appeared to be a judge in the mold of Supreme Court justice John Paul Stevens, a fellow Ford appointee who was widely considered to be one of the court's liberals. In the 1970s, before partisan and ideological polarization, liberal Republicans existed. This was before the conservative legal movement began to enforce ideological discipline on federal court nominees during the Reagan administration in the 1980s.[99]

Legislative intent and biological essentialism dominated the analysis in *Sommers v. Budget Marketing* (1982), a case in which the Eight Circuit unanimously ruled against the Title VII claim of Audra Sommers, who had been fired "because she misrepresented herself as an anatomical female when she applied for the job." The Eight Circuit did not embrace the dynamic interpretation of Title VII presented by Sommers; instead, the court focused on "the privacy interests of . . . female employees" and restroom access for Sommers. The panel comprised two Nixon appointees and one Johnson appointee.[100]

DeSantis v. Pacific Telephone & Telegraph Company, decided by the Ninth Circuit in 1979, represented an appellate court's definitive rejection of the claim that Title VII protections extend to sexual orientation and gender nonconformity. California was a leading center of LGBTQ activism, especially as it related to employment discrimination, and *DeSantis* was a consolidated appeal of three lawsuits brought under Title VII. Two of the lawsuits pitted the Pacific Telephone & Telegraph Company (PT&T) against a group of gay men and a lesbian couple, and the third case involved a male preschool teacher who had been fired for wearing an earring. The decision to bring litigation against PT&T was partly the result of its notorious homophobia. It identified perceived lesbian or gay job applicants with the label "Code 48—Homosexual," rejecting them for fear of negative reactions from customers.[101] At the time, PT&T was the largest employer in California, offering activists a significant and obviously homophobic target. San Francisco's Society for Individual Rights (SIR) first encountered the company's discriminatory practices when PT&T rejected SIR's Yellow Pages ad in 1968. The ad read in part, "HOMO-SEXUALS—Know and protect your rights."[102] Legal successes on behalf of racial minorities and women under the Constitution and Title VII inspired the eventual litigation, which was designed as a test case after political efforts to enact legal protections against discrimination on the basis of sexual orientation stalled. For instance, the attorneys in *DeSantis* invoked "disparate impact," a doctrine created in the context of race-based discrimination in *Griggs v. Duke Power Company* (1971) to refer to discrimination that was not necessarily intentional or explicit but had the effect of perpetuating discrimination.[103] Though not yet nationally coordinated, the *DeSantis* litigation was part of activists' efforts in the 1970s to outlaw employment discrimination. Most of this activism occurred outside the courts, but this litigation was a local, coordinated strategy. As Turk notes, "Advocates began to organize state and federal lawsuits against PT&T to test the legitimacy of workplace equality laws that excluded sexual orientation."[104]

In the third case, teacher Donald Strailey framed his initial complaint with the EEOC as both gender- and sexual orientation–based discrimination, but he dropped the latter claim in federal court. However, as Turk states, "Federal judges presumed his homosexuality, comingling male effeminacy and homosexuality while emphasizing their distinctiveness." Turk also notes that Strailey was part of a group of men who challenged the gendered workplace and turned to the law for protection:

> As working women mobilized around Title VII, a small cohort of men like Donald Strailey tested the boundaries of protected gender and sexual diversity at work. . . . Arguing that new sex equality laws should reshape their working lives as well, men like Strailey challenged the legal and cultural barriers, rooted in gender stereotypes, that rendered feminized work "queer work" for men and prevented them from equal participation in the same pink-collar jobs women were fighting to transform or escape.[105]

Thus, in the minds of LGBTQ individuals and their attorneys, Title VII provided substantial and dynamic protection in the workplace and could be used in the process of social transformation.

The hopes of these litigants and activists ran into the reality of 1970s jurisprudence on LGBTQ rights, as reflected in the Ninth Circuit's *DeSantis* decision. The court found no reason to depart from its approach in *Holloway* and made it clear that sexual minorities had neither federal statutory nor constitutional protection. As judge Herbert Choy, a Nixon appointee, wrote: "We conclude that Title VII's prohibition of 'sex' discrimination applies only to discrimination on the basis of gender and should not be judicially extended to include sexual preference such as homosexuality."[106] He found that the plaintiffs in the case were attempting to bootstrap sexual orientation–based protections onto Title VII, and he deemed Strailey's sex stereotyping claim to be the equivalent of a sexual orientation–based claim. Judge Joseph Sneed, a Nixon appointee, would have allowed the disparate impact argument to proceed because it was possible that there were more gay men than lesbians, resulting in discrimination against men; however, he agreed with the other two judges (the third was Dudley Bonsall, a Kennedy appointee) on the panel that sexual minorities lacked protection under federal statutory or constitutional law, relying on the Supreme Court's 1976 affirmance of a lower court opinion that rejected constitutional challenges to Virginia's sodomy law in *Doe v. Commonwealth's Attorney*. Thus, while some judges in this era could conceive of protections for transgender plaintiffs, none thought that Title VII covered discrimination against sexual minorities.

After decades of government-led oppression, the 1970s were a time of remarkable civil rights activism for a variety of marginalized groups, and the emerging LGBTQ rights movement tapped into this dynamic. In particular, legal and political developments related to sex and gender, such as the enactment of Title VII and passage of the ERA, inspired activism and litigation. However, judges did not see the connections between legal innovations on behalf of racial minorities and cisgender women and those on behalf of LGBTQ individuals. As Chai Feldblum notes in the context of transgender plaintiffs, "By the time transgender individuals started bringing cases under Title VII, . . . two myths were well entrenched: (1) that there was little legislative history regarding the sex discrimination provision and (2) the Congress' sole intent had been to ensure that men and women were not classified differently."[107] These narratives would ultimately be rejected as federal courts and the EEOC created sexual harassment law and interpreted Title VII more dynamically in *Price Waterhouse* and *Oncale*, but they were entrenched for several decades and proved difficult to dislodge, first in the context of gender identity and then in the context of sexual orientation. *Price Waterhouse* and *Oncale* were crucial elements in shifting the legal narrative and dislodging federal judges' interpretative approaches to Title VII in the 1970s.

3. *Price Waterhouse v. Hopkins* and the Shift in Title VII Interpretation

With sexual harassment law, activists, bureaucrats, and judges interpreted Title VII to cover types of discrimination not envisioned or discussed by the legislators who enacted the provision. In 1986 the Supreme Court confirmed this trend in *Meritor Savings Bank v. Vinson*. Three years later, the expansion of Title VII interpretation continued when the Supreme Court held in *Price Waterhouse v. Hopkins* that sex stereotyping related to employment decisions and status is prohibited. This chapter examines the background and dynamics of *Price Waterhouse* and demonstrates how that case was a significant turning point in the interpretation of Title VII. As Susan Gluck Mezey notes, the case "transformed the judiciary's rigid formulation of sex as a binary category and incorporated the concept of discrimination on the basis of gender into discrimination on the basis of sex."[1]

The story of *Price Waterhouse* has been told in several places. Here, the focus is on legal tactics and arguments and the implications of such a significant shift in statutory interpretation. Scholars have extensively debated how powerful a precedent *Price Waterhouse* is or should be, but my primary interest is how it provided a plausible and powerful foundation for LGBTQ litigants and their lawyers. The lawsuit was not designed to fundamentally change the interpretation of Title VII. Ann Hopkins had been denied a partnership, she was angry, so she sued. Her lawyer developed the theory of sex stereotyping early in the litigation, and through his connections in the Washington, DC, legal community and happenstance, he found a crucial witness to prove the theory—yet another "accident" in the life of this case. This theory was affirmed by all three levels of the federal courts and would live on through the *Price Waterhouse* precedent, affecting areas of the law unanticipated by those involved in the litigation.

Less than a decade later, the Supreme Court used *Price Waterhouse* to find that same-sex sexual harassment is prohibited by Title VII. The decision in *Oncale v. Sundowner Offshore Services* (1998) was the product of two streams of Title VII jurisprudence: sexual harassment law and the expanded understanding of gender under *Price Waterhouse*. As discussed in chapter 1, *Oncale* is notable for the approach to statutory interpretation taken by justice

Antonin Scalia in leading the unanimous Supreme Court to its conclusion—
an outcome that would have been inconceivable to those who enacted Title
VII. This chapter discusses how these two cases made it plausible to claim that
Title VII prohibits discrimination on the basis of gender identity and sexual
orientation.

ANN HOPKINS BRINGS A LAWSUIT

Ann Hopkins did not consider herself a feminist, and it did not initially occur
to her that Price Waterhouse had failed to promote her to partner because of
her gender. Her family emphasized traditional gender norms, and she was well
versed in etiquette, but she also rode a Yamaha motorcycle and was fiercely independent and personally forceful. Hopkins attended a women's college and
was proud of this fact, chafing at the notion that it was a "finishing school."
As she notes in her autobiography, "I learned to depend on myself and on the
analytical integrity of an answer to a question or a solution to a problem before I was taught to depend on or defer to members of the opposite sex or their
point of view." She eventually married a man she met at work and had three
children. She was a person of relative economic privilege, but she was not
privileged enough to avoid the oppression of traditional notions of feminine
behavior in the workplace.[2]

Hopkins began her career at IBM, where she helped build NASA computer
systems. She started working at Price Waterhouse in 1978 and eventually became a senior manager. She was assigned to the firm's Office of Government
Services (OGS), which generated and carried out consulting contracts with the
government, and she was instrumental in obtaining a significant contract with
the State Department. When Hopkins applied for partnership in 1982, she had
generated more revenue than any of the other applicants that year. As Gillian
Thomas notes, "Hopkins had generated more business and billed more hours
than any of the other eighty-seven candidates—all of them men."[3] However,
her application was held over until the following year. This was not unusual,
and many holdovers eventually received partnerships, but by 1983, Hopkins
had lost the support of the OGS, dooming her chances. She eventually left
Price Waterhouse in 1984. She had wanted to quit earlier, but her attorney advised her to stay to bolster a claim of constructive discharge, which could potentially lead to reinstatement and higher monetary damages.[4] A constructive

discharge occurs when a person leaves a job due to intolerable circumstances, such as harassment. In other words, the employee is essentially forced out because of the employer's discrimination.

At Price Waterhouse, each senior manager applying for partnership underwent a months-long review process in which feedback was solicited from other employees with knowledge of the candidate's performance. The process was quite subjective, particularly in terms of the evaluation of interpersonal skills. All 662 partners (only seven of whom were women) were invited to submit candidate evaluations: long forms if they had been exposed to the candidate for more than one hundred hours, and short forms if they had less knowledge of the candidate. These evaluations were filtered through the Admissions Committee, which recommended promotion, denial, or holdover to the Policy Board. Of the thirty-two partners who submitted an evaluation of Hopkins, a majority of the votes were not outright positive recommendations: eight voted no, three voted to hold her application until next year, and eight made no recommendation because of a lack of knowledge. Many of the negative votes came from short forms. Hopkins likened another part of the process to a beauty pageant, as applicants engaged in significant socializing at the firm's regional office, where they hobnobbed with partners in the hope of gaining their votes.[5]

Hopkins was angry and confused by her failed application. She knew she had been wronged but was not sure why. As she stated, "This was bullshit. Misery turned to rage."[6] She asked an attorney friend to recommend a lawyer, and she discovered Doug Huron. Then in private practice, Huron had worked in the Civil Rights Division of the Justice Department and in the White House counsel's office under Jimmy Carter.[7] He would eventually file a complaint on Hopkins's behalf with the Equal Employment Opportunity Commission (EEOC) and in federal court, citing Title VII as grounds, but he also filed in DC superior court under the district's antidiscrimination law. At the time, it was not clear whether Title VII could be used in suits involving the denial of partnership, and a case addressing that question was pending before the Supreme Court. That decision, *Hishon v. King & Spaulding* (1984), settled the issue in favor of Title VII's applicability to partnership-based challenges.[8] In her lawsuit, Hopkins asked to be reinstated and made a partner retroactively, with back pay. Initially, she had no intention of changing the interpretation of Title VII. She just wanted to be a partner at Price Waterhouse, and the lawsuit was a way to achieve that goal. According to Cynthia Estlund, "the idea that her gender might have played a role in the partnership decision—indeed in her career at Price Waterhouse—seemed to come utterly out of the blue to Hopkins."[9]

As the lawsuit unfolded, it became clear to Huron that a pattern of sexist attitudes pervaded the review process at Price Waterhouse. It appeared that some sort of discrimination had occurred, given Hopkins's track record and the fact that she had been the only woman up for partner in 1982, but the theory of a Title VII claim evolved during the discovery process. There was no "smoking gun" evidence but something "more subtle," Huron informed Hopkins. Meanwhile, Huron joined a new law firm and brought another attorney, Jim Heller, on board. As Hopkins described Huron's emerging approach: "He did not use the word stereotyping at the time, but he toyed with the idea that perhaps no one person or situation had been decisive in my being rejected. Instead, he hypothesized, the entire selection process had permitted me to be evaluated in terms of how I compared to the conventional image of a woman, rather than how I met the requirements of a manager."[10] In pursuit of this theory, Huron contacted Donna Lenhoff, an attorney for the Women's Legal Defense Fund. Eventually, he was put in touch with a psychology professor at Carnegie Mellon University, Dr. Susan Fiske.[11] The use of Dr. Fiske and her understanding of sex stereotyping would prove to be essential in getting the judges to accept Huron's theory of the case. According to Estlund, "This turned out to be an inspired decision, but it was one that was far from obvious at the time. Such testimony had never been presented in a sex discrimination case."[12] Huron's access to feminist legal networks enriched the litigation, especially given that multiple Price Waterhouse employees made statements to the effect that Ann Hopkins had a difficult personality. For instance, one coworker submitted this comment during the partner review process: "I found her to be (a) singularly dedicated, (b) rather unpleasant. Ann needs a chance to demonstrate people skills. She has a lot going for her but she's just plain rough on people."[13] This would be Price Waterhouse's defense—that Hopkins lacked the social skills to be a partner and that gender had nothing to do with its decision.

However, another body of evidence showed that gender had been a factor, and this evidence proved decisive. After her partnership application was put on hold, Hopkins was told by her mentor Tom Beyer that she needed to "walk more femininely, talk more femininely, dress more femininely, wear make-up, have your hair styled, and wear jewelry." Remarkably, he admitted making that statement both in a deposition and during the trial. Other advice included that Hopkins go to "charm school" and that her swearing was more noticeable and concerning "because it's a lady using foul language." Others commented that she was too "macho" and "masculine" and that she was a "women's libber." The record also reflected that sexist comments had been made about other women denied partnership.[14] Conversely, men with difficult personalities had been promoted to partner. Judges would ultimately view this as clear evidence of discrimination, even if it was unintentional or structural discrimination.

THE TRIAL

The trial lasted for five days. Hopkins's lawyers provided a powerful foundation to support their theory of discrimination, but they also had a receptive audience. In landing judge Gerhard Gesell, they increased their chances of obtaining a potentially law-changing decision, and "Judge Gesell's appreciation of the potentially precedent-setting nature of the case was evident throughout [the trial]."[15] Gesell, appointed to the bench by president Lyndon Johnson in 1967, "was known as a staunch liberal, a strong civil rights jurist and a judge who exerted an imposing command over his courtroom."[16] Four years before *Roe v. Wade*, he ruled that DC's abortion ban was constitutionally invalid. He also played a role in an early challenge to the military's ban on LGB service members. Though critical of the ban, he initially upheld Leonard Matlovich's dismissal from the US Air Force in 1976 but later ordered him reinstated after Matlovich's victory in the court of appeals. As Gesell stated in his 1976 decision: "In the light of increasing public awareness and the more open acceptance of what is in many respects essentially a matter of private sexual conduct, it would appear that the Armed Forces might well be advised to move toward a more discriminatory and informed approach to these problems, as has the Civil Service Commission in its treatment of homosexuality within the civilian sector of Government employment." He noted that the military was an innovator in the context of racial discrimination and held that it was "desirable for the military to reexamine the homosexual problem, to approach it in perhaps a more sensitive and precise way."[17] He felt constrained by judicial deference to military decision making and the lack of supportive federal jurisprudence on LGB rights, but he was sympathetic to Matlovich's plight and the emerging LGB rights movement.

Judge Gesell also realized that the stakes were high in the *Hopkins* case because of its potential to change the interpretation of Title VII. He was not opposed to doing so, but he wanted to be careful and thorough about it. As he declared during the trial: "I can't look at this case as just a case. I've got to think of whatever standard or whatever rule or whatever result I get."[18]

Dr. Fiske and the social science literature on which her testimony was based strongly influenced Judge Gesell. She noted that the lack of women at high levels of management at Price Waterhouse exacerbated sex stereotyping by making the presence of a woman in a leadership role "extremely salient." She also testified that the more subjective elements of the partner-nominee review process, especially those focusing on personality and reputation, allowed such stereotyping. She described gender-based stereotypes and testified that women who violate the stereotypes are punished by negative comments and evaluations. "The overall stereotype for feminine behavior is to be socially concerned and understanding, soft and tender, and the overall stereotype for a man . . . is that they will be competitive, ambitious, aggressive, independent, and active." She observed that women face a "double bind" in the workplace because of these stereotypes. Masculine stereotypes are valued in the workplace, but women are punished for reflecting those same attributes. Justice William Brennan referenced a similar bind in his opinion when the case reached the Supreme Court.[19]

In his decision, Gesell relied on gender-based stereotyping to find that Price Waterhouse had violated Title VII by refusing to make Ann Hopkins a partner. He stated:

> That deep within males and females there exist sexually based reactions to the personal characteristics of one of the opposite sex surely comes as no surprise. It is well documented that men evaluating women in managerial occupations sometimes apply stereotypes which discriminate against women. Indeed, the subtle and unconscious discrimination created by sex stereotyping appears to be a major impediment to Title VII's goal of ensuring equal employment opportunities. . . . One common form of stereotyping is that women engaged in assertive behavior are judged more critically because aggressive conduct is viewed as a masculine characteristic.[20]

Gesell's approach to Title VII relied on the purpose of the statute rather than the intent of its creators, as evidenced by the term "goal." His interpretation of the statute was also dynamic; he was willing to take an expansive view of the law rather than applying a formalistic interpretation that one could violate the law only by intentionally and obviously using sex as an employment factor. He admitted that much of what occurred at Price Waterhouse was unconscious, but he also noted that "maintenance of a system that gave weight to such biased criticisms was a conscious act of the partnership as a whole."[21] In this sense, then, the discrimination was also structural, a result of deeply embedded and biased cultural norms. Gesell found that Price Waterhouse had an obligation under Title VII to keep stereotyped bias out of its evaluation process. He stated, "Price Waterhouse's failure to take the steps necessary to alert partners to the possibility that their judgments may be biased, to discourage stereotyping, and to investigate and discard, where appropriate, comments that suggest a double standard constitutes a violation of Title VII in this instance."[22] Gesell awarded Hopkins a few months back pay (not full compensation since her resignation) and ordered Price Waterhouse to pay her attorneys' fees. He ruled that Hopkins had not demonstrated that her departure from the firm was a case of constructive discharge. But on the larger question of the connection between sex stereotyping and Title VII, Gesell's decision was remarkably innovative.

Gesell was not acting without any intellectual support for these legal innovations. Like the argument about sex discrimination and same-sex marriage in the *Baehr v. Lewin* decision (discussed in chapter 2), the idea was in the legal ether. Gesell cited a 1980 law review article by law professor Nadine Taub that explored the harms inflicted on women by sex stereotyping and argued that sex stereotyping should be prohibited by Title VII. Taub was concerned that Title VII had done little to end the sex-segregated workplace, and she saw a more expansive interpretation of Title VII as a way to address the problem. She tied her arguments to the emerging legal thinking about sexual harassment under Title VII and cited the social science literature confirming the presence of sex stereotyping in the workplace, the same literature Dr. Fiske relied on and Judge Gesell cited in his opinion. Taub noted that this form of discrimination is often unconscious and is more common in workplaces with few women. Finally, the article emphasized the need for expansive employer liability, and on this point, Gesell cited the article directly. Taub's article thus served as a blueprint for Gesell's decision.[23]

VICTORY IN THE APPELLATE COURT

Both sides appealed the split decision. The loss on the constructive discharge issue undermined Hopkins's reason for bringing the lawsuit—reinstatement to the firm—so she appealed that part of the decision. Price Waterhouse appealed the finding that it had violated Title VII in denying Hopkins partnership. There was no such split in the DC Court of Appeals, however. Gesell's decision was affirmed and expanded.

The panel that heard Hopkins's appeal was ideologically divided, with two liberals and one conservative, and this division was reflected in the opinion. Stephen Williams had been appointed to the court by Republican Ronald Reagan in 1986, and Harry Edwards had been appointed by Democrat Jimmy Carter in 1978. The third member of the panel, federal district court judge Joyce Green (appointed by Carter in 1979), was sitting on the appellate case by designation. Edwards and Green sided with Hopkins, while Williams dissented. Consistent with this ideological division, the oral argument appeared to go well for Hopkins. When the attorney for Price Waterhouse argued that the seemingly discriminatory comments in the record were, in fact, neutral, Judge Edwards noted that the court could not make a new factual finding, nor could it make a fresh ruling on liability under Title VII. Judge Green appeared to be skeptical of the argument that Tom Beyer had been speaking only for himself and as a friend when he advised Hopkins to be more feminine.[24]

This dynamic played out in the decision. Judge Green wrote for the majority: "There is ample support in the record for the District Court's finding that the partnership selection process at Price Waterhouse was impermissibly infected by stereotypical attitudes towards female candidates."[25] The majority fully accepted the sex-stereotyping interpretation of Title VII. In particular, the majority held that this type of discrimination need not be intentional and purposeful, noting that "unwitting or ingrained bias is no less injurious or worth[y] of eradication than blatant or calculated discrimination."[26] The decision differed from Gesell's in that the majority held that Hopkins had in fact been constructively discharged, thereby providing a path toward reinstatement and greater monetary damages. As the majority stated, "Price Waterhouse's decision to deny Hopkins partnership status . . . coupled with the OGS's failure to renominate her, would have been viewed by any reasonable senior manager in her position as a career-ending discharge."[27] Unlike the split decision in district court, this was a total victory for Hopkins.

Given that this was a "mixed-motives" case—that is, there was evidence of both legitimate and illegitimate reasons for Hopkins's termination—part of the legal analysis involved the parties' burden of proof. In dispute was the employer's burden to demonstrate that illegitimate reasons for termination were not in play or that it would have made the same decision in the absence of discrimination. Judge Green wrote that the proper standard was to shift the burden to accused employers, requiring them to provide "clear and convincing evidence" that they would have made the same decision in the absence of discrimination, once it was established that prohibited discrimination had been part of the process. As Green explained, keeping the burden on the plaintiff would be too onerous for victims of discrimination and would undermine the purpose of Title VII, making it very difficult for plaintiffs to succeed in a mixed-motives case.[28] This would be the main focus of the litigation once the case reached the Supreme Court.

In dissent, Judge Williams struck at the heart of his colleagues' and Gesell's interpretation of Title VII, describing sex stereotyping as "a novel theory of liability under Title VII" based on an "imaginative" interpretation of the evidence in the case.[29] He objected to the idea that employers have an obligation to prevent sex stereotyping. He thought all the sexist remarks, especially the charm school comment, were "wispy" and "ambiguous."[30] He asserted that Beyer had been speaking only for himself and that his comments were merely "speculations" about how Hopkins ought to change her gender presentation.[31] He rejected Dr. Fiske as biased, calling her "a witness purporting to be an expert."[32] He was also concerned that the majority was inappropriately moving away from the demonstration of intentionality toward an approach that would require employers to be thought police: "The rule turns Title VII from a prohibition of discriminatory conduct into an engine for rooting out sexist thoughts."[33] Critics of sexual harassment doctrine frequently make this argument.[34] In the end, however, Williams's objection to the majority's approach was grounded in a desire to enforce the gender binary and to restrict the interpretation of "sex" in Title VII to one based on legislative intent. "No one argues that Congress intended entirely to overturn Justice Douglas's observation that 'the two sexes are not fungible.' Dismissal of a male employee because he routinely appeared for work in skirts and dresses would surely reflect a form of sex stereotyping, but it would not, merely on that account, support Title VII liability."[35] For Williams, stereotyping was a useful enforcer of strict gender roles and was certainly not legally prohibited. This formalist-intentionalist approach remains quite powerful in contemporary attempts to limit the applicability of Title VII, but it was ultimately rejected in this case.

The appeals court endorsed Huron's legal theory and the dynamic interpretative approach tied to an evolving sexual harassment jurisprudence. Remarkably, as the case moved to the Supreme Court, this issue faded into the background, eclipsed by arguments over burden of proof. As a result, the sex-stereotyping element of the case became muddled, and activists and scholars maintained for decades that only a plurality of the Supreme Court endorsed this theory, that *Price Waterhouse* is not actually a precedent on this question, or that it does not apply to circumstances beyond those faced by Ann Hopkins: a gendered workplace that values societally defined masculine traits but punishes women for exhibiting those same traits. That debate is explored more fully below, but it is worth noting that the dynamic approach reflected in the district court and appellate court decisions was not directly challenged. For instance, Judge Williams's dissent was not taken up as a cause célèbre by the Supreme Court's conservatives, even though it contained many elements of conservative arguments against an expansive interpretation of Title VII. In the long run, the discussion of sex stereotyping in the case was more legally durable and had profound consequences for LGBTQ rights litigation.

THE SUPREME COURT DECISION

Price Waterhouse appealed the appellate decision, but Hopkins's lawyers doubted the Supreme Court would take the case, which they assumed was too narrow. Their thinking was that "the legal issues were technicalities, unlikely to be important enough to warrant review by the highest court in the land."[36] Because this had been a traditional lawsuit designed to get Hopkins her job back and monetary damages, not a test case, there had been no legal incentive to create a transformational precedent. Also, given that Hopkins had won a significant victory in the appellate court, her lawyers were likely hoping that this would be the last major decision in the case. An appeal would only create more uncertainty. Hopkins, too, wanted the litigation to be over, but she kept this sentiment from her attorneys. She later called the Supreme Court's decision to hear the case "one of the worst days of my life." As Thomas notes, "She was eager to get on with her life."[37] However, the lower courts were divided on the issue, and a split in the circuits is often a reason for the justices to take a case. The Supreme Court thus granted the appeal—another accidental aspect of *Price Waterhouse.*

The briefs and oral arguments were dominated by the issue of burden of proof. Notable exceptions were briefs by the American Psychological Association (APA) and another on behalf of prominent women's rights organizations led by the National Organization for Women (NOW). Once certiorari was granted, it became clear that this case would involve more than a technical legal issue for Hopkins's attorneys and feminist activists. In particular, bolstering sex-stereotyping theory and neutralizing Judge Williams's dissent became a focus of amicus briefs submitted to the Supreme Court. Price Waterhouse based its appeal on Williams's dissent, as vividly described by Thomas: "When not quoting him directly, it echoed his sarcasm, such as describing Fiske's conclusions as 'intuitive hunches' and consistently using quotation marks around 'sex stereotyping' as if it were an idiosyncratic concept of Fiske's own invention."[38] The brief from the women's rights organizations was coauthored by Huron's colleague Donna Lenhoff at the Women's Legal Defense Fund, and Nadine Taub was one of its sponsors.[39] Thus, at this stage, the litigation had a strong connection to the women's rights movement, which had a vested interest in a more expansive interpretation of Title VII.

The NOW brief supported the DC Circuit's ruling on burden of proof—requiring "clear and convincing evidence" that Price Waterhouse would have denied Hopkins's promotion based solely on a neutral evaluation process. It also strongly supported Dr. Fiske's testimony and the social science on which it was based. More notably, the brief provided jurisprudential support for the connection between sex stereotyping and the interpretation of Title VII, stating, "To end employers' reliance on outmoded sex stereotypes of the sort present in this case was a primary congressional purpose in enacting Title VII." Interestingly, the brief used the word "purpose" rather than "intent." It then cited Supreme Court and circuit court precedents about sex stereotyping based on "traditional assumptions," referencing *City of Los Angeles Department of Water and Power v. Manhart* (1978). The brief also noted that gender-based stereotyping was present in sexual harassment cases. Emphasizing a broad understanding of the purpose of Title VII and its interpretation over time, the brief declared: "Assumptions based on the sex of the individual constitute intentional discrimination in its classic form. It is true regardless of the precise nature of the sex-based assumptions, which have taken many forms, as the cases demonstrate. Title VII forbids employment decisions that are so tainted." The brief assured the Supreme Court that, from the perspective of leading women's rights organizations, sex stereotyping was nothing new, and ending its use in employment decisions was fully consistent with the purpose of Title VII.[40]

The APA brief emphasized that Dr. Fiske's testimony was consistent with "five decades of research on sex stereotyping" and criticized Price Waterhouse's appellate strategy, which "consistently disparages sex stereotyping theory." The brief compared that approach to the one in *Plessy v. Ferguson*, in which the Supreme Court found that the discrimination claimed by African Americans was simply their own perception. Such a strong position taken by a powerful scientific organization certainly undermined Price Waterhouse's efforts to marginalize Fiske's testimony.[41] The APA brief also helps explain why sex-stereotyping theory was not directly attacked or discredited by the justices. Williams's ridiculing of the theory was a fairly isolated occurrence when the discussion was taken up in the Supreme Court. The brief of the solicitor general came closest to echoing Williams when it emphasized that relying too heavily on sex-stereotyping theory could prohibit thoughts, not actions, under Title VII. As the brief stated, "Title VII bans discriminatory treatment because of sex, not stereotypical thoughts."[42] This position is unsurprising. During the presidency of Republican Ronald Reagan, the Justice Department opposed the expansion of civil rights laws through its legal representation and advocacy.[43]

During oral arguments before the Supreme Court, Price Waterhouse attorney Kathryn Oberly emphasized the conservative position that sex stereotyping is a phantom theory—"an unquantifiable, unconscious, and unintentional element" of Price Waterhouse's decision-making process.[44] Interestingly, conservative justices Kennedy and Scalia observed that gender had played a role in the employment decision, a point that Oberly conceded. However, the discussion quickly turned away from sex-stereotyping theory to arguments over burden of proof, which was the main question on appeal. There was no sustained defense or critique of sex-stereotyping theory by any of the justices, and none of them embraced Judge Williams's analysis in their questioning. Hopkins's attorney, Jim Heller, faced less questioning from the justices than Oberly did, and he even ended his arguments with time to spare—an unusual event when appearing before the Supreme Court.[45]

The decision handed down by the Supreme Court was a bit muddled, opening the door to debate about its relevance as a precedent. Technically, the decision was a victory for Price Waterhouse, in that it invalidated the burden-of-proof standard applied by the DC Court of Appeals. The firm could defend itself using the lower standard of "a preponderance of the evidence" rather than "clear and convincing evidence." Thus, it would be easier for Price Waterhouse to rebut the charge of discrimination by demonstrating that other legitimate factors had led to the decision to deny Hopkins partnership. The dissenters noted that this constituted a change in the law, in that it shifted the burden of proof away from the plaintiff alone in a discrimination case. However, six justices also found that Hopkins had demonstrated that sex-based discrimination was a significant reason for her denial of promotion to partner and that sex stereotyping was part of Price Waterhouse's discriminatory action under Title VII. This, in the end, would allow her to get her job back. In addition, the embrace of a more dynamic interpretation of Title VII meant that the law could potentially protect gender and sexual minorities from discrimination. The six justices in the majority were Harry Blackmun, William Brennan, Thurgood Marshall, Sandra Day O'Connor, John Paul Stevens, and Byron White—all liberal to moderate justices. Conservatives William Rehnquist and Antonin Scalia, along with conservative-to-moderate Anthony Kennedy, were in the minority.

The majority was split on the legal technicalities concerning the burden-of-proof question, but it was not split on the question of whether sex stereotyping was actionable under Title VII. The plurality opinion was authored by Brennan and joined by Blackmun, Marshall, and Stevens (the most liberal justices at the time), and Brennan's opinion fully embraced sex-stereotyping theory:

> In saying that gender played a motivating part in an employment decision, we mean that, if we asked the employer at the moment of the decision what its reasons were and if we received a truthful response, one of those reasons would be that the applicant or employee was a woman. In the specific context of sex stereotyping, an employer who acts on the basis of a belief that a woman cannot be aggressive, or that she must not be, has acted on the basis of gender.
>
> Although the parties do not overtly dispute this last proposition, the placement by Price Waterhouse of "sex stereotyping" in quotation marks throughout its brief seems to us an insinuation either that such stereotyping was not present in this case or that it lacks legal relevance. We reject both possibilities. As to the existence of sex stereotyping in this case, we are not inclined to quarrel with the District Court's conclusion that a number of the partners' comments

showed sex stereotyping at work. As for the legal relevance of sex stereotyping, we are beyond the day when an employer could evaluate employees by assuming or insisting that they matched the stereotype associated with their group. . . . An employer who objects to aggressiveness in women but whose positions require this trait places women in an intolerable and impermissible Catch-22: out of a job if they behave aggressively and out of a job if they do not. Title VII lifts women out of this bind.[46]

Thus, the metaphor of the double bind continued to play a large role in the thinking of judges who supported an expanded interpretation of Title VII. The theory of the case presented by Hopkins's lawyers and feminist activists was embraced by the Supreme Court.

Brennan also dismissed the argument that statements in the record reflected merely the thoughts of Price Waterhouse employees and not concrete, employment-related actions, thereby rejecting the idea that this approach amounted to "thought policing." He stated, "This is not, as Price Waterhouse suggests, 'discrimination in the air'; rather, it is, as Hopkins puts it, 'discrimination brought to ground and visited upon' an employee."[47] Brennan also defended Fiske, criticizing "the dissent's dismissive attitude toward Dr. Fiske's field of study and toward her own professional integrity" but writing that her testimony was "merely icing on Hopkins' cake," given the record established at trial. In a passage dripping with sarcasm and noting the deliberately myopic approach of those who denied that Hopkins had experienced discrimination, Brennan declared: "Nor, turning to Thomas Beyer's memorable advice to Hopkins, does it require expertise in psychology to know that, if an employee's flawed 'interpersonal skills' can be corrected by a soft-hued suit or a new shade of lipstick, perhaps it is the employee's sex, and not her interpersonal skills, that has drawn the criticism."[48]

The two concurring opinions either directly or indirectly affirmed the plurality's interpretation of Title VII and sex stereotyping. Justice White's brief concurrence addressed only the burden-of-proof issue and did not refute Brennan's substantive interpretation of Title VII, as the dissenters did. It is possible that he disagreed with this interpretation but wanted to overturn the DC Circuit on the issue of burden of proof, but this seems unlikely. Justice O'Connor's support for a sex-stereotyping analysis was more explicit, but she appeared to be worried about giving too much weight to isolated or extraneous statements. In her view, Hopkins had provided enough evidence of discrimination without Dr. Fiske's testimony, and she denied that the stereotype-reinforcing statements made by a range of actors during the review process were, in isolated circumstances, proof of discrimination. However, O'Connor asserted that Hopkins and her lawyers had provided "direct evidence that decisionmakers placed substantial negative reliance on an illegitimate criterion in reaching their decision."[49] Given that this "illegitimate" standard was linked to a binary notion of gender, O'Connor accepted the more dynamic interpretation of Title VII, at least in part. As a result, I agree with Thomas that this was a 6-to-3 decision on the issue of sex stereotyping and Title VII: "Six justices—Brennan, Blackmun, Marshall, O'Connor, Stevens, and White—had ruled that gender stereotyping was sex discrimination."[50]

This becomes more apparent when these opinions are contrasted with Justice Kennedy's dissent. Kennedy argued that the burden of proof should always remain with the plaintiff in a Title VII case, fearing that any departure from this standard would harm employers and open the door to more litigation. In the future, he claimed, "almost every plaintiff is certain to ask for a *Price Waterhouse* instruction, perhaps on the basis of 'stray remarks' or other evidence of discriminatory animus."[51] In other words, thoughts could become the basis for proving discrimination, rather than obvious, intentional discrimination. The majority was inappropriately expanding the application of Title VII in the context of sex or gender discrimination, according to Kennedy and the other dissenters. They also rejected the entire approach to Title VII embraced by the lower courts and the Supreme Court majority. As Kennedy plainly and emphatically stated, fully embracing Judge Williams's dissent:

> Title VII creates no independent cause of action for sex stereotyping. Evidence of use by decisionmakers of sex stereotypes is, of course, quite relevant to the question of discriminatory intent. . . . Our cases do not support the suggestion that failure to "disclaim reliance" on stereotypical comments itself violates Title VII. Neither do they support creation of a "duty to sensitize." As the dissenting judge in the Court of Appeals observed, acceptance of such theories would turn Title VII "from a prohibition of discriminatory conduct into an engine for rooting out sexist thoughts."[52]

Thus, given this narrow interpretation of Title VII, it is unclear whether Kennedy would have been an ally of LGBTQ rights in the context of Title VII had he remained on the Supreme Court and not been replaced by Brett Kavanaugh.

With the decision in *Price Waterhouse*, three levels of federal courts endorsed sex-stereotyping theory and a more dynamic approach to the interpretation of Title VII. The most conservative judges in the process dissented vigorously from this legal innovation. As noted earlier and discussed more fully below, scholars have debated the direct implications of this decision, but it clearly represents an important and consequential development in the interpretation and application of Title VII. Gender norms and roles could now potentially be part of the legal analysis in a range of claims under Title VII, a development not anticipated by those who debated the provision in 1964. The Supreme Court's ruling on burden of proof was overturned by Congress in the Civil Rights Act of 1991, thus making the sex-stereotyping element of the case its most enduring legacy.

ANN HOPKINS GETS HER JOB BACK

The Supreme Court sent the case back to the district court to apply its decision on burden of proof. Judge Gesell found that Price Waterhouse failed to demonstrate by a preponderance of the evidence that its decision had been based on legitimate criteria, as the company did not present any new evidence or try to reframe the facts from the original trial to make its case. Gesell also declared that his theory of the case, largely grounded in an analysis of sex stereotyping, had been validated by the Supreme Court. He stated, "The existence of sex discrimination originally found by this Court was affirmed."[53] Thus, he saw the majority decision as ruling on the question of the substantive interpretation of "sex" in Title VII, not simply on burden of proof. Because the issue of constructive discharge was not appealed to the Supreme Court (recall that the court of appeals found that Hopkins had been constructively discharged), Gesell granted Hopkins back pay plus interest, based on the difference between her actual income and what she would have earned as a partner at Price Waterhouse. Including attorneys' fees, this amounted to $371,175. Hopkins eventually received a cash award of $389,207 after Gesell's second decision was confirmed on appeal. More dramatically, Gesell ordered what Hopkins had wanted all along: she was made a partner at Price Waterhouse.[54]

Ann Hopkins went back to work at Price Waterhouse in February 1991, seven years after she sued. She was eventually transferred back to the OGS, where her job involved attaining and managing federal government contracts.

It was quite clear to her that Price Waterhouse did not want her back, but she was unmoved by this opposition. She called her time away from the firm a "sabbatical." In 1990 the *New York Times* described Hopkins's typical no-nonsense style: "She said it would be fine to be a partner in a firm where it had been established, for the record, that she was not wanted, because she was sure of her abilities as a management consultant and wanted a chance to use them at a top-notch concern. In any case, she added, many of the people who criticized her are no longer in the Washington office." Hopkins retired in 2002 and died in 2018 at age seventy-four. She was an accidental but highly consequential plaintiff—one of the most important in the history of Title VII and the struggle to make sense of its language and purpose.[55]

THE IMMEDIATE LEGACY OF *PRICE WATERHOUSE V. HOPKINS*

Price Waterhouse was the product of decades of liberal and feminist thinking about Title VII, as reflected by the movement to expand its scope beyond the types of discrimination envisioned by its congressional supporters. But the case was also influenced by conservative opposition to the expansion of civil rights, and it was one of a series of decisions by the same Supreme Court that limited civil rights law. While conservative academics and judges in the 1980s tried to limit civil rights laws and their interpretation, Congress, controlled by Democrats until 1995, opposed these efforts. Congress enacted the Civil Rights Act of 1991, which largely overruled these negative Supreme Court decisions, thus limiting the long-term legacy of *Price Waterhouse* as a precedent.

Debate among the judges involved in *Price Waterhouse* was influenced by how legal interpretations could either incentivize plaintiffs to bring private lawsuits under Title VII or discourage them from doing so. The position of the DC Court of Appeals was the most plaintiff-friendly, as that court created a high burden for employers to defend themselves against charges of discrimination, which made plaintiffs more likely to sue. The Supreme Court dissenters hoped that keeping the burden on plaintiffs would discourage lawsuits. The majority of Supreme Court justices ended up in the middle, shifting the burden to employers while lowering the standard they were required to meet. As Sean Farhang describes the 1989 cases, "A new conservative majority on the Supreme Court issued a series of five decisions leveling a frontal assault on Title VII's private enforcement regime, and one clearly intended to curtail private enforcement levels."[56] The phrase "private enforcement regime" refers to the fact that the Civil Rights Act of 1964 largely relied on private parties, such as employees claiming discrimination, to enforce the law, rather than legal action by a governmental agency such as the EEOC. Indeed, the EEOC's direct enforcement power was sharply limited by the 1964 law, largely because of pressure from Republicans and southern Democrats. *Price Waterhouse* was one of the least conservative decisions among these five cases, as reflected by the fact that the most conservative justices were in the minority. The Civil Rights Act of 1991 included language that bolstered plaintiffs' ability to sue employers for discrimination—just one of many provisions encouraging civil rights lawsuits. The votes in Congress were bipartisan and overwhelmingly in favor of the act: 93 to 5 in the Senate and 381 to 38 in the House.[57] Thus, Congress did not share the Supreme Court's concern about making it easier for victims of workplace discrimination to bring and win civil rights lawsuits. This strong policy statement by Congress made the legacy of *Price Waterhouse* less powerful and less independently relevant on the question of burden of proof. According to Philip McGough, the 1991 law "makes a defendant with a discriminatory motive liable even with proof that absent that motive, the same action would have been taken."[58] The statutory language allowed for liability, even in the face of this defense. The case's more long-term legacy would relate to the question of how broadly "sex" should be interpreted in Title VII, and that is the primary topic in the chapters that follow.

However, scholars and commentators disagree about the implications of *Price Waterhouse* for sex- or gender-based discrimination. Some argue that it should have a very limited impact, given that Brennan's was a plurality, not a majority, opinion. For instance, according to McGough, "the only holding in *Price Waterhouse* on gender stereotypes is that the trial court was not clearly erroneous in admitting evidence of stereotyping as part of the evidence to prove discrimination."[59] Similarly and more recently, Melnick is quite dismissive of the case's power as a precedent. He argues that judges who use it to expand the interpretation of Title VII are legally incorrect, as their approach "relie[s] almost entirely on dicta in a plurality opinion announced by the Supreme Court in 1989, *Price Waterhouse*."[60] As noted in chapter 1, Melnick is a critic of judicial policymaking in the realm of civil rights. Additionally, he is strongly critical of dynamic statutory interpretation, arguing that it gives far too much power to judges. In doing so, he takes the position of Scalia's dissent in *Romer v. Evans* (1996). In a 6-to-3 ruling, the Supreme Court found that a popularly approved Colorado constitutional amendment barring the enactment of antidiscrimination laws based on sexual orientation violated the equal protection clause of the Constitution. Justice Anthony Kennedy wrote for the majority that even under the traditionally deferential rational basis test, the Colorado law was unconstitutional because it singled out a group for disfavor based not on a legitimate policy motivation but on hostility toward that group. Scalia argued that such hostility could indeed be the primary basis for a law and that the amendment was perfectly reasonable and certainly not prohibited by the equal protection clause:

> Today's opinion has no foundation in American constitutional law, and barely pretends to. The people of Colorado have adopted an entirely reasonable provision which does not even disfavor homosexuals in any substantive sense, but merely denies them preferential treatment. Amendment 2 is designed to prevent piecemeal deterioration of the sexual morality favored by a majority of Coloradans, and is not only an appropriate means to that legitimate end, but a means that Americans have employed before. Striking it down is an act, not of judicial judgment, but of political will.[61]

Noting that judges engage in nonmajoritarian activism in their pro-LGBTQ decisions in both constitutional and statutory cases, Melnick is critical of both types of interpretation. When the Supreme Court "expanded its reading of the Equal Protection Clause to invalidate not only laws containing explicit sex classifications, but policies *allegedly* based on 'animus' against sexual minorities, these constitutional arguments migrated to interpretations of" civil rights statutes. "'Dynamic' statutory interpretation," Melnick continues, "is a younger, less familiar sibling of 'living constitution' jurisprudence. By smuggling novel constitutional claims into statutory rulings, judges can claim to follow rather than confront popularly elected legislators."[62]

An examination of the historical record in Colorado finds evidence of real, as opposed to alleged, animus against sexual minorities. Indeed, as discussed in chapter 2, the events in Colorado were part of a decades-long process by the religious right to use popular initiatives and referenda to undermine civil rights protections for sexual and gender minorities. A majority of the Supreme Court ruled that the Constitution applies to this process, but Melnick and Scalia disagreed. Melnick is also quite skeptical of using federal civil rights laws to expand transgender rights, especially in public schools. This normative position against judicial policymaking can obscure a full understanding of the courts' role in expanding civil rights policy. For instance, although Melnick's study condemns the use of judicial and bureaucratic politics in the expansion of transgender rights—indeed, calling the movement an "experiment"—it does little to explore the history of the LGBTQ rights movement and its connection to employment discrimination and attempts to combat that discrimination. Melnick describes the link between transgender discrimination and educational opportunity as "attenuated at best" and states that the "tiny" number of transgender students have "not been denied access to anything vaguely curricular in nature."[63] This attempt to minimize or outright dismiss LGBTQ discrimination claims is central to conservative opposition to contemporary LGBTQ rights and the conservative strategy of containing and rolling back legal advances that protect those rights.

Another way to limit the influence of *Price Waterhouse* is to assert that it should apply only to women in Ann Hopkins's "double bind" situation.[64] Under this reading of the case, it should apply not to LGBTQ individuals but only to straight, cisgender women who are discriminated against for exhibiting traits deemed by society to be masculine. As discussed in later chapters, courts have varied in their application of *Price Waterhouse*, but none of the attempts to limit its use as a precedent were fully successful. Federal judges have generally read it broadly and applied it especially aggressively in the context of transgender rights.

ONCALE AND THE EXPANSION OF TITLE VII

Oncale v. Sundowner Offshore Services, Inc. is a short and unanimous opinion, but the litigation was significant because it involved expanding the interpretation of Title VII to include sexual harassment and sex stereotyping and addressed the emerging legal question of the rights of sexual minorities. In the process of deciding whether same-sex sexual harassment is actionable under Title VII, justice Antonin Scalia authored a passage that eventually set the stage for Title VII's support of LGBTQ rights. This passage solidified the notion that the Supreme Court would not be concerned with legislative intent when interpreting the phrase "because of . . . sex." This, along with the sex-stereotyping analysis from *Price Waterhouse*, created a powerful legal foundation for the application of Title VII to LGBTQ rights—an approach previously viewed as legally absurd, as evidenced by the 1970s cases discussed in chapter 2. As Mary Anne Case notes, "Justice Scalia's *Oncale* opinion may have been a catalyst in finally pushing courts to reexamine their precedent on the coverage under Title VII of sexual minorities and gender-nonconforming employees in light of *Hopkins*."[65]

Joseph Oncale, a straight man, was hired in August 1991 as a roustabout on an oil-drilling platform owned by Chevron and located in the Gulf of Mexico, eighty miles off the coast of Louisiana. Only men were employed on the platform, and they worked long shifts (one week on, one week off) in close quarters. He experienced persistent, jaw-dropping sexual harassment from his fellow employees, including the threat of rape; many of these incidents would likely be considered sexual assault today. For example, one coworker said to Oncale: "You know you got a cute little ass, boy. If I don't get you now, I'm going to get you later. I'm going to get you."[66] Oncale was also assaulted in the shower when a coworker and his supervisor grabbed him and placed soap between his buttocks and into his anus, threatening rape, before he was able to get away. At the time, Oncale's direct employer, Sundowner Offshore Services, considered this a harmless case of "boys being boys." Many federal judges shared this view, and this was a common refrain in the defense of early sexual harassment claims by women. Oncale complained to supervisors, but nothing was done about the situation. He quit the job in November 1991, and soon thereafter he filed a sexual harassment complaint with the EEOC.

These stunning facts were consistently downplayed and dismissed by Oncale's employer and its attorneys. It was normal horseplay, according to this narrative. Technically, the legal argument was that Title VII did not, and was not intended to, cover this situation because Oncale was a man harassed by other men, and dismissing the extent of the harassment went hand in hand with this claim. Ultimately, however, the Supreme Court was unable to ignore the severity of the abuse Oncale suffered. Legal scholars note that "fact freedom" can influence legal arguments.[67] This involves picking and choosing among facts in a case, emphasizing some and de-emphasizing others, to attain the desired legal outcome. In its brief to the Supreme Court, Sundowner acknowledged only "three incidents" of harassment, including the shower incident, even though the brief described additional occurrences, such as comments and "goosing," and simply ignored others in the record. The brief asserted that one of the attackers "did not have any physical contact with Oncale" after the incident in question. The brief then stated that other men on the rig had been subjected to harassing behavior, reemphasizing the "boys will be boys" point. Violent hazing was simply a fact of life on an oil rig, according to Sundowner; it was certainly not a hostile work environment under Title VII. The brief also asserted that Oncale had quit after being reprimanded for taking an unauthorized smoke break.[68] However, the Supreme Court ultimately ruled that he had been constructively discharged, just like Ann Hopkins.

Lower courts unanimously sided with Sundowner, largely out of fear of opening the door to sexual orientation–based claims under Title VII; their reliance on direct and indirect precedents reflected the same fear. Indeed, lawyers and judges who argued against protecting Oncale under Title VII cited the negative 1970s precedents on sexual orientation discussed in chapter 2. Judge G. Thomas Porteous Jr. referred to "acts and assaults," but he found no possible recourse under Title VII.[69] (At the time, Porteous was a recent Clinton appointee, but he was impeached and removed from office in 2010.) He felt bound by Fifth Circuit precedents that relied on a 1988 case, *Goluszek v. Smith*, from the Northern District of Illinois. In *Goluszek*, another case of same-gender sexual harassment, judge Ann Williams declared that "the defendant's conduct was not the type of conduct Congress intended to sanction when it enacted Title VII."[70] The Fifth Circuit affirmed Porteous's decision in *Oncale*.[71]

The Supreme Court granted certiorari in *Oncale*, likely because there was a conflict between the Fifth Circuit's position and that of the Seventh Circuit. In 1997, in *Doe v. City of Belleville*, a Seventh Circuit panel ruled that same-gender sexual harassment was actionable under Title VII and largely adopted the approach later taken by the Supreme Court—rejecting legislative intent and focusing on the text. The Seventh Circuit judges in the majority strongly rejected the *Goluszek*–Fifth Circuit approach, asserting, "It is, ultimately, the plain, unambiguous language of the statute upon which we much focus."[72]

Amicus briefs submitted on behalf of Oncale cited *Doe* and created a powerful narrative, grounded in sexual harassment law, by liberally referencing *Price Waterhouse* and emphasizing the need for a textual or purposeful approach to interpretation of the statute, rather than a dependence on legislative intent. Some of the briefs authored by leading feminist legal scholars such as Catherine Mackinnon, Katherine Franke, and Nan Hunter also made connections between gender and sexuality and argued that "*Price Waterhouse* represented an important advance in Title VII law, one that provided the undergirding for the Seventh Circuit's decision in *Doe*."[73] Although many of the briefs reassured the court that *Oncale* did not need to be about sexual orientation, the brief authored by Mackinnon argued in favor of this: "In practical terms, harassment because of homosexuality cannot be separated from harassment because of sex."[74] (In 2020 this would become the Supreme Court's position in the context of employment discrimination.) In comparison, the brief submitted by Lambda Legal was more constrained and focused on linking the case to sexual harassment law and *Price Waterhouse*, signaling to the court that it was not asking for a dramatic expansion of LGBTQ rights through Title VII; however, a win for Oncale, combined with *Price Waterhouse*, clearly had implications for future LGBTQ rights litigation. Another important signal came from the EEOC and the Clinton administration's Justice Department. The EEOC declared: "Title VII's coverage is sex-neutral. . . . There is no exemption from . . . coverage for cases of sexual harassment."[75] In contrast, a brief from the Texas Chamber of Commerce for Sundowner argued that by recognizing same-sex sexual harassment, "courts may ultimately be encouraging all alleged harassers to claim that they are bi-sexual."[76] In general, the amicus briefs in support of Oncale (which significantly outnumbered the briefs submitted for Sundowner) laid out the approach the unanimous Supreme Court would eventually take: a rejection of legislative intent and the application of sexual harassment doctrine regardless of gender, supported by sex-stereotyping theory from *Price Waterhouse*.

During oral arguments, the Supreme Court justices expressed strong skepticism toward Sundowner's arguments, although the conservative justices seemed to struggle with the concept of same-sex sexual harassment when questioning Oncale's attorney. For instance, Scalia asked, reflecting a common critique of sexual harassment law, "Is this a dirty word law, or something?" Seeming to buy into the "harmless hazing" narrative, Rehnquist asserted: "But just the hazing by itself, unless you can show that men are treated differently than women, doesn't make out a claim." However, the justices seemed to be united in their reservations about Sundowner's extreme position that Title VII had no connection to the case because Congress did not intend it to apply in such situations. For instance, less than two years after he authored the majority opinion in *Romer*, Kennedy asked Harry Reasoner, Sundowner's attorney: "You would have us hold that if a homosexual supervisor trades favors with people of his own sex for advancement, that is not a violation of the statute?" Reasoner replied, "Yes, Your Honor." Scalia appeared to be reluctant to totally exclude men from Title VII's sexual harassment protections. He pushed Reasoner on hypothetical examples of sexual and nonsexual harassment of men in a workplace, but not of women in that same workplace. Reasoner would not budge from his position that Title VII did not apply, and he relied on the fact that Congress had not enacted the Employment Nondiscrimination Act. However, Scalia declared, "discriminatory hazing is discriminatory hazing, whether the hazing has sexual allusions mixed into it or not," previewing the textualism that would be central to his opinion. In response to Reasoner's argument that the Equal Pay Act (enacted a year before the Civil Rights Act) bolstered the assertion that Title VII was intended to protect only women, Rehnquist, echoing Scalia, retorted, "The statute doesn't say either women or men. It says sex."[77]

Price Waterhouse and sex stereotyping played a significant role in the oral arguments, and Edwin Kneedler, the deputy solicitor general, addressed both. Scalia asked whether someone like Oncale had been singled out "because they didn't like his maleness." Justice Ginsburg echoed this by asking, "Did they want to demean him because they didn't consider him sufficiently male, or was it just that they didn't like him and they used this disgusting way of showing it." Later, combining *Price Waterhouse* with *Phillips v. Martin Marietta* (1971), an early Title VII case touching on gender stereotypes, she asked Reasoner:

> Why couldn't it [the harassment] be because you're not the right kind of man, just as with respect to women, and wasn't there, at least in one case, a statement to the effect of what title VII is aimed at is getting rid of stereotypical notions about the way men are or the way women are, so . . . we know that an employer can't say, as in *Martin Marietta*, how could I discriminate against women, most of the people I hire are women, but I won't take the ones who have children.[78]

Clearly, this legal terrain was quite different from that explored by the lower courts. The entire Supreme Court considered a more dynamic and less intent-driven approach, as demonstrated by the oral arguments.

Furthermore, the justices were not obsessed with the issue of bootstrapping sexual orientation—a concern expressed by Reasoner. He declared, before being interrupted by Justice Stevens: "Once you've cut loose from the moorings of the two sexes, because of sex, are we then going to get into homosexuality—." Stevens then broke in, "Of course, there's another way of looking at it. Instead of saying it's expanding the statute, say the statute's always covered discrimination, and you're asking to cut out of the general field of discrimination in this one area." This statement reflected a focus on purpose, rather than intent, or a dynamic textualism. Justice Breyer followed by making a similar point and a vivid analogy: "It seems to me that it's sufficient to look at the sexual harassment law as being in effect a kind of evidentiary gloss on the statute, that when this kind of conduct occurs, as Thoreau put it, you know, there's a trout in the milk." The court had already done the heavy lifting in creating sexual harassment law, and now it was simply applying that law to the case at hand. Something was seriously wrong, and the court could forthrightly address the problem within existing, albeit recent, legal frameworks. "A trout in the milk" replaced "boys will be boys," even if there were only boys in the workplace.[79]

Relying heavily on sexual harassment precedents and those holding that men are covered by Title VII, Scalia declared for the unanimous majority that "nothing in Title VII necessarily bars a claim of discrimination 'because . . . of sex' merely because the plaintiff and the defendant . . . are of the same sex."[80] After briefly summarizing conflicting approaches taken by the lower courts, Scalia made the most consequential statement from the Supreme Court on the issue of statutory interpretation in relation to LGBTQ rights:

> We see no justification in the statutory language or our precedents for a categorical rule excluding same-sex harassment claims from the coverage of Title VII. As some courts have observed, male-on-male sexual harassment in the workplace was assuredly not the principal evil Congress was concerned with when it enacted Title VII. But statutory prohibitions often go beyond the principal evil to cover reasonably comparable evils, and it is ultimately the provisions of our laws rather than the principal concerns of our legislators by which we are governed.[81]

He went on to note that harassment need not be motivated by sexual desire to run afoul of Title VII. What happened to Joseph Oncale was harassment based not on sexual orientation but on sex. Scalia was careful to note, especially given his earlier comment about "a dirty word law," that "the prohibition of harassment on the basis of sex requires neither asexuality nor androgyny in the workplace; it forbids only behavior so objectively offensive as to alter the 'conditions' of the victim's employment."[82] Thoroughly grounded in sexual harassment law, the decision was a clear statement that the applicability of

Title VII should not be restricted by the intent of legislators. In fact, the opinion does not discuss the legislative history of Title VII, which is common in many cases considering the application of Title VII beyond cisgender women. Ultimately, the court was worried less about leapfrogging than about not leapfrogging and leaving this type of harassment untouched by federal law. Although the legal narrative of the amicus briefs for Oncale did not dominate the court's ultimate analysis, the narrative of the employer and the lower court judges was thoroughly rejected.

Ann Hopkins's quest for justice interacted with evolving interpretations of Title VII. This, combined with Scalia's rejection of legislative intent in *Oncale*, set the stage for LGBTQ rights activists and litigators to use Title VII to remedy the rampant discrimination faced by gender and sexual minorities. Many of the standard conservative approaches to Title VII employed today were not embraced by the Supreme Court in either case. It applied existing legal frameworks to new questions.

4. Transgender Rights and *Price Waterhouse*

The legal foundation created by *Price Waterhouse v. Hopkins* and *Oncale v. Sundowner Offshore Services* was consequential for transgender rights, even though the transgender rights movement was less developed than the LGB rights movement at the time. Because of the conscious decision to downplay sexual orientation in *Oncale*, in addition to the bleak federal legal terrain that started to change only with *Romer* in 1996, the relevance for LGB rights litigation was less immediate. Indeed, legal arguments for LGB rights under Title VII would piggyback on arguments for transgender-based protections. Many transgender legal activists did not immediately recognize the relevance of *Price Waterhouse* and generally did not embrace the case and its implications in the 1990s. However, soon after *Oncale*, legal activists began to deploy *Price Waterhouse* in litigation, and the first federal court to accept this line of argument did so in 2000. This chapter explores the legal evolution of transgender rights litigation using Title VII, including a landmark decision by the Equal Employment Opportunity Commission (EEOC), and illustrates the emergence of a strong legal consensus that transgender and gender nonconforming individuals are protected from employment discrimination under federal law.

THE MOVEMENT FOR TRANSGENDER RIGHTS

Transgender people have always existed, but the development of an organized political and legal movement for trans rights and equality is fairly recent. As Jami Taylor, Daniel Lewis, and Donald Haider-Markel note, "A collective transgender political identity developed in the late 1980s and early 1990s, but gender variant people have existed throughout time and across cultures."[1] Although there were earlier events, activists, and associations, a fully developed movement—that is, sustained and coordinated activism and organization—did not form until the 1990s. This lag was partly the result of social marginalization and partly the result of marginalization within the LGBTQ rights movement itself. This section highlights developments in the movement's growth and the challenges it faced.

In the 1960s transgender individuals were beginning to challenge the legal regime regulating their existence. In particular, laws prohibiting cross-dressing led to invasive enforcement practices and harassment. In addition, police routinely viewed transgender individuals as sex workers and used laws against prostitution to harass and arrest them. The homophile movement also enforced the gender binary and marginalized transgender and gender-variant individuals. For instance, at the homophile demonstrations led by Frank Kameny, there was a strict dress code: women in skirts and dresses, and men in traditional suits. However, instances of civil disobedience sometimes united the emerging LGBTQ rights movement. In 1965 patrons of Dewey's restaurant in Philadelphia engaged in several forms of protest, including a sit-in, to challenge the restaurant's denial of service based on perceived gender nonconformity and sexual orientation. The local LGBTQ rights organization, the Janus Society, used its newsletter to point out the connections between gender identity and sexual orientation and the inclination to downplay the former:

> All too often there is a tendency to be concerned with the rights of homosexuals as long as they somehow appear to be heterosexual, whatever that is. The masculine woman and the feminine man often are looked down upon by the official policy of homophile organizations. . . . What is offensive today we have seen become the style of tomorrow, and . . . there is no reason to penalize such non-conformist behavior unless there is direct anti-social behavior connected with it.[2]

A year later, in 1966, transgender patrons of Compton's cafeteria in San Francisco rioted in reaction to police harassment. This was three years before transgender individuals, including Marsha P. Johnson and Sylvia Rivera, became central players in the more famous Stonewall riots in New York City. The Compton's riot led to more activism in San Francisco around transgender and poverty issues, but it did not create a national movement. It was, however, a product of the unique setting of political activism in the late 1960s. As Susan Stryker notes, the riot was fostered by many factors, including "discriminatory policing practices that target members of minority communities, urban land-use policies that benefit cultural elites and displace poor people, the unsettling domestic consequences of US foreign wars, access to health care, civil rights activism aiming to expand individual liberties and social tolerance on matters of sexuality and gender, and political coalition building around structural injustices that affect many different communities."[3] Yet social marginalization continued to constrain the rise of a transgender political and legal movement. For instance, while Johnson and Rivera were involved in New York–based LGBTQ activism in the 1970s and 1980s, LGB activists generally did not reciprocate due to discrimination against gender-variant people within the movement. Pathbreaking organizations such as Street Transvestite Action Revolutionaries (STAR) and STAR House (both focused on transgender youth, poverty, and homelessness) lasted only a few years due to a lack of financial resources. In these decades, Stryker notes, "transgender people made only small, erratic strides toward a better collective resistance."[4]

By the late 1960s and 1970s, gender affirmation surgery became more common, especially for those who could afford medical care and could navigate the strict clinical protocols.[5] This resulted in legal challenges to the discrimination faced by transitioning individuals, such as the lawsuits brought by Paula Grossman and Karen Ulane (see chapter 2). However, these cases were not coordinated and were not the product of a movement-based strategy. By the 1990s, transgender activists and lawyers began to envision a legal strategy, leading to a decade of rapid mobilization and organization of the transgender rights movement. Influenced by feminist arguments and queer theory, many theorists began to argue for a distinct but broad transgender political and legal identity. Formal lobbying and advocacy increased, organizations were formed, publications were created, and regional and national conferences were held. Most of these organizations were nonlegal and focused on media, culture, and political advocacy, however.[6]

Litigation is a lengthy process and requires significant time, information, expertise, and money, especially when litigation strategies move beyond uncoordinated local and pro bono legal representation. These barriers impeded the emerging transgender rights movement's access to the legal arena, beyond the negative case law. Historically, transgender rights organizations have been resource poor in comparison to LGB organizations, making them heavily dependent on the financial support of groups such as Lambda Legal, the National Center for Lesbian Rights, GLBTQ Advocates & Defenders (GLAD), and the American Civil Liberties Union (ACLU). In addition, transgender issues have been marginalized within the LGB rights movement, especially given its attention to marriage equality activism and litigation. Even so, leading transgender rights litigators admit that LGB-based litigation strategies helped build a foundation for transgender rights cases. Shannon Minter, one of the central figures in early transgender rights and marriage equality litigation, asserts that without these resources, litigation efforts for transgender rights "would be sunk."[7] For instance, in the midst of GLAD's successful New England–based marriage equality litigation, it established a powerful trans-supportive precedent in 2000 (discussed in more detail later).

Whereas judges in the 1970s often conflated gender identity and sexual orientation, by the 1990s, the creation of distinct movements led to separate legal discussions. Increasingly, activists reinforced this distinction: sexual orientation is about romantic and sexual attraction, while gender identity is about one's relationship to the gender binary. State and local antidiscrimination laws increasingly created separate legal categories of protection as the legal and political understanding of these categories became more sophisticated. For instance, Minnesota's landmark 1993 law—the first statewide law to offer gender identity–based protections—defined gender identity as a subset of sexual orientation, a legacy of the 1970s approach to the law in Minneapolis.[8] When states added gender identity protections in the 2000s, the definition of gender identity was distinct from sexual orientation. In litigation, these parallel legal tracks largely persisted until the Supreme Court combined both forms of discrimination in *Bostock*. Legal activists saw promise in linking gender identity discrimination to gender stereotyping after *Price Waterhouse*, and this separation from sexual orientation, without as much potential bootstrapping, would benefit transgender plaintiffs.

The International Conference on Transgender Law and Employment Policy (ICTLEP) was the most prominent transgender legal organization in the 1990s. It focused not on litigation but on education and political advocacy and hosted six annual conferences starting in 1992. It eventually merged with the National Lesbian and Gay Law Association and its Lavender Law Conference, as that organization began to address transgender issues more substantively. The ICTLEP conferences did not get much media coverage, but prominent transgender activists attended, including Leslie Feinberg, Susan Stryker, Dallas Denny, and Shannon Minter.[9] According to Stryker, in addition to influencing the attendees, the conferences "did much to inspire a new burst of transgender legal activism and to connect activists at the national level."[10] The records of these conferences provide an excellent means of examining how transgender lawyers and their allies viewed their potential pathway to reform through the courts. Starting only three years after *Price Waterhouse*, the conference proceedings illustrate how these activists viewed the relevance and potential of that case. In short, *Price Waterhouse* did not figure prominently in the discussions, as its importance was not yet recognized. These activists were demoralized by the negative federal precedents and were more focused on enacting local, state, and federal protections for gender identity.

Phyllis Frye, the first openly transgender judge in the United States, was the primary organizer of the ICTLEP conferences. Frye transitioned in the 1970s, lost her job as an engineer as a result, and developed a strong legal conscious-ness that led her to become an attorney. She lobbied against the Houston city council's ordinance banning cross-dressing, and it was repealed in 1980. She eventually became involved in national marches on Washington and lobbying for a trans-inclusive Employment Nondiscrimination Act (ENDA). She was outspoken on transgender exclusion from various events and initiatives, and her activism was serious and multifaceted. In particular, she saw a distinct lack of activism surrounding legal strategies, which led her to found the ICTLEP. She observed that the annual conferences "allowed transgenders to discuss and formulate future strategies, on both a grassroots and national scope, for changing the laws that adversely effect [*sic*] the lives of transgenders."[11] Con-sistent with the proliferation of transgender rights activism in the 1990s, Frye declared at an early ICTLEP meeting, "This is our decade."[12] Future Houston mayor Annise Parker, the first openly lesbian mayor of a major city, attended ICTLEP meetings and appointed Frye to the bench.

The International Bill of Gender Rights was one of the more enduring leg-acies of the ICTLEP. After several years of revisions, it was formally adopted at the 1996 meeting. Whereas other, more radical legal critiques question a rights-based framework, this document was steeped in the language of rights, and it viewed transgender rights in the larger context of expanding the rights of all marginalized groups in the United States. The document defined the right to self-definition and expression, the right to be free from employment discrimination, the right to access gendered spaces and activities, the right to bodily integrity and control, the right to affirmative health care and pro-tection from coercive and unprofessional care, the right to sexual expression regardless of gender identity or sexual orientation, the right to marry, and par-enting rights.[13] Thus, the transgender rights movement substantially adopted the framework initiated by the civil rights movement and used by most iden-tity-based political and legal movements in the latter decades of the twentieth century, one that "created a collective identity as victims of discrimination deserving equal rights."[14]

In this approach, lawyers were central. For instance, a presentation at the first ICTLEP conference was entitled "Cherish the Lawyers Who Protect Your Freedom."[15] Initiating litigation was a strong theme of the conferences, in addition to legislative lobbying. Despite the negative case law, activists still had a strong sense that the courts *could* be avenues for change, but significant pessimism remained. Sex-stereotyping theory and *Price Waterhouse* were, for the most part, not elements of the ICTLEP strategy. Instead, presenters at the conferences repeatedly condemned and bemoaned the federal case law and focused on the need to add gender identity to local, state, and federal antidiscrimination laws. Participants were urged to work with and educate their employers if they planned to transition or come out, and as a strategy to prevent dismissal, they were advised to "establish their value . . . before they go out trying to establish their identity."[16] They were encouraged to sue their employers, if necessary. This was a fairly defensive position that placed much of the burden on transgender individuals, but it was a product of the negative state of the law.

At the 1993 meeting, Laura Skaer, the ICTLEP's employment law director, speculated that the lack of success in using Title VII was due to the premature timing of the cases: "I really wonder, if they came up today, if we might not have different results if we have the right preparation for the case."[17] She was on to something. Federal courts began to change their approach less than a decade later, but Skaer assumed that a more enlightened judicial approach would be the result of a general cultural change, not the power of a new precedent. Helen Cassidy, staff attorney of a Houston state appellate court, noted at the 1992 meeting that "sex" had been included in Title VII as a joke. She went on to say, "With 80% of our federal judges in this country now appointed by Presidents Reagan and Bush and with the Neanderthal Supreme Court, you're not going to get a court interpretation that says that sex also includes gender identification. Simply don't hold your breath for that. But we need to keep insisting that it should be that way."[18] At the same meeting, Frye noted that the negative precedents were based on "a very interesting legal fiction" of "plain meaning" devised by law clerks: "you cannot discriminate against men because they are men and you cannot discriminate against women because they are women but you can discriminate against transsexuals because they are transsexuals."[19] Thus, rather than arguing that inclusion of gender identity was an interpretative stretch or an approach that could lead to leapfrogging, Frye argued that the approach taken by judges in the 1970s and 1980s was the real stretch. Further evidence of the dearth of federal jurisprudential support was contained in a 1993 report about the state of the law. In discussing legal strategies, it argued that "the best solution to the dilemma of the transgendered employee is not court battles for legal protections, rather awareness, education and the development of a mutually beneficial, common sense policy [in workplaces]."[20]

At the 1993 ICTLEP conference, regional EEOC attorney Jim Sacher saw the creation of sexual harassment jurisprudence, combined with the appointment of new judges (Democrat Bill Clinton had been elected president in 1992), as a potential model for the expansion of transgender rights. He stated, "Even the concept that we now take for granted, that it violates the law to be sexually harassed at work, that wasn't in the statute. That was something the commission said constituted a violation of the law and the Supreme Court chose to agree. There's a new generation of judges that are going to be appointed, at least now on the federal side."[21] This too reflected the primary stance of ICTLEP presenters on the question of Title VII: hopelessness in the past, a lack of recognition of the importance of *Price Waterhouse*, and cautious optimism about the future. This did not change significantly during the remaining years of the ICTLEP's existence.

A paper presented at the 1993 conference, almost by accident, was a notable exception to this approach. Sharon Kahn, a recent law school graduate, was a last-minute replacement at a session titled "The Education in Transgender Issues Project." She had previously contacted Frye about a paper she wrote in law school about the potential use of *Price Waterhouse* as a precedent for transgender rights. Kahn briefly discussed *Price Waterhouse* in her presentation, but it was not the focal point of an extended discussion in 1993 or in any year thereafter. Kahn reenvisioned the approach to transgender employment discrimination, relying on *Loving v. Virginia* (1967) and *Price Waterhouse* as she declared, "There is some hope in the law." She agreed with Frye that federal judges had intentionally ignored or distorted the text of Title VII by artificially limiting the definition of sex, to the detriment of transgender plaintiffs. As she noted, "The judiciary has done some interesting tap dancing to change definitions."[22]

Kahn relied on *Loving* to argue against the biological essentialism and crude formalism undergirding the precedents of the 1970s and 1980s. She wrote, "The court explicitly found that the anti-miscegenation laws constituted race discrimination because a permissible behavior (marriage) was only prohibited when persons of different races attempted to engage in it. This precisely mirrors the situation . . . where men are not allowed to engage in behavior considered acceptable for women, such as wearing feminine attire." *Price Waterhouse* expanded this interpretation because it prohibited sex stereotyping and addressed "gender nonconformity," according to Kahn. She did not assert that change would happen immediately using these precedents, and she recommended a selective legal strategy focused on liberal, activist judges who would be most open to expanding the interpretation of Title VII. As she argued, "Care should be taken to choose a forum where judicial activism is the norm as opposed to judicial conservatism. A judicially active court will be more willing to expand protection based on sex."[23] Kahn also saw connections among between sex discrimination, sexual harassment law, and sexual orientation discrimination. She cited Catherine Mackinnon and a law review article by Samuel Marcosson discussing sexual orientation–based harassment. In addition, she noted the Hawaii Supreme Court's ruling that the state's ban on same-sex marriage likely violated the state constitution's prohibition on sex discrimination.

This approach, however, did not influence discussions in subsequent years. In fact, *Price Waterhouse* does not appear in the formal records of the ICTLEP conference after 1993, based on my examination of the proceedings. For instance, at the 1995 meeting, a report submitted on employment discrimination focused on an equal protection–based legal strategy, not Title VII, and lobbying for the enactment of legislative protections.[24] The controversial approach of using disability rights, especially the Americans with Disabilities Act (1990), to further transgender rights was much more prevalent in the discussions. Barriers to the use of Title VII made this a potential path in the eyes of some activist lawyers.[25] It is likely that *Oncale* provided another crucial step in the evolution of Title VII interpretation—a case decided after the last ICTLEP conference. As discussed in chapter 3, Scalia severed legislative intent from Title VII analysis, allowing activists to seriously reenter the legal arena on behalf of transgender rights, freed from the burden of legislators' intentions in 1964. The issue of legislative intent weighed heavily on the lawyers attending the ICTLEP conferences, however, and it was difficult for them to see a legal path through Title VII that was not blazed by changes in state and federal law.

This perception led to a focus on federal legislation, but the barriers were enormous. The mainstream LGBTQ rights movement saw the embrace of transgender rights as a threat to its emerging clout. Transgender rights activists were routinely excluded from public events and calls for legislative protection. Frye and other activists were sidelined at the 1979, 1987, and 1993 marches on Washington. Interestingly, Chai Feldblum, the leading legal strategist behind ENDA, supported the exclusion of gender identity protections in the 1990s. Feldblum represented the view of mainstream activists well into the 2000s, perhaps most visibly represented by opposition to a trans-inclusive bill by congressman Barney Frank and the Human Rights Campaign (HRC). Frye attempted to use ICTLEP as a springboard to congressional activism, but she was rebuffed by the HRC. She had planned to speak at a hearing for ENDA in 1994 but "could only watch as ENDA was discussed."[26]

Success in the bureaucracy was blocked as well. Although the EEOC was somewhat sympathetic, it was locked into its position from the 1970s. When asked to change its interpretation of Title VII to include transgender protections, it declined. Specifically, Frye and other activists met with EEOC commissioners and staff in 1995, where activists "argued that with rule-making power, the EEOC could find that Title VII protected transgenders and essentially override the *Ulane* trio. The commissioners understood, but declined, noting that the Republican Congress would retaliate by reducing appropriations for the EEOC in the next budget."[27] Realistically, there was neither a legislative nor a bureaucratic route to achieve the protection of transgender rights in the 1990s and 2000s. Ultimately, the federal courts represented the best hope.

EARLY *PRICE WATERHOUSE*–INSPIRED CASES

The year 2000 was pivotal for judicially protected transgender rights. In that year, two federal appellate courts applied the logic of *Price Waterhouse* and *Oncale* to cases of discrimination brought by transgender plaintiffs: *Rosa v. Park West Bank and Trust Company* and *Schwenk v. Hartford.* Beyond the two favorable Supreme Court decisions, two developments supported this new phase of transgender rights litigation. First, legal scholars began to frame arguments about transgender rights in the context of these decisions, in an attempt to attract the attention of activist lawyers and judges. Some of these scholars were directly involved in the litigation process, advising lawyers and filing amicus briefs. Second, LGBTQ rights organizations began to focus more of their litigation efforts and resources on transgender plaintiffs. For instance, GLAD took a test case in 1998 that resulted in the Second Circuit's decision in *Rosa*. This was a carefully calibrated and orchestrated strategy designed to reverse the negative jurisprudence on gender identity under Title VII. The strategy was grounded in gradualism, and according to GLAD attorney Jennifer Levi, "advocates may have to wait to tackle head-on the most difficult cases until some smaller victories can be secured."[28]

Feminist legal scholars Katherine Franke and Mary Anne Case were central to the rethinking of Title VII interpretation that would allow a more dynamic and realistic understanding of sex and gender. They both published influential articles in 1995 that placed *Price Waterhouse* at the center of their analysis. Relying on gender theorists such as Judith Butler, Franke advocated a move away from biological essentialism, which had dominated legal thinking about gender equality for much of the twentieth century. Connecting theory to practice, she would work with GLAD on the *Rosa* litigation and submitted an amicus brief in the case. Franke pointed out the potential of *Price Waterhouse* and sex-stereotyping theory to change the legal reality, noting that "bodies have been dropped out of the equation. The law, therefore, should no longer require . . . that discriminatory conduct be directed exclusively at one or the other biological sex. Any adverse action in the workplace on account of a person's gender should be cognizable under Title VII, regardless of the body parts of the plaintiff or defendant."[29] Case called for a "reconceptualization of existing law" related to Title VII to expand its reach, including "sex-specific clothing regulations, stereotypically feminine behavior by both men and women, sexual harassment of both men and women, jobs seen to require either predominately masculine or predominately feminine traits, single-sex education, sexual orientation, and transsexuality."[30]

In July 1998 Lucas Rosa, a trans person, was refused an application for an automobile loan at a Holyoke, Massachusetts, branch of Park West Bank because a bank official deemed that Rosa was not wearing sufficiently masculine clothing. The loan officer told Rosa to leave the bank, change clothing, and then return to fill out the application. The bank official, Norma Brunelle, told Rosa "that he [the courts used male pronouns for Rosa, as did GLAD, whereas Rosa preferred the gender-neutral 'they' and 'their'] had to be dressed like one of the [three] identification cards [Rosa presented] in which he appeared in more traditionally male attire before she would provide him with a loan application to process his loan."³¹ When Rosa approached GLAD, the organization saw an opportunity to chip away at the well-established anti-LGBTQ Title VII jurisprudence. First, there was clearly no reason for the bank's action, other than bias. Second, the case could be based on the Equal Credit Opportunity Act (ECOA) rather than Title VII, avoiding a direct challenge to established precedent. The ECOA, enacted in 1974 as part of the expansion of civil rights laws in the 1960s and 1970s, prohibited discrimination in the credit process based on sex as well as other factors, including marital status. A key rationale for the law was to give women financial independence. As Bella Abzug's biographer Leandra Ruth Zarnow notes, "Before this landmark law, women were in a sense non-persons economically, for it was assumed that fathers or husbands handled their financial affairs."³² Abzug was a leading force behind the law's enactment.

At the bank, Rosa was, of course, humiliated. This was the first time their forms of identification had been questioned in the context of their physical presentation. Rosa contacted an attorney, who then contacted GLAD attorney Jennifer Levi, who had been adding to the organization's transgender rights portfolio since 1998, after working on transgender rights in Chicago through Lambda Legal. Attending ICTLEP conferences had awakened her interest in pursuing transgender rights. "That was a transformative experience," she said, "one that motivated me to become increasingly involved in the legal struggle."³³ About *Rosa*, Levi stated, "We took this case, because, in other cases, justifications had sometimes been offered about why someone had to look stereotypically masculine or stereotypically feminine that were tied to customer preferences [such as the PT&T litigation discussed in chapter 2] or appropriate ways to look in the workplace. . . . It was really a great case strategically to bring forward, because it was stripped of any kind of business-oriented justifications for the discrimination."³⁴ With the facts of this case, the ECOA, and the precedents of *Price Waterhouse* and *Oncale*, Levi saw an indirect path to establishing transgender rights in federal law.

The trial court judge was quite dismissive of Rosa's claims, agreeing with the bank that transgender persons were excluded from the ECOA's protections. Levi and GLAD argued that this discrimination was actionable under sex discrimination and sex-stereotyping theory, relying on *Price Waterhouse*. Judge Frank Freedman, a Nixon appointee, ruled from the bench after only thirty minutes of deliberation in an unusually dismissive move. Freedman declared: "The issue in the case is not sex, but rather how he chose to dress when applying for a loan."[35] On appeal, *Price Waterhouse* was central to GLAD's argument, and it viewed the case as identical to what had happened to Ann Hopkins. As the brief stated, "In Norma Brunelle's eyes, Lucas Rosa did not look the way a 'real man' should."[36] For the appeal, GLAD arranged for Franke to author an amicus brief under the auspices of the NOW Legal Defense and Education Fund, and in this brief too, *Price Waterhouse* played a critical role. Franke argued that *Price Waterhouse* was the culmination of the Supreme Court's dynamic thinking about gender in its equal protection analysis, with a particular focus on cases brought by men: "The Supreme Court's modern sex discrimination jurisprudence has primarily taken aim at two forms of sex stereotyping: policies and practices that reward conformance to certain over-broad and unfounded class-based assumptions about the relative strengths and weaknesses of men and women, and policies and practices that punish men and women for their failure to conform to stereotypic expectations about who men and women are or should be."[37] Indeed, Franke's role in the case was "to reassure the First Circuit that this case fit comfortably within the scope of well-established sex discrimination jurisprudence that dealt with sex stereotypes."[38]

In this case and others that followed, it made strategic sense for the litigators to frame the issue as instances of men, rather than trans women, being discriminated against because of sex stereotyping. No court had yet ruled that transgender discrimination was a violation of Title VII, so they "framed their cases in the way most likely to fit within the *Price Waterhouse* theory."[39]

These strategies worked. A unanimous First Circuit panel reversed Freedman's decision, finding that *Price Waterhouse*, bolstered by *Oncale*, made the bank's actions potentially violative of the ECOA because, when "interpreting the ECOA, this court looks to Title VII case law, that is, to federal employment discrimination law."[40] Two of the judges had been appointed by Bill Clinton and one by George H. W. Bush, reflecting a generational if not a purely ideological difference from Judge Freedman. With this decision, GLAD succeeded in creating a new federal precedent that could chip away at federal judicial hostility to transgender rights claims under Title VII.

The First Circuit was not alone in taking a more dynamic approach. Earlier in the year, the Ninth Circuit departed significantly from precedents established in the 1970s and 1980s, marking 2000 as a year of significant legal change for transgender rights under federal law. In *Schwenk*, the Ninth Circuit found that the Gender Motivated Violence Act, enacted in 1994 as part of the

Violence against Women Act, was applicable to the sexual assault of transgender inmate Crystal Schwenk by a Washington state prison guard. Judge Stephen Reinhardt asserted that the legal reasoning in cases such as *Holloway* and *Ulane* "have been overruled by the language and logic of *Price Waterhouse.*" In particular, sex was not limited to "anatomical sex" but also included notions of gender, such as "socially-constructed gender expectations," according to Reinhardt. The decision also embraced the "plain language" approach of *Oncale,* thereby diminishing the effect of legislative intent, despite using that line of reasoning to justify a broad and inclusive "gender-neutral" interpretation of the law.[41] All three judges on the panel had been appointed by Jimmy Carter, and Reinhardt was considered one of the most liberal members of the federal judiciary. Frye saw great potential in the reasoning of *Schwenk,* and she wrote later that year that trans individuals "who have been fired should go to the EEOC with a copy of *Schwenk.*"[42]

Given that they were not Supreme Court decisions, *Rosa* and *Schwenk* were not definitive, yet they profoundly destabilized the precedents of the 1970s and 1980s by rejecting legislative intent as the only way to interpret federal statutes protective of sex and by rejecting a rigid gender binary. They established the foundation of a jurisprudence that would spread to most other circuits, the EEOC, and, ultimately, the Supreme Court.

A LEGAL CONSENSUS EMERGES

After 2000, federal courts began to apply the logic of *Schwenk* and *Rosa* to Title VII, creating a significant consensus that Title VII prohibits discrimination on the basis of gender identity, either as a form of sex stereotyping or as sex discrimination per se. Under this approach, discriminating against individuals who challenge the gender binary is, on its face, sex discrimination, because gender is inappropriately used to make an employment decision. Either approach, however, required a more dynamic interpretation inspired by *Price Waterhouse* and facilitated by *Oncale.* This legal consensus led to the EEOC's ruling in 2012 that gender identity discrimination is actionable under Title VII.

However, in the early 2000s, federal courts continued to reject Title VII claims made by transgender plaintiffs.[43] For example, in the 2002 case of *Oiler v. Winn-Dixie Louisiana, Inc.,* newly minted George W. Bush appointee Lance Africk rejected the application of *Price Waterhouse,* instead relying on *Ulane* in a particularly transphobic opinion. Peter Oiler, who had been employed by Winn-Dixie since 1979, was fired after telling supervisors that he occasionally cross-dressed. Winn-Dixie admitted that Oiler had been fired due to concern about customers' reaction to seeing Oiler dressed as a woman outside of work. Africk, who is still on the federal bench as of 2021, distinguished Oiler's situation from that of Ann Hopkins by tapping into the trope about transgender people "disguising" themselves: "Plaintiff was not discharged because he did not act sufficiently masculine. . . . Rather, the plaintiff disguised himself as a person of a different sex and presented himself as a different sex and presented himself as a female for stress relief and to express his gender identity."[44] Reflecting his ignorance, Africk discussed the case in the context of sexual orientation–based discrimination, even though Oiler was heterosexual. He asserted that the legislative history of Title VII did not allow for the protection of "gender identity disorder" or sexual orientation.[45] Ultimately, Africk simply could not escape the gender binary, and he asserted, "This is a matter of a person of one sex assuming the role of a person of the opposite sex."[46] *Schwenk* and *Rosa* were not mentioned in Africk's opinion, as if the Title VII–related analysis and discussion of the implications of *Price Waterhouse* in those cases had never been uttered. Africk would prove to be an outlier in the coming years, even among some Republican appointees, but his approach demonstrates the strength of the interpretations of Title VII forged in the 1970s and 1980s.

The legal narrative was quite different in *Smith v. City of Salem* (2004), in which the Sixth Circuit became the first federal court to validate gender identity–based protections under Title VII. This important precedent directly influenced the case of Aimee Stephens, which was eventually adjudicated in the same circuit (see chapter 6). One of the remarkable aspects of litigation from the 2000s is the ease with which employers, including public officials, engaged in obvious discrimination against transgender employees. In this case, Smith was a firefighter in Salem, Ohio, who transitioned while working in that capacity. Smith informed supervisors of their plans to transition, and this information was passed along to city officials, including the mayor. These officials attempted to constructively discharge Smith by requiring that they submit to three psychological evaluations. Soon thereafter, Smith contacted the EEOC and received a right-to-sue letter from that agency. Smith's lawsuit was initially dismissed by federal district judge Peter Economus (interestingly, a Clinton appointee), who noted "tension" between *Ulane* and *Price Waterhouse*, referred to sex stereotyping as a "term of art," and asserted that "transsexuals are not protected by

Title VII."[47] He cited neither *Rosa* nor *Schwenk*, eschewing any form of judicial innovation. The Sixth Circuit panel (consisting of two Clinton appointees and one Ford appointee) unanimously overturned that decision, holding that discrimination against transgender individuals is actionable under Title VII. The appellate judges faulted the lower court judge for relying on pre–*Price Waterhouse* precedents. Directly citing *Schwenk*, the Sixth Circuit held: "the approach in *Holloway*, *Sommers*, and *Ulane*—and by the district court in this case—has been eviscerated by *Price Waterhouse*."[48] The court also admonished the trial judge and the city for constantly placing the term "sex stereotyping" in quotation marks. Given this admonition and language such as "eviscerated," *Smith* represented an important moment in the evolution of transgender rights. Now, three federal circuits had applied the reasoning of *Price Waterhouse* to federal laws prohibiting discrimination on the basis of sex and gender.

Smith was "orphaned" litigation, as it was unsupported by any regional or national LGBTQ rights organizations. However, the next significant victory for transgender rights, *Schroer v. Billington* (2008), was supported by the ACLU. In 2004 Diane Schroer applied for the position of specialist in terrorism and crime at the Congressional Research Service of the Library of Congress. She had impressive military and intelligence credentials and was the top applicant. She was offered the position, and she accepted it. However, Schroer then informed a library official that she was transitioning. The job offer was rescinded out of concern that her transition would affect her security clearance, that she would be unable to maintain a good working relationship with the military after transitioning, and that she would not be credible when testifying before Congress.

After the Library of Congress withdrew the job offer, Schroer contacted the ACLU in late 2004. The ACLU attorneys working on LGBTQ rights realized that this would be a good test case, but they were also encouraged by the Sixth Circuit's ruling in *Smith* just a few months earlier. As lead attorney Sharon McGowan stated, "Had the courts not yet decided *Smith* and *Barnes* [*Barnes v. City of Cincinnati* (2005)], there likely would have been greater resistance among my ACLU colleagues to bringing a case on Ms. Schroer's behalf."[49] The ACLU attorneys abandoned the previous approach of framing the issue as discrimination against men, based on sex stereotyping. Thus, the tactics were evolving as the jurisprudence expanded, starting with the incrementalism of GLAD. Only a decade after the hopelessness expressed at ICTLEP meetings, transgender plaintiffs could use Title VII to address the blatant employment discrimination they faced.

Judge James Robertson, a Clinton appointee, found the Library of Congress's reasons for rescinding the job offer to be pretextual and ruled that it had discriminated against Schroer in violation of Title VII, citing both sex stereotyping and per se discrimination on the basis of sex. Library staff had never tried to validate their concerns and simply assumed them to be true, an approach that was "facially discriminatory as a matter of law. Deference to the real or presumed biases of others is discrimination, no less than if an employer acts on behalf of his own prejudices," Robertson declared.[50] Initially, Robertson had been unsure whether the factual record supported a sex-stereotyping claim and "expressed reservations about the Sixth Circuit's reading of *Price Waterhouse*," but he became more convinced of its relevance as the litigation proceeded.[51] Noting that it is difficult to differentiate between sex stereotyping and discrimination per se, Robertson asserted that both forms of discrimination were present in this case. In his analysis of the latter, Robertson used an analogy to religious discrimination:

> Imagine that an employee is fired because she converts from Christianity to Judaism. Imagine too that her employer testifies that he harbors no bias toward either Christians or Jews but only "converts." That would be a clear case of discrimination "because of religion." No court would take seriously the notion that "converts" are not covered by the statute. Discrimination "because of religion" easily encompasses discrimination because of a change of religion. But in cases where the plaintiff has changed her sex, and faces discrimination because of the decision to stop presenting as a man and to start appearing as a woman, courts have traditionally carved such persons out of the statute by concluding that "transsexuality" is unprotected by Title VII. In other words, courts have allowed their focus on the label "transsexual" to blind them to the statutory language itself.[52]

Robertson then invoked *Oncale* for the proposition that the Supreme Court had "applied Title VII in ways Congress could not have contemplated," and he rejected the argument that Congress's failure to add gender identity to the Civil Rights Act or to enact separate protections for gender identity in federal employment law should be interpreted as the intent of Congress. This was a strong repudiation of the 1970s and 1980s precedents and their legal frameworks. Schroer was eventually awarded nearly $500,000 in damages in 2009, and a stronger federal precedent had been established.[53] The Obama administration did not appeal, thus leaving the powerful decision in place. As other scholars have noted, this decision was a return to the per se approach of Judge Grady's district court opinion in *Ulane*. "Judge Robertson's 2008 *Schroer* decision, having followed in the footsteps of decisions such as *Price Waterhouse*, *Oncale*, and *Smith*, was the next logical legal step in the development of Title VII case law, and it set the groundwork for the next stage in Title VII 'because of . . . sex' jurisprudence."[54]

Despite these victories, between 2000 and 2008, the federal judiciary was inconsistent on the question of gender identity and Title VII. For instance, federal judges in Utah and the Tenth Circuit ruled against Krystal Etsitty, who was fired as a bus driver with the Utah Transit Authority after transitioning. District judge David Sam, a Reagan appointee, noted that "there is currently a great deal of tension between *Ulane* and *Price Waterhouse*," but he cited *Ulane* and *Oiler* to defend his strong notions of a gender binary and his reliance on legislative intent. He declared, "This complete rejection of sex-related conventions was never contemplated by the drafters of Title VII and is not required by the language of the statute or the Supreme Court opinion in *Price Waterhouse*."[55] Although the Tenth Circuit panel (composed of two Clinton appointees and one George W. Bush appointee) also ruled against Etsitty, its approach was less dismissive of her claims, especially under *Price Waterhouse*. The judges rejected out of hand the argument for per se discrimination with regard to transgender individuals (making their ruling before the 2008 decision in *Schroer*), but they were open to the idea of applying *Price Waterhouse*. However, in a factually questionable ruling, the Tenth Circuit found that the actual reason for Etsitty's firing had nothing to do with sex stereotyping; rather, it was connected to concerns about restroom use: "However far *Price Waterhouse* reaches, this court cannot conclude it requires employers to allow biological males to use women's restrooms."[56] The ACLU, Lambda Legal, and the National Center for Lesbian Rights filed an amicus brief with the Tenth Circuit grounded in an analysis of *Price Waterhouse* and *Oncale*, indicating that these organizations were engaging with this type of litigation around the country.[57]

Cases out of Texas during this period also reflected federal judges' willingness to embrace the new jurisprudential approach. In 2008, in *Lopez v. River Oaks Imaging, Inc.*, Clinton appointee Nancy Atlas used *Price Waterhouse* to find in favor of a discrimination claim by Izza Lopez in a case supported by Lambda Legal.[58] In 2009 magistrate judge Nancy Stein Nowak ruled in favor of a transgender plaintiff under Title VII.[59] Magistrate judges are appointed by a committee of mostly federal district court judges; they have fixed terms, and they typically deal with early phases of civil litigation, easing the workload of federal district courts. As a result, magistrate judges tend not to be aggressive legal innovators, making Nowak's ruling even more notable and a strong indicator of the evolving jurisprudence of Title VII.

As discussed in chapter 1, overlap exists between statutory and constitutional analysis of discrimination issues. *Glenn v. Brumby* (2011), from the Eleventh Circuit, centered on an analysis of equal protection, but it was grounded in sex-stereotyping theory. This sex-stereotyping approach was accepted by both the district court judge (a Clinton appointee),[60] and all three judges on the appellate panel (including William Pryor, a George W. Bush appointee widely considered to be quite conservative, as well as Carter and Clinton appointees). "The Eleventh Circuit's decision, issued within a week after oral argument, is particularly noteworthy in that it emanated from a circuit that is generally considered conservative in the area of employment law and LGBTQ rights."[61] It was a significant jurisprudential development and, coming from a conservative circuit, demonstrated that the legal momentum was building.

As was the case in *Smith*, Vandiver Elizabeth Glenn was fired by a governmental entity after transitioning. She was employed by the Georgia legislature as an editor in the Office of Legislative Counsel. A few weeks after informing her supervisor that she was transitioning, Glenn was called into the office of Sewell Brumby, senior legislative counsel. He asked, "Do I understand correctly that you have formed a fixed intention of becoming a woman?" When Glenn responded affirmatively, Brumby replied, "I wish you well, but that just can't happen simultaneously with your employment here, and I have to dismiss you." Knowing that this outcome was likely, Glenn had already been in contact with Lambda Legal, and a lawsuit was filed.[62] Glenn's employer claimed that legislators would react negatively to her, referred to being transgender as "unnatural," and deemed it immoral to employ her.[63]

Despite the conservative reputation of the Eleventh Circuit, the litigation was quite one-sided. Glenn and her attorneys had been concerned about Pryor as a potential negative vote, but during the oral argument, Pryor told Brumby's lawyer, "You have a big problem under *Price Waterhouse*." It went so poorly for Brumby that Glenn's attorney decided to skip a prepared argument and just reply to questions from the judges. In a twist on the standard legislative intent approach, Pryor told Brumby's attorney to "take it up with Congress" if he objected to viewing transgender people as a "protected class."[64] Pryor seemed to be indicating that the law compelled him to protect against transgender discrimination and that only an explicit act of Congress could lead to a contrary result. His application of *Price Waterhouse* required a recognition that transgender discrimination was prohibited by the equal protection clause of the Constitution. Relying in part on *Schwenk, Rosa, Smith,* and *Schroer,* Pryor signed off on a decision that declared: "Ever since the Supreme Court began to apply heightened scrutiny to sex-based classifications, its consistent purpose has been to eliminate discrimination of the basis of gender stereotypes."[65] In support of its position, the Eleventh Circuit cited law review articles arguing for the protection of transgender individuals under sex stereotyping, including a prominent 2007 article by Ilona Turner.[66] Turner eventually worked for the Transgender Law Center as its legal director, illustrating the interplay among legal scholarship, activism, and judging in an evolving area of the law.[67]

The court noted that a Title VII analysis would have established illegal discrimination, but it was required to consider the "exceedingly persuasive justification" under a standard equal protection analysis when considering semisuspect classifications. It rejected the formal reason provided by Brumby: other employees' concerns about using the restroom. The court deemed that this was based solely on "speculation," and it noted that "only single-occupancy restrooms" were available in the Office of Legislative Counsel. The opinion, authored by Rosemary Barkett, was quite dismissive of Brumby's legal position: "Brumby has advanced no other reason that could qualify as a governmental purpose, much less an 'important' governmental purpose, and even less than that, a 'sufficiently important governmental purpose' that was achieved by firing Glenn because of her gender non-conformity."[68]

Thus, by 2011, a decade after *Rosa* and *Schwenk,* there was significant federal jurisprudence supporting the notion that Title VII protected transgender and gender nonconforming employees. This facilitated a major policy change by the EEOC, spearheaded by newly appointed commissioner Chai Feldblum.

THE EEOC ALTERS THE LEGAL LANDSCAPE

Barack Obama's appointments to the EEOC, including Feldblum, gave Democrats a three-to-two majority on the commission, allowing policy change in a liberal direction. Feldblum was the first openly LGBTQ person to serve as an EEOC commissioner. She was also a law professor with an extensive policy and advocacy background, having worked on the Americans with Disabilities Act and ENDA. Feldblum and the other commissioners and staff had an agenda to expand protections on the basis of gender identity and sexual orientation under Title VII, and they worked with LGBTQ legal advocacy organizations to do so. However, even before Feldblum began her tenure in 2010, the EEOC had been considering changing its approach to, and interpretation of, Title VII in relation to gender identity. Obama's nominee as general counsel, David Lopez, worked closely with Feldblum on this policy change. By 2012, the commission had fully shifted its direction, represented by the groundbreaking decision in *Macy v. Holder.* The EEOC would extend its new policy by asserting that sexual orientation–based discrimination was prohibited by Title VII in *Baldwin v. Foxx* (2015). These decisions both reflected and accelerated the federal jurisprudential changes that had been taking place since 2000. The EEOC's stance on sexual orientation is explored more fully in the next chapter.

Reflecting the changes in interpretation since 2000 and the fight over a trans-inclusive ENDA, the EEOC issued a letter in 2007 indicating that it was revisiting its decades-long position that Title VII does not cover transgender individuals. This change in policy accelerated once Feldblum arrived at the agency.[69] In 2011 the EEOC noted that its approach to Title VII and transgender claimants was "evolving," and it petitioned to file (unsuccessfully) an amicus brief in favor of a transgender plaintiff claiming discrimination under Title VII.[70] According to Braden Campbell, Feldblum initiated this evolution:

> Feldblum came to the EEOC from academia, where she had pushed a theory
> that Title VII's plain language covered gay and transgender workers. The new
> appointment allowed her to turn that theory into official policy through the
> commission's role deciding appeals from decisions in job bias cases against
> federal employers. "My first year I just asked to see every single decision dealing
> with sex that came out of the federal sector," Feldblum said. "I was just doing my
> job, from my perspective, as commissioner. But then I realized that this was an
> important avenue in which the EEOC could speak."[71]

This was a fairly rapid process, given the EEOC's decades-long policy stance against an expanded interpretation of Title VII. New appointments facilitated the change. As Feldblum writes, "With a full complement of commissioners and a general counsel, the EEOC took to its work with gusto—finishing work on a series of regulations and actively engaging in approving amicus briefs, reviewing subpoena determinations, approving litigation requests, and voting on opinions dealing with claims of discrimination brought by federal employees."[72]

Like Feldblum, Lopez viewed Title VII through an expansive lens. For instance, after departing the EEOC in 2016, he gave a lecture at Harvard Law School titled "Title VII: A Magna Carta of Human Rights." He noted the EEOC's innovative role in expanding the reach of Title VII in the context of LGBTQ rights, stating, "It's on, folks, this battle [for LGBTQ rights under Title VII] is on, this battle is on, okay. This is going to the Supreme Court of the United States. It's on." Lopez also stressed the influence of *Price Waterhouse* and *Oncale*, with a particular emphasis on Scalia's rejection of legislative intent in the latter decision.[73]

The ambition of the EEOC project is clear from the text of the *Macy* decision. Mia Macy applied for, and was tentatively offered (pending a background check), a position as a ballistics investigator with the federal Bureau of Alcohol, Tobacco, Firearms, and Explosives (ATF). At the time, she was a police detective, and she was transitioning. When Macy's transition came to light, an ATF official informed her that there was no longer any funding for the position. Macy filed a complaint with the EEOC and was represented by Ilona Turner and the Transgender Law Center. Finding in favor of Macy, the EEOC asserted that "intentional discrimination against a transgender individual because that person is transgender is, by definition, discrimination 'based on . . . sex,' and such discrimination therefore violates Title VII."[74] The opinion cited and discussed *Price Waterhouse, Oncale, Schwenk, Rosa, Smith, Glenn,* and *Schroer,* noting how the courts in these cases had applied the theory of sex stereotyping. The agency also argued that Title VII prohibited per se discrimination, analogizing discrimination on the basis of gender identity to discrimination based on religion, which is also prohibited by Title VII. It relied substantially on the argument in *Schroer* that a religious conversion triggering an adverse employment action would be prohibited. As the EEOC declared, "A transgender person who has experienced discrimination based on his or her gender identity may establish a prima facie case of sex discrimination through any number of different formulations. These different formulations are not, however, different claims of discrimination. . . . Rather, they are simply different ways of describing sex discrimination."[75] Minus the religion analogy, this would also be the approach taken by Justice Gorsuch and the majority in *Bostock v. Clayton County*, but it would take a carefully crafted litigation strategy to get there. In 2012, however, it was significant that a major civil rights policymaker had fundamentally changed federal policy on employment protections for transgender individuals in a manner that built on, and confirmed, the jurisprudential currents at play since *Price Waterhouse*.

The EEOC soon turned to aggressive enforcement of its new approach, including initiating the legal proceedings for Aimee Stephens (see chapter 6). The agency viewed this as part of its new plan, adopted in late 2012, to make discrimination on the basis of gender identity and sexual orientation "an enforcement priority."[76] In this endeavor, the agency acted in tandem with LGBTQ rights organizations, which knew they had a strong ally when they filed EEOC complaints on behalf of their clients. Rather than only adjudicating disputes within the federal government or providing private claimants with right-to-sue letters, the EEOC commenced independent enforcement actions against employers accused of gender identity–based discrimination. More broadly, employers were put on notice that discrimination on the basis of gender identity could result in legal action.

After 2012, no federal court ruled that discrimination on the basis of gender identity was *not* covered by Title VII (although the conservative Fifth Circuit argued in 2019 that gender identity was not covered, the court made its ruling on a separate basis).[77] A federal magistrate judge in Georgia held in 2015 that a claim of gender nonconformity was actually a claim based on sexual orientation. On appeal, the Eleventh Circuit dismissed the claim based on sexual orientation but held that discrimination on the basis of gender nonconformity was "actionable" in *Evans v. Georgia Regional Hospital* (2017).[78] This case is explored more fully in chapter 5, but in this context, it illustrates that a rejection of the EEOC's approach to gender identity (affirmed by the Eleventh Circuit, with Judge Pryor again acknowledging that a gender nonconformity claim is actionable) would have required a fairly aggressive repudiation of this line of reasoning by the Supreme Court and a return to the pre-2000 jurisprudence.

Even in the previously reluctant Tenth Circuit, a district court judge distinguished Southeastern Oklahoma State University's blanket reading of *Etsitty* and relied on *Smith* to dismiss the university's motion for summary judgment in a case brought by the Obama Justice Department in 2015 (the administration had adopted the EEOC's position on Title VII and gender identity–based discrimination in 2014). In that case, Rachel Tudor, the first openly transgender person on the faculty at Southeastern, had been denied tenure. In a set of facts relevant to the discussion of religious exemptions to Title VII, Douglas McMillan, the vice president for academic affairs, asked the human resources department whether Tudor could be fired for being transgender. According to the complaint, McMillan's sister, who also worked at the university, told Tudor that he "considered transgender people 'to be a grave offense to his [religious] sensibilities.'"[79] The university refused to settle with the EEOC, and this led to the lawsuit brought by the Justice Department's Civil Rights Division. District judge Robin Cauthron, a George H. W. Bush appointee, ruled against the university's motion to dismiss, arguing that, under *Etsitty*, discrimination based on gender nonconformity is actionable, even though discrimination on the basis of "transgender status" is not. She stated, "The factual allegations raised by Dr. Tudor bring her claims squarely within the Sixth Circuit's reasoning [in *Smith*] as adopted by the Tenth Circuit in *Etsitty*."[80] A jury awarded Tudor more than $1 million. Citing the fact that *Bostock* overruled *Etsitty*, the Tenth Circuit ordered her reinstated with tenure in 2021.[81]

Widely considered the most conservative federal circuit, the Fifth Circuit reaffirmed its support for the 1979 precedent of *Blum v. Gulf Oil Corporation* (involving discrimination on the basis of sexual orientation), without directly applying that decision, in *Wittmer v. Phillips 66 Company* (2019). This decision is the most significant rhetorical challenge to the new jurisprudence from a federal appellate court. Although the lower court judge, a George H. W. Bush appointee, found the new Title VII jurisprudence "persuasive," he ruled that the plaintiff provided insufficient evidence that discrimination had occurred. The appellate panel narrowly upheld this decision, while opining on the relevance of *Blum*. One of the judges on the all-Republican panel, Patrick Higginbotham, hinted that *Blum* was undermined by *Lawrence v. Texas*, while judge James Ho strongly defended *Blum* and challenged the post-2000 jurisprudence in what proved to be a preview of justice Samuel Alito's dissent in *Bostock*. Ho is considered one of the most conservative of the conservative Trump appointees. His opinion for the court was narrow, focused on the question of evidence; however, in dicta, he asserted the validity of *Blum* and then wrote a separate concurring opinion expanding on this position. In his concurring opinion, Ho emphasized legislative intent, discussed restrooms at length (even though this was not at issue in the case), sharply limited the precedential value of *Price Waterhouse*, and argued that only Congress could change Title VII.

Adding this concurrence to his own majority opinion was a breathtaking example of conservative judicial aggressiveness. If we categorize the expansion of initial understandings of legislative enactments as leapfrogging, we must also recognize and identify when judges refuse to incorporate consensus-based expansions of interpretations. Here again, we see a split among Republican appointees, with some recognizing the jurisprudential changes and others ignoring them out of obvious ideological commitments. Remarkably, in Ho's view, little had changed since 1979. *Bostock* undermined Ho's approach, but he made President Trump's list of potential Supreme Court nominees for second-term vacancies.[82]

NEW JUDICIAL CONSENSUS EXTENDS TO TITLE IX AND HEALTH CARE

The emerging legal consensus about transgender rights is also evident in areas of federal law dealing with the word "sex." Federal courts, especially appellate courts, have sided overwhelmingly with transgender students claiming discrimination under the Education Amendments of 1972, or Title IX. The relevant language of Title IX reads: "No person in the United States shall, on the basis of sex, be excluded from participation in, be denied the benefits of, or be subjected to discrimination under any education program or activity receiving Federal financial assistance." Transgender students have been guaranteed access to school facilities, including restrooms and locker rooms, based on their gender identity. Federal judges have also found that denying health care coverage to transgender employees is illegal discrimination. Reasoning under Title VII is generally applicable to, and interchangeable with, other areas of federal law with similar statutory language, as evidenced by the importation of legal reasoning from *Schwenk* and *Rosa* to Title VII cases. Only strongly conservative judges have challenged the trend of expanding the interpretation of these provisions.[83]

Under Title IX, transgender students seeking to use school facilities consistent with their gender identity have found nearly uniform success in federal court. As the Eleventh Circuit noted in a 2020 case, *Adams v. School Board of St. Johns County*, "Every court of appeals to consider bathroom policies like the School District's agrees that such policies violate Title IX." The schools in St. Johns County, Florida, prohibited students from accessing facilities based on their gender identity and required them to use facilities inconsistent with that identity or separate, gender-neutral bathroom facilities. The two Democratic appointees in the majority relied on the circuit's own precedent in *Glenn* and the Supreme Court's decision in *Bostock* to find that this policy violates the equal protection clause of the Constitution and Title IX. It noted that the "gender stereotypes the School Board imposed on Mr. Adams track the stereotypes this Court ruled unconstitutional in *Glenn*." Further, the court asserted, "With *Bostock*'s guidance, we conclude that Title IX, like Title VII, prohibits discrimination against a person because he is transgender, because this constitutes discrimination based on sex."[84]

Remarkably, the dissent came from William Pryor, the author of *Glenn* and, at that point, the chief judge of the Eleventh Circuit. He denied the relevance of both his previous decision and *Bostock*, focusing instead on standard conservative objections to transgender rights in workplaces, schools, and other public accommodations. This approach involves (1) denying the existence of gender identity diversity (calling it "gender ideology") and transgender individuals because sex and gender are biologically determined, and (2) identifying a physical, harassing, or privacy threat to cisgender individuals in gender-segregated spaces such as restrooms, based on the mere presence of transgender persons in those spaces. Largely due to the work of Ryan Anderson, the protégé of Princeton political scientist Robert George, this has become a common conservative political and legal narrative.[85] This perspective has reached the most conservative realms of the federal judiciary, and as the majority in *Adams* noted, "Our dissenting colleague believes that the term 'sex' cannot encompass any conception of gender identity."[86] Reflecting this approach, Pryor began his decision with a political statement: "Not long ago, a suit challenging the lawfulness of separating bathrooms on the basis of sex would have been unthinkable. This practice has long been the common-sense example of an acceptable classification on the basis of sex. And for good reason: it protects well-established privacy interests in using the bathroom away from the opposite sex."[87] Pryor also misgendered Adams, referring to him as "a female who identifies as a male," reflecting the view of many strongly conservative judges that sex assigned at birth is more important than self-defined gender identity. For instance, Fifth Circuit Trump appointee Kyle Duncan argued that using the preferred gender pronouns of a litigant would amount to bias in favor of that litigant. Judge Ho also misgendered a litigant in a 2019 opinion.[88] George W. Bush appointee Timothy Corrigan was the district judge who ruled in favor of Adams, citing "the Eleventh Circuit's clear statement in *Glenn*." He grounded his analysis in the new Title VII and Title IX consensus, all of which stemmed from *Price Waterhouse*.[89] Corrigan's decision was based on this jurisprudence and on expert testimony at trial, not ideological analysis. Pryor's more conservative approach apparently motivated an en banc review of *Adams* that was pending as of 2021.[90]

In the years-long case of Gavin Grimm, who also sued for restroom access on the basis of his gender identity, the Fourth Circuit ruled in his favor twice, in 2016 and 2020, despite notable objections from Republican-appointed judges challenging the gender identity jurisprudential consensus. In 2021 the Supreme Court denied an appeal from the school board in the 2020 case, leaving a powerful precedent in place and providing Grimm a victory. In the 2016 case, two Democratic appointees overturned a district court decision against Grimm, with a dissent by Republican appointee Paul Niemeyer. Niemeyer was consistent and persistent: he was the only judge to dissent from an en banc denial of a rehearing in that round of litigation, and he dissented from another decision by two Obama appointees in 2020.[91] Reflecting the consensus represented by the Eleventh Circuit's decision, the Fourth Circuit panel noted: "At the heart of this appeal is whether equal protection and Title IX can protect transgender students from school bathroom policies that prohibit them from affirming their gender. We join a growing consensus of courts in holding that the answer is resoundingly yes." In a powerful concurring opinion, judge James Wynn compared the segregation of transgender students to racial segregation, noting that the "'transgender predator' myth echoes similar arguments used to justify segregation along racial lines." In his dissent from this decision and the consensus, Niemeyer relied on a definition of sex based on genitalia alone, discounted *Bostock*, and elevated cisgender privacy concerns over antidiscrimination principles. He noted that Title IX allows for gender-segregated facilities, a point not contested by Grimm and other plaintiffs, who asked not for unisex facilities but for access to facilities based on their gender identity. This, however, was sufficient for Niemeyer to limit the interpretation of Title IX to the "intent" behind the law rather than the interpretation of the text, bolstering his essentialist view of sex and gender. "In short," he declared, "the physical differences between males and females and the resulting need for privacy is what the exceptions in Title IX are all about."[92]

Despite the approach taken by Pryor and Niemeyer, federal judges have generally been quite skeptical of arguments from parents and school boards that allowing access to facilities based on gender identity violates the privacy and equality rights of cisgender students. Often, these claims are deemed to be speculative or insufficient to reach the legal threshold of sexual harassment when that claim is made. Generally, equality mandates outweigh privacy concerns. Thus, the new Title VII–Title IX jurisprudence has proved to be more powerful than conservative arguments mobilized in opposition to transgender rights.[93]

Texas district court judge Reed O'Connor, a favorite among conservative litigators, is another notable ideological exception to the consensus. Conservatives hoping to achieve national injunctions against policies they oppose, including those that support transgender rights, have forum-shopped for sympathetic jurists like O'Connor. A *Texas Tribune* profile describes O'Connor as a hard-charging legal conservative:

> Active in the conservative Federalist Society, O'Connor is a former aide to U.S. Sen. John Cornyn, R-Texas, and a former federal prosecutor in North Texas who has been rumored to be on the short list for a promotion to a federal appeals court. O'Connor, a 2007 appointee of President George W. Bush, worked in relative obscurity until 2015, when Texas' litigation force began to frequent his courtroom. Since then, he's earned a reputation as a no-nonsense conservative darling.[94]

In 2018 he invalidated the Affordable Care Act, and his decision was widely criticized across the ideological spectrum. In 2016 O'Connor imposed a nationwide injunction against the Obama administration's policy of including gender identity in Title IX. In support of this aggressive use of judicial power, he declared: "It cannot be disputed that the plain meaning of the term sex . . . meant the biological and anatomical differences between male and female students as determined at their birth."[95] The Obama policy was undone by the Trump administration, rendering that particular case moot.

Relying in part on the Seventh Circuit's Title VII and Title IX precedents of *Hively* and *Whitaker v. Kenosha Unified School District*, Obama appointee William Conley challenged Wisconsin's ban on coverage of certain forms of transgender health care under Medicaid and state employee health plans and ruled that this was discriminatory under section 1557 of the Affordable Care Act. This section invokes Title VII and Title IX to prohibit discrimination on the basis of sex.[96] His approach was grounded significantly in sex-stereotyping analysis. Similarly, Obama appointee Rosemary Márquez ruled that Arizona's ban on state employee transgender health care funding ran afoul of Title VII. Another Obama appointee made a similar ruling with regard to North Carolina's ban, based on Title IX and section 1557. All these decisions were handed down before *Bostock*, and one would expect this approach to expand with the Supreme Court's decision. These judges also found equal protection violations, applying intermediate scrutiny. Again, Judge O'Connor was something of an outlier on this question. He ruled against an Obama administration regulation interpreting section 1557 as prohibiting discrimination on the basis of gender identity.[97]

When transgender rights activists turned to a formal litigation campaign, *Price Waterhouse* and *Oncale* provided the foundation. In fact, *Price Waterhouse* served as the inspiration for the rethinking of Title VII jurisprudence in the context of transgender rights. This resulted in a remarkable shift from the precedents of the 1970s and 1980s. The EEOC, controlled by Democrats, embraced this shift and accelerated the trend. Judges appointed by both parties, though driven largely by Democratic appointees, accepted this change in interpretation and recognized the clear implications of *Price Waterhouse*, with the exception of the most conservative holdouts. In just a few years, the hopelessness articulated by transgender activists and their attorneys in the mid-1990s was replaced by a strong judicial consensus that Title VII and similar provisions offer protection for transgender and gender nonconforming individuals.

5. Sexual Orientation, *Price Waterhouse,* and *Oncale*

Claims made under Title VII for sexual orientation–based discrimination were uniformly rejected by federal courts in the 1970s and 1980s, but unlike gender identity–based discrimination claims, there was no clear post–*Price Waterhouse* change in jurisprudence. Fear of bootstrapping and assertions that Congress did not intend to protect sexual orientation in 1964 or later, as evidenced by its inaction, dominated the analysis. After *Oncale,* same-sex sexual harassment claims were sometimes found to be actionable, but nonsexualized discrimination claims, such as being fired or not hired for being LGB, were largely rejected.[1]

Some district court judges began to challenge the status quo in the mid-2010s, followed by the Equal Employment Opportunity Commission (EEOC) and the appellate courts. Until the Seventh Circuit's 2017 decision (discussed in chapter 1), no federal appellate court found in favor of sexual orientation protections; however, building on its 2012 *Macy* decision, the EEOC found sexual orientation–based discrimination to be actionable in 2015 in *Baldwin v. Foxx.* The EEOC's more textualist approach, severed from legislative intent, combined with a more sophisticated understanding of the relationship between sex and sexual orientation, grounded in the analysis of *Price Waterhouse,* destabilized the prior judicial consensus and emboldened federal judges to challenge that consensus. Even after the initial Seventh Circuit and EEOC decisions, other appellate courts declined to use Title VII for sexual orientation–based claims, leading to the circuit split settled by the Supreme Court in *Bostock v. Clayton County.*

The Second Circuit was particularly notable during this transitional period because it had clear recent precedents holding that, outside of sexual harassment claims, sexual orientation was not covered by Title VII. Some judges called for these precedents to be overturned, and the full circuit changed its approach in 2018 in *Zarda v. Altitude Express.* The 2018 shift is explored in chapter 6, while this chapter examines the transitional dynamics within the Second Circuit. *Price Waterhouse* also allowed LGB plaintiffs to challenge negative employment decisions based on sex-stereotyping theory, even if the courts were reluctant to rule that sexual orientation–based discrimination is prohibited by Title VII. By 2019, when the Supreme Court agreed to enter the fray and address the issue, it had become much more legally unsettled. The Supreme Court's 2020 ruling confirmed a much shorter and more contested trend in statutory interpretation, even though the court had been expanding constitutional protections for LGB individuals for decades, and public opinion strongly favored protections against employment discrimination.

CONGRESSIONAL ACTIVITY AND PUBLIC OPINION

Reliance on a litigation-based strategy stemmed from Congress's failure to enact protections based on sexual orientation, despite overwhelming public support and decades of activism. This, of course, refutes the narrative that the legislative branch is most responsive to public sentiment and that unelected judges should refrain from civil rights policymaking. Republican opposition to the expansion of civil rights policy to protect LGBTQ individuals, combined with Republican control of the federal veto power for much of the past several decades, prevented public sentiment from being translated into policy. In the 2000s Democrats were divided over the inclusion of gender identity–based protections, which also constrained policymaking in this area. In addition, although Democrats controlled all levers of federal policymaking in the first two years of the Obama administration, they were intent on repealing "Don't Ask, Don't Tell." The Obama administration was wary of too strong a focus on LGBTQ policy, and House Speaker Nancy Pelosi did not push for a vote on workplace discrimination legislation. Attention to marriage equality also eclipsed antidiscrimination policy.[2]

In 2013 the Democrat-controlled Senate passed a gender identity–inclusive Employment Nondiscrimination Act (ENDA) with ten Republican votes to overcome a filibuster. However, in the House, Republican Speaker John Boehner refused to consider the bill.[3] Its passage by the Senate demonstrates what Congress *could* do, if not for legislative leaders' enormous power to control which bills are considered, often in opposition to clear public sentiment but in line with party interests.

With the introduction of the Equality Act in 2015 and its passage by the House of Representatives in 2019, along party lines, Democrats and activists abandoned the compromise of ENDA and embraced an assertive approach to

LGBTQ civil rights policy. However, because Republicans now controlled the Senate and the White House, the Supreme Court was the lead policymaker, not Congress. The Equality Act would amend Title VII to add sexual orientation and gender identity and eliminate ENDA's broad religion-based exemptions. It would also add these categories to Title II, which prohibits discrimination in public accommodations, and to a range of other federal statutes prohibiting discrimination. Thus, if enacted, it would go beyond the ruling in *Bostock.* The bill passed the House in 2019 by a vote of 236 to 173—with no defections from Democrats and eight Republicans voting in favor of it. In 2021 the bill passed the House by a narrower vote, 224 to 206, reflecting the smaller Democratic majority; this time, only three Republicans voted for the bill. With only fifty Democrats in the Senate after the 2020 elections, the bill faced a Republican-led filibuster as of the summer of 2021, and it was not clear whether support by other Republicans would be sufficient to overcome it.[4]

Since the 1970s, there has been consistent support for policies banning discrimination on the basis of sexual orientation, with support increasing over time. Polling on the question of gender identity does not go back that far, but more recent surveys show support for bans on gender identity–based employment discrimination. According to Jeremiah Garretson, "The trends reveal a more-or-less even liberalization in support of employment protections from the 1970s onward. The amount of change is fairly consistent across question and decade, although rising support for nondiscrimination may have leveled off in the mid-2000s." A 2019 poll conducted by the Public Religion Research Institute found 71 percent of respondents in favor of and 25 percent opposed to "laws that would protect gay, lesbian, bisexual, and transgender people against discrimination in jobs, public accommodations, and housing." If individuals are asked only about employment discrimination on the basis of sexual orientation, the percentage of respondents supporting protection is higher. For instance, in a 2017 poll from Quinnipiac University, 89 percent of respondents answered "illegal" when asked: "Do you think it should be legal or illegal for an employer to discriminate against an employee based on their sexual orientation?" In a 2016 survey, 71 percent of respondents agreed with the statement: "Congress should pass laws to protect transgender people from job discrimination."[5]

Thus, it is clear that congressional inaction is inconsistent with public opinion. As the next chapter outlines, Republican opposition to transgender rights has increased in recent years and was a focal point of the party's messaging in the 2020 campaigns for Congress and the White House. It is also possible that the Supreme Court's decision in *Bostock* will diminish the incentive for Congress to legislate in this area. As Neal Devins notes, "It is often the case . . . that lawmakers are quite happy to leave a contentious social policy issue in the Court's hands. . . . Lawmakers have little incentive to risk their political futures by staking out a position on a volatile political issue."[6]

CONSTITUTIONAL CASES CREATE INSTABILITY IN TITLE VII INTERPRETATION

The Supreme Court's holding that sexual orientation and gender identity are protected under Title VII occurred against the backdrop of the court's increasing protection for the constitutional rights of sexual minorities but less so for gender minorities. Despite the robustness of the constitutional jurisprudence surrounding sex, the Supreme Court has not applied it to transgender and gender nonconforming individuals, although lower courts have done so. The almost uniform rejection of the employment rights of LGBTQ individuals in the 1970s and 1980s coincided with a jurisprudence that refused to apply constitutional protections, such as the right to privacy and equal protection, to such individuals. In fact, the Supreme Court has exhibited hostility toward sexual minorities, culminating in the constitutional legitimacy of sodomy laws in *Bowers v. Hardwick* in 1986. This legal state of affairs was destabilized by the Supreme Court's break with this nonapplication of protection, starting with *Romer v. Evans* in 1996. Many federal judges noted this shift in constitutional jurisprudence when ruling in favor of LGB plaintiffs under Title VII or when calling for higher courts to overturn precedents that excluded sexual orientation. Given the court's marriage equality mandate in *Obergefell*, it was not possible to allow employment discrimination, they argued. As I have stated elsewhere, part of this shift was a turn toward the notion of positive rights, or a conception of rights that include egalitarian in addition to libertarian elements. Under this approach, antidiscrimination principles are as important as principles of freedom from government restraint and coercion.[7]

Justice Anthony Kennedy facilitated this shift, starting with his opinion in *Romer*. As part of the religious right's campaign against antidiscrimination laws protecting sexual orientation, voters in Colorado narrowly approved a state constitutional amendment (known as amendment 2) invalidating and prohibiting such laws. This effort began as soon as the first laws were enacted in the mid-1970s, and it was made famous by Anita Bryant's "Save Our Children" campaign. An important element of Kennedy's decision was his assertion that discrimination is harmful and not simply someone's choice. He was not a conservative who downplayed or dismissed the harm cause by discrimination. Rather, he recognized that identifying the harm was essential for the preservation and protection of civil rights. He noted that amendment 2 "inflicts on them [sexual minorities] immediate, continuing, and real injuries that outrun and belie any legitimate justification that may be claimed for it." Condemning amendment 2 as a violation of the equal protection clause, Kennedy declared: "It is not within our constitutional system to enact laws of this sort."[8] Kennedy echoed this defense of antidiscrimination laws in another case out of Colorado, *Masterpiece Cakeshop v. Colorado Civil Rights Commission* (2018), which some mistakenly interpret as providing a religious exemption to antidiscrimination laws (it does not). Kennedy stated: "Our society has come to the recognition that gay persons and gay couples cannot be treated as social outcasts or as inferior in dignity and worth. For that reason the laws and the Constitution can, and in some instances must, protect them in the exercise of their civil rights. The exercise of their freedom on terms equal to others must be given great weight and respect by the courts." While he noted that there may be narrow exemptions based on religious claims, "it is a general rule that such objections do not allow business owners and other actors in the economy and in society to deny protected persons equal access to goods and services under a neutral and generally applicable public accommodations law."[9] For Kennedy, it was not sufficient for the government to merely leave citizens alone; it must afford all citizens equal dignity and respect, including sexual minorities. Kennedy's decision in *Lawrence v. Texas* (2003), which completely repudiated *Bowers,* also reflected this approach. In particular, he held that Tyron Garner and John Lawrence, who had been arrested in the privacy of Lawrence's apartment, "are entitled to respect for their private lives. The State cannot demean their existence or control their destiny by making their private sexual conduct a crime."[10]

The marriage equality cases were supported by this new jurisprudential foundation. In *United States v. Windsor* (2013), Kennedy emphasized the discriminatory purpose of the Defense of Marriage Act (DOMA): "The avowed purpose and practical effect of the law here in question are to impose a disadvantage, a separate status, and so a stigma upon all who enter into same-sex marriages made lawful by the unquestioned authority of the States. . . . The differentiation demeans the couple, whose moral and sexual choices the Constitution protects and whose relationship the State has sought to dignify."[11] From here, it was just a short jurisprudential leap for the court to strike down state bans on same-sex marriage, as it did in *Obergefell* in 2015. Again, Kennedy emphasized the harm inflicted on same-sex couples and their families. He explicitly noted the evolution of the new jurisprudence relating to sexual minorities and stated, "While *Lawrence* confirmed a dimension of freedom that allows individuals to engage in intimate association without criminal liability, it does not follow that freedom stops there. Outlaw to outcast may be a step forward, but it does not achieve the full promise of liberty." Only the recognition of same-sex marriage would fulfill that promise: "Just as a couple vows to support each other, so does society pledge to support the couple, offering symbolic recognition and material benefits to protect and nourish the union," Kennedy wrote.[12]

Before 2010, marriage equality activists avoided federal litigation, fearing an unresponsive judiciary based on conservative ideology and negative case law. Activists decided on a gradualist strategy, first targeting DOMA and then using a favorable decision to attack state bans on same-sex marriage. The strategy worked. After *Windsor*, a legal dam burst, and federal judges across the ideological spectrum applied that precedent to strike down state bans.[13] Public opinion was also moving rapidly toward acceptance of same-sex marriage. By 2014, national polls consistently showed majority support for the legal recognition of same-sex marriages.[14] With the popular wind at their backs and a powerful Supreme Court precedent, federal judges facilitated activists' desire to eliminate the thirty state constitutional bans on same-sex marriage. And although an EEOC decision does not have the same weight as a Supreme Court decision, *Baldwin* was a powerful legal tool, particularly for Democratic appointees, to oppose and overturn the established approach of fencing sexual orientation out of Title VII's protections.

EARLY POST-*ONCALE* CASES

For nearly two decades after *Oncale*, federal courts refused to apply the logic of that case to find that sexual orientation–based discrimination unconnected to sexual harassment was prohibited under Title VII. Some judges were open to LGB plaintiffs' arguments that they were subjected to discrimination due to sex stereotyping, but this was sporadic and did not provide blanket protections based on sexual orientation. By 2014, it could accurately be stated that "each of the 12 circuit courts of appeals have held that discrimination based on sexual orientation is not actionable under Title VII."[15] A 2013 Lambda Legal amicus brief reflected the relative timidity of legal activists on this question. Not until 2014 did this uniform approach start to break down with the DC court's decision in *TerVeer v. Billington.* The EEOC's consequential 2015 decision in *Baldwin* soon followed.

Emblematic of the post-*Oncale* refusal to allow sexual orientation–based claims under Title VII, the First Circuit's panel of Republican appointees went out of its way in *Higgins v. New Balance* (1999) to dismiss the plaintiff's claims of harassment and discrimination because they were ultimately grounded in his sexual orientation. The court did not deny the severity of the harassment and discrimination faced by Robert Higgins, who "toiled in a wretchedly hostile environment." However, this was no reason to engage in bootstrapping, according to the court: "We hold no brief for harassment because of sexual orientation; it is a noxious practice, deserving of censure and opprobrium. But we are called upon here to construe a statute as glossed by the Supreme Court, not to make a moral judgement—and we regard it as settled law that, as drafted and authoritatively construed, Title VII does not proscribe harassment simply because of sexual orientation." To the First Circuit, *Price Waterhouse* and *Oncale* were irrelevant. Indeed, it referred to the plaintiff's use of these cases pejoratively as "riding this horse for all it is worth."[16] These cases had changed nothing for LGB plaintiffs under Title VII, according to the First Circuit. Ironically, this case helped inspire GLAD's gender identity–based litigation discussed in chapter 4. In a footnote, the First Circuit noted that *Oncale* expanded the reach of *Price Waterhouse* and held that "a man can ground a claim of evidence that other men discriminated against him because he did not meet stereotyped expectations of masculinity."[17]

In 2000 the neighboring Second Circuit took a similar approach in *Simonton v. Runyon.* That panel, consisting of two Clinton appointees and one George H. W. Bush appointee, cited *Higgins* and was similarly appalled by the workplace conduct in question. But the court maintained that the text of the statute (lacking the words "sexual orientation") and legislative intent, bolstered by congressional inaction, provided no cause of action: "Title VII does not prohibit harassment or discrimination because of sexual orientation."[18] In this analysis, the court repeatedly cited *DeSantis v. Pacific Telephone & Tele-graph*. Like the First Circuit in *Higgins*, the Second Circuit refused to apply *Oncale* because that case applied only to harassment based on sex. And ac-cording to the Second Circuit, the record in the case did not establish that one sex had been singled out for discrimination and harassment. It declared, "We are unable to infer that the alleged conduct would not have been directed at a woman."[19] Interestingly, the court asserted that a sex-stereotyping claim might have succeeded, but the plaintiff had not made this argument. This would have been an acceptable interpretation under *Price Waterhouse*, not judicial innovation: "This would not bootstrap protection for sexual orientation into Title VII because not all homosexual men are stereotypically feminine, and not all heterosexual men are stereotypically masculine. But it would plainly afford relief for discrimination based upon sexual stereotypes."[20] One judge on the panel, Clinton appointee Robert Katzmann, would eventually lead the Second Circuit's interpretative shift. Here, we can see the door leading to that change cracking open.

In 2001 the Ninth Circuit found a sex-stereotyping claim to be valid in *Nichols v. Azteca Restaurant Enterprises*. In doing so, the court chipped away at its own precedent of *DeSantis*, holding that it had been undermined by *Price Waterhouse*: "To the extent that it conflicts with *Price Waterhouse*, as we hold it does, *DeSantis* is no longer good law."[21] The Ninth Circuit also cited its 2000 holding in *Schwenk v. Hartford*, forbidding discrimination on the basis of gender role expectations. The panel consisted of all Democratic appointees: two recent Clinton appointees, along with liberal stalwart Stephen Reinhardt, appointed by Carter.

In *Prowel v. Wise Business Forms* (2009), the Third Circuit took a similar approach and, according to Susan Gluck Mezey, "provided an opening for gay and lesbian plaintiffs."[22] This case indicates that federal appellate judges, in-cluding some Republican appointees, had moved away from a blanket refusal to consider the claims of LGB plaintiffs under Title VII and that sex-stereo-typing analysis was becoming more accepted. All the judges on this panel had been appointed by George W. Bush, including Thomas Hardiman, the author of the decision, who would later be on Donald Trump's short list of possible Supreme Court nominees.[23] The district court had dismissed Prowel's claims outright, asserting that it was a sexual orientation case "repackaged as a gen-der stereotyping claim in an attempt to avoid summary judgement." Noting that "the line between sexual orientation discrimination and discrimination 'because of sex' can be difficult to draw," the appellate court ruled that a gay plaintiff could bring a case based on sex stereotyping: "It is possible that the harassment Prowel alleges was because of his sexual orientation, not his effeminacy. Nevertheless, this does not vitiate the possibility that Prowel was also harassed for his failure to conform to gender stereotypes."[24] Hardiman relied on the Third Circuit precedent of *Bibby v. Philadelphia Coca Cola Bottling Co.* from 2001, in which a unanimous panel had declared that a gay male plaintiff could bring a sex-stereotyping claim. That panel's two Democratic appointees included Donald Trump's sister, Maryanne Trump Barry, who authored the opinion, and a judge appointed by George H. W. Bush.[25] Hardiman and his colleagues were thus bound by the precedent of a less conservative panel.

Trump ultimately chose Neil Gorsuch for the Supreme Court over Hardiman, begging the question: would Hardiman have ruled that the text of Title VII requires the inclusion of gender identity and sexual orientation, as Gorsuch did? His position in 2009 was that it did not. In another ironic twist, the third judge on Trump's short list was William Pryor, who opposed the inclusion of sexual orientation but clearly believed that gender identity–based protections were mandated by *Price Waterhouse.*

In the cases cited above, district court judges typically ruled in favor of employers, declining to expand the interpretation of Title VII. Thus, *TerVeer v. Billington,* a 2014 case involving discrimination by the Library of Congress, was notable for two reasons: the decision expanded sex-stereotyping analysis in the context of LGB plaintiffs, and it was made by a district court judge. Up to that point (prior to the EEOC's ruling in 2015), it was the clearest embrace of the idea that an LGB plaintiff was protected by Title VII. While the decision was based on a sex-stereotyping analysis, the plaintiff's sexual orientation was central to both his claims of discrimination and the judge's assessment. Peter TerVeer was subjected to lectures and statements by his religiously conservative supervisor in the Office of the Inspector General, and his complaints about this behavior went unaddressed by officials at the Library of Congress. For instance, the decision chronicles the following interaction between TerVeer and his supervisor, John Mech:

> On June 21, 2010, Mech called an unscheduled meeting, lasting more than an hour, for the stated purpose of "educating [Plaintiff] on Hell and that it is a sin to be a homosexual . . . [, that] homosexuality was wrong[,] and that [Plaintiff] would be going to Hell." Mech began reciting Bible verses to Plaintiff and told

Plaintiff "I hope you repent because the Bible is very clear about what God does to homosexuals." Four days later, on June 25, 2010, Plaintiff received his annual review from Mech. Plaintiff found the review did not accurately reflect the quality of his work and believed the review was motivated by Mech's religious beliefs and sexual stereotyping. That day, Plaintiff confronted Mech regarding the purpose of his religious lecturing and "the unfair treatment that began after Mech learned [Plaintiff] was homosexual." Mech was greatly angered by Plaintiff's questioning, vehemently denied that Plaintiff's homosexuality and personal religious views had impacted his impartiality with regard to Plaintiff's work and performance, and accused Plaintiff of trying to "bring down the library."[26]

Judge Colleen Kollar-Kotelly, a Clinton appointee, agreed that this amounted to sex stereotyping stemming from Mech's disapproval of TerVeer's sexual orientation. This discrimination was not based on TerVeer's gender nonconforming behavior, as previous courts had conceived of it; rather, it was based on direct discrimination because of his sexual orientation. This alone constituted sex stereotyping, according to Kollar-Kotelly. Previous courts had generally required some form of gender norm transgression, beyond a disapproval of sexual orientation, to find a violation of Title VII. Thus, this was a significant judicial "breakthrough," as described by Mezey.[27] Kollar-Kotelly was not obsessed with bootstrapping, as judges had been for decades, and she was comfortable protecting LGBTQ rights. In 2017 Kollar-Kotelly issued a preliminary injunction against the Trump administration's ban on transgender members of the military as a likely violation of the equal protection clause in a "strongly worded" decision.[28]

The success in *TerVeer* was connected to activists' attempts to push federal judges to expand their approach to Title VII and sexual orientation. Their strategy was to use test cases and the submission of amicus briefs, with the goal of "bringing each of the federal circuits around, one by one, to the correct interpretation of Title VII." They also knew that the EEOC was a strong ally in these efforts.[29] The brief by Lambda Legal in *TerVeer* emphasized that a plaintiff's LGB status did not preclude Title VII protection, stressed the issue of relational or associational discrimination, and argued that discrimination on the basis of sexual orientation is sex discrimination per se. The brief's overarching objective was to counter the phenomenon of "immunizing sexual orientation discrimination." The brief also countered a common argument by judges and employers: that Congress was speaking through its inaction when it failed to add sexual orientation to federal civil rights law. Lambda Legal invoked Scalia's opinion in *Oncale* to make this counterargument: one "can be reasonably sure that Justice Scalia and a unanimous Court, in dismissing the relevance of the 88th Congress that passed Title VII, were not inviting courts deciding coverage issues to shift their focus to what later sessions of Congress did not enact into statutory law."[30] The EEOC also worked with Lambda Legal, encouraging test cases such as *Hively*, in which Lambda Legal filed an appeal in 2015. According to journalist Braden Campbell, in addition to bringing transgender rights cases in the wake of *Macy*, the EEOC "enlisted the help of LGBTQ legal rights group Lambda Legal to develop more worker-friendly case law on the sexual orientation issue."[31]

Thus, by the middle of the 2010s, there was a concerted effort, buoyed by *Windsor* and *Obergefell,* to move the federal judiciary beyond recognizing same-sex sexual harassment and certain cases of discrimination based only on sex stereotyping of LGB plaintiffs. The goal was to get the federal courts where the Supreme Court would eventually be in 2020—acceptance of the proposition that discrimination on the basis of sexual orientation is clearly discrimination because of sex and thus prohibited by Title VII. The courts had been moving in a more expansive direction, but the outcome of this legal advocacy was far from clear in 2014 and 2015. The EEOC's adoption of this position was a clear turning point, resulting in a consequential shift in the interpretation of Title VII.

THE EEOC EMBRACES LGBTQ RIGHTS AGAIN

Before the *Baldwin* decision in 2015, no federal court had ruled that discrimination on the basis of sexual orientation per se was covered by Title VII's protections. Using *Price Waterhouse* and sex-stereotyping analysis, some had pointed in that direction, but none had ruled definitively and broadly. After *Baldwin*, courts began to take this approach to sexual orientation and Title VII, but not uniformly. Clearly, the EEOC decision was a catalyst, and it validated the arguments that activists such as Lambda Legal had been making. It was a split 3-to-2 decision, with the Democrats voting in favor of the expanded interpretation and the Republicans opposed. As discussed in chapter 4, Chai Feldblum was the driving force behind this change in interpretation, and legal journalist Mark Joseph Stern describes her as "a one-woman legal powerhouse who helped enshrine equal dignity for LGBTQ people into law."[32] *Baldwin* was part of the same strategy to expand LGBTQ rights that resulted in *Macy*, and the EEOC used that decision as a springboard for the inclusion of sexual orientation.

David Baldwin was an air traffic controller at Miami International Airport. Although he had been promoted to a temporary management position, he was not given a permanent position. Because Baldwin was an employee of the Federal Aviation Administration, the EEOC possessed direct jurisdiction over his claim of discrimination. As the EEOC decision described the facts: "Complainant stated that in May 2011, when he mentioned that he and his partner had attended Mardi Gras in New Orleans, the supervisor said, 'We don't need to hear about that gay stuff.' He also alleged that the supervisor told him on a number of occasions that he was a distraction in the radar room when his participation in conversations included mention of his male partner."[33]

In its reasoning, the EEOC largely followed Lambda Legal's approach in the *TerVeer* brief and declared, "We conclude that sexual orientation is inherently a 'sex-based consideration,' and an allegation of discrimination based on sexual orientation is necessarily an allegation of sex discrimination under Title VII." The decision found that sex and sexual orientation are "inseparable." The EEOC offered an analogy that would also be used by the Seventh Circuit in *Hively v. Ivy Tech Community College*: "Assume that an employer suspends a lesbian employee for displaying a photo of her female spouse on her desk, but does not suspend a male employee for displaying a photo of his female spouse on his desk. The lesbian employee in that example can allege that her employer took an adverse action against her that the employer would not have taken had she been male." The EEOC also argued that discrimination on the basis of sexual orientation is associational discrimination and grounded in inappropriate sex stereotyping. It relied on *Oncale* for the proposition that congressional intent or lack of action is not dispositive when interpreting Title VII. Further, the EEOC rejected that argument that its approach would "create a new class of covered persons." The EEOC asserted that it was simply applying statutory language to new situations connected to discrimination: "When courts held that Title VII protected persons who were discriminated against because of their relationships with persons of another race, the courts did not thereby create a new protected class of people in interracial relationships. And when the Supreme Court decided that Title VII protected persons discriminated against because of gender stereotypes held by an employer, it did not thereby create a new protected class of 'masculine women.'"[34]

The decision was a sweeping embrace of the theories offered by activists in the context of LGBTQ rights and made possible by *Price Waterhouse* and *Oncale.* Lambda Legal noted the success of its strategy: "For years, Lambda Legal has been explaining to courts that Title VII, when properly understood, protects LGBT employees. Three of Lambda Legal's successful efforts in 2014, in federal courts in Seattle, Chicago and Washington D.C., were cited by the EEOC in *Baldwin v. Foxx.*"[35]

Immediate reaction to the decision was muted and uncertain, definitely not commensurate with the influence the decision would ultimately have. However, given the relatively low profile of the EEOC compared with the Supreme Court, this was not unexpected. As law professor and former LGBTQ rights litigator Suzanne Goldberg states, "There is often not a lot of publicity for agency determinations even when those determinations are extremely important."[36] Given the negative precedents in the circuit courts, some commentators were unsure whether the EEOC decision would make a difference. As one attorney described the future legal uncertainty, "This has to work its way through the courts, and we don't know if they are going to accept this theory."[37]

EEOC INFLUENCE, A CIRCUIT SPLIT, AND A NEW APPROACH

After the EEOC decision in *Baldwin*, there was a significant but not uniform trend among federal judges to endorse the approach in a manner that rejected the previous fear of bootstrapping. Generally, Democratic appointees expanded the interpretation of Title VII in the wake of *Baldwin*, while Republican appointees were more divided, especially in the circuit courts, as reflected in the discussion of *Hively* in chapter 1. In particular, between 2015 and 2017, when the en banc panel in *Hively* rendered its decision, district court judges could either follow the EEOC or fall back on the uniformly negative appellate court precedents related to the inclusion of sexual orientation under Title VII. Notably, several chose to follow the EEOC. The agency's decision was a new and powerful resource for judges who were willing to use it.

The EEOC wasted little time in trying to shape the outcome of future litigation. It quickly turned to enforcing its new position by bringing actions against private employers, in tandem with Lambda Legal. For instance, in *EEOC v. Scott Medical Health Center*, the ACLU and Lambda Legal, along with other regional and national organizations, filed an amicus brief. Judge Cathy Bissoon, an Obama appointee, embraced the EEOC's approach laid out in *Baldwin* and declared: "There is no more obvious form of sex stereotyping than making a determination that a person should conform to heterosexuality." Bissoon did so despite Third Circuit precedents such as *Bibby* and *Prowel*, which rejected a discrete sexual orientation protection, demonstrating the extent to which the legal ground had shifted by 2016. She distinguished those cases because they did not present precisely the same arguments; instead, she relied on other recent federal district court decisions such as *TerVeer*. Bissoon noted that the precedents had become destabilized, particularly in the wake of *Obergefell*: "The Supreme Court's recent opinion legalizing gay marriage demonstrates a growing recognition of the illegality of discrimination on the basis of sexual orientation."[38] Bissoon's approach was not uniform among district court judges, however. George W. Bush appointee Joel Slomsky noted the same legal shifts but refused to depart from the Third Circuit precedents in *Doe v. Parx Casino* (2019), even after other circuits had started to change their approach.[39] Judging is about choices reinforced by ideology, as evidenced by two district court judges in the same circuit applying that circuit's precedents in such a diametrically opposed manner.

In late 2015 and 2016 other district court judges followed the EEOC and ruled that sexual orientation is protected by Title VII. Although all these innovators were appointed by Democrats, not all Democratic appointees would take this position. In *Isaacs v. Felder Services* (2015), Myron Thompson, a Carter appointee, agreed "with the view of the Equal Employment Opportunity Commission that claims of sexual orientation–based discrimination are cognizable under Title VII."[40] Obama appointee Mark Walker did not embrace the EEOC's analysis in its entirety, but he held in *Winstead v. Lafayette County Board of County Commissioners* (2016) that "discrimination of the basis of sexual orientation is necessarily discrimination based on gender or sex stereotypes" and thus prohibited by Title VII.[41] Johnson appointee and senior district judge Jack Weinstein offered a "times have changed" argument similar to that of judge Richard Posner (see chapter 1). In an opinion evocative of a mid-twentieth-century analysis based on legal realism, Weinstein acknowledged the legal changes reflected by the EEOC decision and the line of cases ending with *Obergefell,* but he also engaged in an extensive discussion of public opinion and policy shifts in favor of sexual orientation–based protections, complete with figures, tables, and a map. As he asserted, "The nation continues to seek equality, understanding, and acceptance of lesbian, gay, and bisexual members of our community."[42] In *Boutilier v. Hartford Public Schools* (2016), Carter appointee Warren Eginton noted the negative precedent in the Second Circuit but agreed with the EEOC's approach. He believed the Second and Seventh Circuits were likely reconsidering their interpretations and asserted, "Straightforward statutory interpretation and logic dictate that sexual orientation cannot be extricated from sex; the two are necessarily intertwined in a manner that, when viewed under the Title VII paradigm set forth by the Supreme Court, place sexual orientation discrimination within the penumbra of sex discrimination."[43] Illustrating the connection between Title VII and similar areas of federal law, judge Dean Pregerson, appointed by Clinton, ruled that discrimination on the basis of sexual orientation is prohibited by Title IX in *Videkis v. Pepperdine University* (2015), citing *Baldwin.*[44]

Some Republican-appointed district court judges were reluctant to follow the EEOC. For instance, in *Hinton v. Virginia Union University* (2016), Robert Payne, appointed by George H. W. Bush, explicitly refused to follow the agency or any of its reasoning. He asserted that any changes in the understanding of Title VII's protections should come from Congress: "It is not the province of unelected jurists to effect such an amendment."[45] Other judges, appointees of both parties, acknowledged the shift on the question of sexual orientation but felt constrained by precedents in their circuits.

Courts of appeals began to hear the new crop of lawsuits starting in 2016. Generally, three-judge panels were reluctant to embrace the new approach, with Democratic appointees dissenting or pointing out the need to update their circuit's interpretation (joined by some Republican appointees, especially in the Seventh Circuit). However, courts sitting en banc adopted the new approach in *Hively* and in *Zarda* (*Zarda* is discussed in chapter 6).

Kimberly Hively sued Ivy Tech Community College on her own, but Lambda Legal took the case after she lost in district court in 2015. In that decision, Reagan appointee Rudy Lozano held that a Seventh Circuit precedent precluded a sexual orientation–based claim under Title VII. His decision came a few months before the EEOC ruling in *Baldwin.*[46] A three-judge panel of the Seventh Circuit upheld this decision, but it was overturned by the full court. The initial appellate panel consisted of Republican appointees who were conflicted about the relatively new instability in the law, especially in light of the EEOC decision. According to judge Ilana Rovner, the EEOC "created a groundswell of questions about the rationale for denying sexual orientation claims while allowing nearly indistinguishable gender non-conformity claims, which courts have long recognized as a form of sex discrimination under Title VII." Rovner also noted the irony of the Supreme Court allowing same-sex marriage but not protecting sexual minorities from discrimination. Indeed, Rovner blamed the high court for this inconsistency, despite strong precedents supporting antidiscrimination protections. She stated:

> Curiously, however, despite *Price Waterhouse* and *Oncale*, the Supreme Court has opted not to weigh in on the question of whether Title VII's prohibition on sex-based discrimination would extend to protect against sexual orientation discrimination. Even in the watershed case of *Obergefell*, when the Court declared that "laws excluding same-sex couples from the marriage right impose stigma and injury of the kind prohibited by our basic charter," it made no mention of the stigma and injury that comes from excluding lesbian, gay, and bisexual persons from the workforce or subjecting them to un-remediable harassment and discrimination. Perhaps the majority's statement in *Obergefell* that "[i]t demeans gays and lesbians for the State to lock them out of a central institution of the Nation's society" could be read as a forecast that the Supreme Court might someday say the same thing about locking gay men and lesbians out of the workforce—another "central institution of the Nation's society." But, as we noted earlier, in the same-sex marriage case, the Court was presented with the opportunity to consider the question as one of sex discrimination but declined to do so and thus far has declined to take any opportunity to weigh in on the question of sexual orientation discrimination under Title VII.

Ultimately, Rovner argued that the panel's hands were tied by Supreme Court and congressional inaction, in addition to the legacy of *Ulane* and its power in the Seventh Circuit. Although the EEOC's ruling and other federal court decisions outside of the Seventh Circuit reflected the "writing on the wall," that was not enough. "Until the writing comes in the form of a Supreme Court opinion or new legislation, we must adhere to the writing of our prior precedent," she declared. Subsequently, the writing was enough for the full court, or at least for a significant number of its judges. Rovner and another judge from the initial panel, Kenneth Ripple, joined the en banc decision, while the third member of the panel, William Bauer, dissented. In the mostly Republican Seventh Circuit, this debate largely took place among Republican appointees. It was an indication of how quickly things were moving in Title VII interpretation and how foundational *Price Waterhouse* and *Oncale* were to this shift.[47]

A similar dynamic occurred in the Second Circuit. Appellate court judges could see the law evolving in a powerful way, but they felt restricted by circuit precedents and called for en banc rulings. In *Anonymous v. Omnicom Group* (2017), a panel of two Democratic appointees and one Republican overturned a district court's ruling that a gay man could not pursue a claim based on gender stereotyping. The appellate court argued that circuit precedent barred it from also accepting a claim of sexual orientation–based discrimination. A concurring opinion, written by one of the Democratic appointees and joined by the other, called for a full panel to reconsider the issue. This judge was none other than chief judge Robert Katzmann, who was now calling for his own precedent of *Simonton* to be overturned. As he opined seventeen years later, "I write separately to express my view that when the appropriate occasion presents itself, it would make sense for the Court to revisit the central legal issue confronted in *Simonton* . . . , especially in light of the changing legal landscape that has taken shape in the nearly two decades since *Simonton* [was] issued."[48] In doing so, he relied heavily on the EEOC ruling, other favorable court decisions, and the Supreme Court's pro–LGB rights jurisprudence, taking an approach almost identical to Rovner's. Katzmann would soon write the full court's opinion in *Zarda*, which did exactly what he recommended (see chapter 6).

More conservative than the Second and Seventh Circuits, the Eleventh Circuit refused to embrace the new interpretation of Title VII. In *Evans v. Georgia Regional Hospital* (2017), it held firm to the view that sexual orientation discrimination was not actionable, and the full court denied a review of, and potential change to, this position. The Supreme Court also rejected an appeal from Lambda Legal in this case. In the Eleventh Circuit, William Pryor was part of the effort to bracket sexual orientation from gender identity under Title VII (recall that he had endorsed the inclusion of gender identity protections). The appellate court in this case overturned the lower court's ruling that Jameka Evans could not bring a gender nonconformity claim, while agreeing that a sexual orientation claim was foreclosed by the circuit's precedents. By this time, Lambda Legal was representing Evans, and the EEOC filed an

amicus brief in the appeal. However, the court disregarded the agency's arguments, relying on its own precedents and older case law from various circuits,
including *Blum* (see chapter 4). Although *Blum* was a Fifth Circuit decision,
the Eleventh Circuit had been created from a division of the Fifth in 1981, so
pre-1981 precedents were applicable.

In a concurring opinion, Pryor elaborated on the differences between
gender identity and sexual orientation under Title VII. The core of Pryor's
argument was that some lesbians and gay men (he did not address bisexual
persons) may not engage in same-sex sexual activity or relationships or that
they may not appear to be LGB by contravening traditional gender roles. He
utilized a common conservative approach to sexual orientation—divorcing
"behavior" from "status." He stated, "A gay individual may establish with
enough factual evidence that she experienced sex discrimination because her
behavior deviated from a gender stereotype held by an employer, but our review of that claim would rest on behavior alone." Thus, if a person is celibate
or does not challenge traditional gender stereotypes, Title VII does not protect
that individual. Remarkably, he cited a brief from the *Obergefell* litigation submitted by an "ex-gay" organization to support the proposition that "gay individuals choose to enter mixed-orientation marriages." Of course, such entities
came out on the losing side in *Obergefell* and were, to say the least, an unusual
source of legal authority. Unlike his fellow Republican appointee Rovner from
the Seventh Circuit, Pryor was uninterested in and unconcerned with recent
changes in interpretation grounded in *Price Waterhouse* and *Oncale*; rather,
he based his analysis on standard socially conservative understandings of sexual orientation. For him, *Price Waterhouse* had no bearing on the question of
LGB "status." As he noted, "The only possible 'status' in *Price Waterhouse* was
the employee's status as an 'aggressive' woman." He could envision a direct
connection between Ann Hopkins and transgender individuals, but he could
not make the same link to LGB individuals, except through their "behavior."
Remarkably, he framed this approach through the lens of diversity, citing "the
diversity of experiences of gay individuals."[49]

This appears to be a fairly clear instance of ideology trumping legal analysis (similar to the analysis of judge James Ho discussed in chapter 4). Pryor's
obsession with "behavior" is not a position driven by competing approaches
to statutory interpretation; it is more likely connected to his views on sexual
diversity, as exhibited by his citation of "ex-gay" perspectives. One can envision a different dynamic in *Bostock* had Donald Trump nominated Pryor to

the Supreme Court instead of Neil Gorsuch. Pryor had been one of Trump's final three candidates, and ironically, it was likely his decision in *Glenn v. Brumby* that led to him being passed over. Eliana Johnson and Shane Gold-macher described the behind-the-scenes lobbying taking place in 2017—an obvious example of boundary maintenance: "As Gorsuch's fortunes have risen, Pryor's have dimmed. A 2006 George W. Bush appointee, Pryor is currently the subject of raging debate on an off-the-record group email list that includes many in the conservative legal and political communities, including many Republican Senate staffers, thanks to his decision to join the majority in *Glenn v. Brumby,* a 2011 opinion that protected transgender people from workplace discrimination."[50] A textualist path to sexual orientation protection might not have been viable in the presence of Pryor's socially conservative take on the issue.

In a direct critique of Pryor, Obama appointee Robin Rosenbaum placed *Price Waterhouse* back in the center of the analysis in her dissent. She described that precedent as "revolutionary" and declared that it had "rocked the world of Title VII litigation." Rather than trying to explain it away, she argued that it was the start of a path leading to the inclusion of sexual orientation in Title VII interpretation, including *Glenn v. Brumby.* She called the distinction between discriminating on the basis of stereotypes and sexual orientation "arbitrary." Most notably, she extensively critiqued Pryor's concurrence, arguing that he "tries to use this case as a do-over of that one [*Glenn*]." She was especially critical of Pryor's emphasis on "behavior," noting that the "distinction between 'behavior' and 'being' is a construct that is both illusory in its defiance of logic and artificial in its lack of legal basis." Calling Pryor's discussion of this distinction "irrelevant," Rosenbaum wrote that Pryor's "argument seems to fundamentally misunderstand what it means to be a lesbian. Lesbians are women who are sexually attracted to other women. That's not a stereotype; it's a definition." She also pointed out that her approach was in line with the EEOC and other recent court decisions.[51]

REJECTION OF THE FIRST COORDINATED
SUPREME COURT APPEAL

By 2017, LGBTQ rights litigators were ready to take the issue to the Supreme Court, and they appealed the Eleventh Circuit's *Evans* decision in September.

Lambda Legal coordinated with Stanford Law School's Supreme Court Litigation Clinic, which would lead the oral arguments in *Bostock* two years later. Stanford professors Pamela Karlan and Jeffrey Fisher were on the petition for certiorari, along with Lambda Legal attorneys. Coming only two years after the EEOC's *Baldwin* decision, the timing reflected the depth of the Lambda Legal–EEOC strategy and the fear that Justice Kennedy might soon retire from the Supreme Court, leaving the fifth pro-LGBTQ rights vote in limbo. Indeed, Chicago-Kent law professor Anthony Kreis argued that a Kennedy retirement would be detrimental to LGBTQ rights cases and that Neil Gorsuch would be an "unreliable vote." Greg Nevins of Lambda Legal was more optimistic about Gorsuch, who would become central to advocates' litigation strategies in the Supreme Court in 2019 and 2020.[52] Further supporting the strategy, the Seventh Circuit had ruled en banc in *Hively* in April, and in May the Second Circuit signaled that it was ready to take up Judge Katzmann's plea by agreeing to hear *Zarda* en banc. In doing so, the court requested an amicus brief from the EEOC. The legal ground was shifting rapidly, but the Supreme Court was potentially moving in a more conservative direction. The window of opportunity appeared to be closing, despite the shift in accepted jurisprudence.[53]

This early attempt to get the Supreme Court's attention was not as well developed in terms of amicus support, for instance, as the successful attempt commenced in 2019, but the legal foundation was clear. The EEOC's 2015 decision was highly consequential for the shift in legal analysis. The sporadic decisions supporting this shift became much more regular, and judges called for a change in the law from "higher powers" even when they voted to uphold the pre-*Baldwin* approach. The issue was not a legal or a prudential one; rather, it was an issue of judicial politics and timing. On a policy level, Lambda Legal emphasized the need for uniformity, given the uneven application of the new approach to Title VII and sexual orientation. But the organization also leveraged the Supreme Court's marriage equality jurisprudence, targeting Justice Kennedy in particular: "Ours is a national economy, and basic protections in the workforce should not depend on geography. More fundamentally, lesbian, gay, and bisexual Americans will not enjoy true legal equality until their sexual orientation is irrelevant not only to their right to enter into consenting relationships and to marry but also their ability to maintain jobs and pursue their livelihoods." Here, the right to intimacy and marriage and the right to earn a livelihood were framed by Lambda Legal and the Stanford clinic as equally important. However, the Supreme Court denied the petition in December.

It would take up the issue in 2019 without Kennedy and with a new strategy focused on Gorsuch.[54]

When activists campaigned to prohibit sexual orientation–based discrimination through Title VII, the results from federal judges were mixed, despite the EEOC's support. For many judges, especially Republican appointees, this required too much bootstrapping. *Price Waterhouse* was too far removed to be applicable, and existing precedents emphasized that only Congress could change the law, despite the guidance provided by Scalia in *Oncale*. Democratic appointees, in contrast, saw the connection to the evolving jurisprudence on gender identity and applied a similar approach to sexual orientation. Ultimately, the latter approach would be the one embraced by the Supreme Court.

6. *Bostock*, Stephens, and *Zarda* in the Lower Federal Courts

Bostock v. Clayton County, R. G. & G. R. Harris Funeral Homes v. EEOC, and *Zarda v. Altitude Express* percolated in the legal environment surrounding the issue of LGBTQ employment discrimination. These cases were the direct result of strategies designed to change the federal legal interpretation of Title VII, grounded in an analysis derived from *Price Waterhouse* and *Oncale*. The outcomes in district and circuit courts were connected to judicial ideology, but they also reflected the emerging legal consensus on statutory interpretation with regard to gender identity and sexual orientation under Title VII. Given the strong legal consensus on the issue of gender identity, the discrimination case of Aimee Stephens was strong and was only temporarily derailed by the claim of a religious exemption. The outcomes of the cases brought by Gerald Bostock and Donald Zarda, involving sexual orientation–based discrimination, were mixed, but the newer jurisprudence had a clear effect, propelled by *Hively*. Despite several legal twists and turns in the lower courts, the Supreme Court ultimately narrowed the scope of inquiry and used these cases to examine the legacy of its own pathbreaking, though accidental, precedent in *Price Waterhouse*.

STEPHENS: A CLEAR CASE TEMPORARILY DERAILED

Aimee Stephens was a funeral director in Michigan when she decided to transition in 2013. She sent her employer, Thomas Rost, and her colleagues a letter outlining her plans to transition. It stated in part: "I will return to work as my true self, Aimee Australia Stephens, in appropriate business attire. I hope we can continue my work at R. G. and G. R. Harris Funeral Homes doing what I always have, which is my best!"[1] She had worked at the funeral home since 2007, but because of this letter and her desire to express her gender identity, she was fired. She declined a severance package, which would have required her silence, and contacted the American Civil Liberties Union (ACLU) chapter in Michigan. "I decided to fight," she said. "When I was fired it made me mad, to say the least . . . that's when it finally hit home that we weren't treated the same as everybody else and it's time that somebody stood up and said enough is enough."[2] The ACLU filed a Title VII discrimination complaint with the Equal Employment Opportunity Commission (EEOC). The timing was excellent, as the EEOC was looking for cases it could use to enforce its new stance on Title VII and gender identity.

After an investigation, the EEOC found that the funeral home had discriminated against Stephens and had run afoul of Title VII. In 2014 the EEOC found that this discrimination was based on sex stereotyping as well as the fact that Stephens was transgender and transitioning. Rost initially defended her termination by arguing that the dismissal was due to Stephens's refusal to wear traditionally masculine attire. Rost and his attorneys relied on case law that allows gender-based dress codes, but this interpretation was increasingly being challenged and ultimately was not accepted by the Sixth Circuit.[3] During the investigation, it was discovered that the funeral home gave a clothing allowance to men but not to women employed at the business, and the EEOC found this to be discriminatory as well.[4]

Rost was initially represented by a local solo-practitioner law firm, supported by the strongly anti-LGBTQ Alliance Defending Freedom (ADF). The early rulings were not favorable to the funeral home. Rost's attorneys argued that the EEOC was acting beyond its scope of authority, that "gender identity disorder was not a protected class under Title VII," and that the business was allowed to enforce its dress code under Title VII.[5] They also requested to see Stephens's genitalia as part of the discovery process, but she was granted a protective order to prevent this.[6] Realizing that their initial approach was not working, Rost's attorneys tried a new strategy: they claimed his actions were protected by the Religious Freedom Restoration Act (RFRA). This new claim was added in June 2015, after a negative ruling in April and after the ADF joined Rost's defense team.[7] This change in tactics resulted in a significant shift in the litigation before district court judge Sean Cox, appointed to the bench by George W. Bush. However, this approach did not prove useful in the Sixth Circuit and was dropped before the case reached the Supreme Court.

The RFRA was enacted by Congress in 1993 in reaction to the Supreme Court's decision in *Employment Division v. Smith* (1990). In a decision authored by Justice Antonin Scalia, the court held that a governmental policy that burdened a religious practice—in this case, the use of peyote by Native Americans—was constitutional under the free exercise clause, as long as the law applied neutrally and did not specifically target religious practices. Scalia was concerned that ruling otherwise would open the door to a plethora of exemptions that would undermine all kinds of laws and their application.[8]

Before the RFRA claim, Cox had felt constrained by Sixth Circuit precedents such as *Smith v. City of Salem* (2004), but the RFRA argument gave him the opportunity to rule against a transgender claimant. He thought the EEOC was going too far in asserting that Title VII protected against discrimination based on gender identity, despite decisions supporting that position in other federal courts; instead, he viewed the case through a *Price Waterhouse*–sex-stereotyping lens. However, Cox foreshadowed a central tenet of the emerging conservative judicial opposition to Title VII protections for LGBTQ people: discrimination may be prohibited by Title VII, but it is allowed under statutory or constitutional protections for religious freedom. In this case, Cox argued that the EEOC ran afoul of the RFRA: "The funeral home is entitled to a[n] RFRA exemption from Title VII, and the body of sex-stereotyping case law that has developed under it, under the facts and circumstances of this unique case."[9]

Applying the Supreme Court precedent of *Burwell v. Hobby Lobby* (2014), Cox found the funeral home to be a "closely-held" business and allowed Rost to assert his theological claim that sex is "biological" and that a rigid gender binary is ordained by God. He ruled that the EEOC's actions had created a "substantial" burden on Rost's religious views, compelling him "to allow an employee who was born a biological male to wear a skirt while working as a funeral director for this business."[10] Cox adopted and elevated the framing of the issue of gender identity as one of biology. For instance, he emphasized Stephens's prior name and legal designation as "male" at the time she was hired.[11] In Cox's telling, Stephens's transition was not an affirmation of her dignity but evidence that Rost was justified in reacting negatively to her transition. Cox used male pronouns when referring to Rost but never referred to Stephens as "she" or "her" in his opinion, only "Stephens," despite the EEOC's use of these pronouns in the litigation. Cox painted Stephens as someone who had fundamentally changed in a manner that could be legitimately objectionable, but he portrayed Rost as a person of deep and long-standing faith: "Rost has been a Christian for over sixty-five years," Cox declared.[12] The bulk of the opinion consisted not of how Stephens had been treated unfairly by Rost but of how Rost had been treated unfairly by the EEOC.

Judging is clearly about making choices. Cox's framing of and reliance on religious freedom allowed him to undo the legacy of *Price Waterhouse* and set aside the clearly evolving jurisprudence concerning gender identity and Title VII. His decision was much more critical of the EEOC than of Rost. He denied that the agency had a compelling interest in enforcing Title VII and asserted that its remedy was not the "least restrictive means" of enforcement. Instead of requiring the funeral home to allow Stephens to express her gender identity at work, Cox asserted that the proper remedy was to impose a gender-neutral dress code.[13] The real injustice in this case, according to Cox, was the EEOC's treatment of Rost and his business, not the discrimination Stephens faced. Absent the RFRA defense, Rost would have lost, as Cox could not deny the power of Sixth Circuit precedent (although he wanted to cabin it), but the new argument allowed Cox to give the funeral home a victory.

The legal terrain Cox created, especially the positive narrative of Rost and his business, was called into question on appeal. This was evident during oral arguments before the Sixth Circuit appellate panel consisting of three women: Bernice Bouie Donald (an Obama appointee), Karen Nelson Moore (a Clinton appointee), and Helene White (a George W. Bush appointee). They expressed skepticism about the RFRA defense, questioning whether the RFRA could be used in a sex discrimination context when an employer had a religious objection to men and women working together or wished to hire only men for religious reasons. When the ADF attorney representing the funeral home, Douglas Wardlow, invoked *Price Waterhouse,* one of the judges asked, while laughing, "How does *Price Waterhouse* help you?" Overall, the judges appeared to be much less critical of the arguments made by the EEOC and ACLU lawyers on behalf of Stephens. They viewed the issue as one of sex discrimination and were uncertain whether the RFRA could be invoked as a defense for Title VII discrimination.[14]

During the oral argument, ADF attorney Wardlow misgendered Stephens, a common occurrence in ADF litigation. It is the largest conservative Christian legal advocacy organization in the country; it is deeply opposed to LGBTQ rights and does not recognize the concept of gender identity.[15] For instance, in 2020, when a federal judge ordered the ADF to use proper pronouns, the organization "asked the judge to disqualify himself."[16] The Southern Poverty Law Center (SPLC) labels the organization a hate group. Supreme Court justice Amy Coney Barrett was part of the ADF-led Blackstone legal fellowship when she was a faculty member at Notre Dame. Journalist Chris Johnson notes:

Alliance Defending Freedom's legal positions would be consistent with the personal views expressed by Barrett, who in 2015 co-signed a letter with other Catholic women to religious leaders affirming marriage is between a man and a woman and the sexual difference between men and women was significant, and called the Obama administration interpreting transgender protections under Title IX of the Education Amendments of 1972 . . . a "strain" on the statute.[17]

Defenders of the ADF, including Barrett, focus almost exclusively on its success in winning religious liberty cases. Often ignored in their defense is the ADF's stated hostility to LGBTQ rights. Daniel Bennett, a scholar of the religious right's legal activism, summarizes the ADF's stance on and approach to LGBTQ rights as follows:

> One of ADF's founders once said that the organization "gives Christians a unique way to fight back against the radical attacks of groups like the ACLU, homosexual activists, and anti-family activists." In its litigation activities, outreach strategies, partnerships with like-minded groups, and attorney training programs [such as the Blackstone legal fellowship], ADF has striven to create a well-balanced, multipronged proactive attack against groups and interests it perceives to be threatening Christian conservatives in American society.[18]

According to the SPLC, the ADF distributed a letter advising school districts how to oppose the rights of transgender students. "The letter misrepresented trans identity and gender identity in general. . . . It also echoes the frequent claim of other anti-LGBT groups that suggest that trans women are just male 'predators' seeking access to women's bathrooms and locker rooms."[19]

Wardlow, a former state legislator in Minnesota, was involved in the ADF's litigation and advocacy efforts against the rights of transgender students. When he ran for Minnesota attorney general as a Republican in 2018, his work for the ADF became an issue in the campaign, which began soon after he presented his oral argument before the Sixth Circuit. During the race, a former high school classmate accused Wardlow of antigay bullying, a claim he denied.[20] He lost the election to Democrat Keith Ellison.

The unanimous decision by the Sixth Circuit panel—reversing Cox's decision—reflected the lopsided oral argument. Writing for the court, Judge Moore crafted an entirely different narrative than the one presented by Cox. His was a restrictive understanding of the legacy of *Price Waterhouse*, and he ignored *Oncale* in his opinion, thus facilitating the limitation of *Price Water-house.* In contrast, the Sixth Circuit cited *Oncale,* as well as other decisions expanding LGBTQ rights under Title VII. Relying on cases such as *Hively* and *Schroer,* Moore created a narrative that was fully consistent with the emerging jurisprudence, and she recentered Stephens as the true victim of discrimination. Moore's opinion also referred to Stephens as a transgender woman and used feminine pronouns to refer to Stephens.[21] During the appeal, Stephens had asked to be a direct party along with the EEOC, given the Trump adminis-tration's opposition to transgender legal protections and the possible negative effects on the EEOC. Indeed, the Trump administration and the EEOC took different positions on the Title VII LGBTQ rights cases that reached the Su-preme Court, with the EEOC maintaining the stances articulated in *Macy* and *Baldwin.*

Moore wrote for the court that, in addition to a sex-stereotyping analysis, "it is analytically impossible to fire an employee based on that employee's sta-tus as a transgender person without being motivated, at least in part, by the employee's sex."[22] She asserted that although it might have been unclear in *Smith* that discrimination on the basis of gender identity was per se discrim-ination, not simply a form of sex stereotyping, "we now directly hold: Title VII protects transgender persons because of their transgender or transitioning status, because transgender or transitioning status constitutes an inherently gender non-conforming trait."[23] The EEOC's analysis in *Macy* was thus fully embraced by the court. On the question of the RFRA, Moore denied that the funeral home was a religious institution, held that Rost had not established that his religion was burdened by the EEOC, and found that even if the RFRA applied, the government had a compelling interest in eliminating sex-based discrimination in employment. The Sixth Circuit's framing was quite differ-ent from Cox's. For instance, Moore wrote: "At bottom, the fact that Rost sincerely believes that he is being compelled to make such an endorsement [of the 'mutability of sex'] does not make it so."[24] As previously noted, the defeat on the RFRA question was so complete that Rost's lawyers dropped that ele-ment of the litigation in their appeal to the Supreme Court. The two questions granted review by that court were whether Title VII prohibits discrimination against transgender people based on (1) their status as transgender or (2) sex stereotyping under *Price Waterhouse.*[25]

ZARDA: A CASE CONSIDERED DURING AN ONGOING LEGAL SHIFT

Donald Zarda was a skydiving instructor for Altitude Express, a Long Island–based company. During a tandem skydive, Zarda would be strapped to the client, and when that client was a woman, he would tell her that he was gay to lessen any potential concern about the intimacy. In this case, Zarda told the client, "Don't worry about me, I'm gay and have the ex-husband to prove it." The woman's boyfriend complained about this statement and also claimed that Zarda had touched his girlfriend inappropriately, a claim Zarda denied. He was fired soon thereafter and consulted leading New York civil rights attorney Gregory Antollino. They eventually brought claims of sexual orientation–based discrimination in federal district court under state and federal law. The judge ruled against the federal Title VII claim and presided over a jury trial on the state claim, which resulted in a verdict in favor of Zarda's employer in 2015. Zarda had died in 2014 at age forty-four in a BASE-jumping accident in Switzerland, but his estate and one of the estate's executors, his former partner Bill Moore (the other executor was Zarda's sister Melissa), continued the litigation. Antollino attributed the trial loss to having a deceased plaintiff who could "testify" only through prior sworn statements.[26] The ruling against the Title VII claim was appealed, ultimately leading to an en banc decision from the Second Circuit in Zarda's favor after a three-judge panel affirmed the district court judge on the Title VII question.

Judge Joseph Bianco, who ruled against Zarda's Title VII claim in 2014, had been appointed by George W. Bush to the district court and was elevated to the Second Circuit in 2019 by Donald Trump. The Trump administration relied heavily on the conservative Federalist Society to screen judicial nominations, so it was unlikely that a judge perceived to be moderate would be elevated to a higher court. In fact, Bianco is a member of the Federalist Society. Although New York's Democratic senators opposed his elevation, the "blue slip" process was not being honored by the Senate Judiciary Committee in 2019.[27] Zarda's estate requested that his Title VII claim be reinstated after the EEOC's decision in *Baldwin*, but Bianco refused.[28]

As discussed in chapter 5, similar litigation in the Second Circuit had led judge Robert Katzmann to call for an en banc ruling to change that circuit's interpretation of Title VII. He had felt constrained by Second Circuit precedents, especially *Simonton v. Runyon* (2000), as did the three-judge panel that heard Zarda's appeal: Dennis Jacobs (a George H. W. Bush appointee), Robert Sack (a Clinton appointee), and Gerard Lynch (an Obama appointee). They declined to overturn *Simonton* because they lacked the power of an en banc panel. By the time this case reached the appellate court, national LGBTQ rights groups were involved, and several of them submitted amicus briefs, including the ACLU and Lambda Legal. The appellate opinion was per curiam, or for the court, with no individual authorship. The judges noted the similar Second Circuit litigation and the Seventh Circuit's approach in *Hively*, but they did not engage in much independent analysis of sexual orientation and Title VII, beyond a reference to their lack of authority. Compared with other appellate opinions, it was quite brief. This, along with the per curiam approach, may have indicated a divided or conflicted court. Lynch would eventually vote to uphold the panel's approach during the en banc proceeding, but he wrote a much more developed analysis of why Zarda should lose the case. Interestingly, Jacobs and Sack were part of the en banc majority that found in favor of Zarda, but they did not fully join Katzmann's expansive opinion.[29]

In 2018 an en banc panel of the Second Circuit, led by chief judge Katzmann, changed its interpretation of Title VII to include discrimination based on sexual orientation and overruled precedents to the contrary. In contrast to the Seventh Circuit's en banc panel consisting of a majority of Republican appointees, this panel was dominated by Democratic appointees, nine to four. The Republicans were divided—two were in the majority and two dissented—and the Democrats split eight to one, with a notable dissent from Judge Lynch. Thus, with the exception of the one Democratic defector, this fits the trend noted earlier—that is, a strong consensus on this issue among Democratic appointees. The judges in the majority, however, were quite divided over their interpretive approaches; some joined Katzmann's broad approach, while others preferred to rule on narrower grounds, such as associational discrimination.

By the time the case reached the full court in 2017, both LGBTQ rights advocates and opponents were fully engaged, including the Trump Justice Department arguing in opposition to the EEOC. LGBTQ litigation groups were already prepared for a high-level fight in the Supreme Court in *Evans v. Georgia Regional Hospital* (see chapter 5). The Second Circuit invited Lambda Legal to argue along with Zarda's lead attorney and the EEOC, and it invited conservative legal scholar Adam Mortara, justice Clarence Thomas's former law clerk, to argue the other side along with Altitude Express and the Department of Justice (DOJ). In addition, a wide array of groups submitted amicus briefs in support of Zarda: Democrats in Congress (including openly lesbian senator Tammy Baldwin and openly gay congressman David Cicilline), Democratic state attorneys general, and corporations such as Microsoft, Sun Life Financial, Ben & Jerry's, CBS, Citrix Systems, Dropbox, Google, Levi Strauss, Lyft, Pinterest, Salesforce, and Spotify. The much smaller number of amicus briefs submitted by conservative and religious right groups illustrates the extent to which elite opinion was in favor of this expansion of Title VII and the extent to which LGBTQ legal advocacy groups were willing and able to deploy this support.[30]

During oral arguments, a majority of the thirteen judges appeared to favor protections for sexual orientation, based on their questions and comments. Many of the judges were perplexed by the DOJ's presence in opposition to the EEOC, especially given the fact that the DOJ had not opposed the EEOC in *Hively*. Judge Rosemary Pooler inquired of DOJ attorney Hashim Mooppan, "Can I . . . ask a question about why you are here?" Subsequent questioning attempted to nail down the process by which the DOJ had decided to oppose the EEOC, but Mooppan was evasive. There was laughter in the courtroom when a judge referenced the 2016 election. Mooppan asserted that sex was "physiological" and attempted to characterize race-based discrimination as something far more serious than discrimination based on sexual orientation. He also emphasized fears that bathroom use in the workplace would be disrupted by a different interpretation of Title VII—the standard conservative legal argument. He claimed the EEOC position would require the resegregation of bathrooms in the workplace based on race. Mortara echoed these arguments. Judge Lohier responded: "I don't understand how bathrooms are critical to Title VII." Ultimately, a majority of the court followed the advice of Antollino in urging the judges not to allow bathroom arguments to "swallow the issue" of sexual orientation protection.[31]

Relying on *Price Waterhouse* and *Oncale* (and bolstered by *Hively*), Katzmann's opinion ratified the EEOC's position in *Baldwin*, repeatedly referring to sexual orientation as a "subset" of sex under Title VII and overturning the circuit's precedents on that question. According to Katzmann, sexual orientation–based discrimination involves sex stereotyping and is therefore a form of per se discrimination. He wrote, "A woman who is subject to an adverse employment action because she is attracted to women would have been treated differently if she had been a man and attracted to women." Katzmann also found that associational discrimination is involved in sexual orientation–based employment decisions, thus affirming all three arguments presented by the EEOC in *Baldwin.* Responding to the argument that associational discrimination analysis should not apply because, unlike racial discrimination, there may be legitimate reasons for discriminating against sexual minorities, he declared, "We see no principled basis for recognizing a violation of Title VII for associational discrimination based on race but not on sex. Accordingly, we hold that sexual orientation discrimination, which is based on an employer's opposition to association between particular sexes and thereby discriminates against an employee based on their own sex, constitutes discrimination 'because of . . . sex.' Therefore, it is no less repugnant to Title VII than anti-miscegenation policies." Katzmann rejected the argument that legislative history or subsequent legislative inaction can compel a particular interpretation of a statute. Embracing purposivism or broad textualism, and rejecting legislative intent by citing *Oncale,* he wrote: "because Congress could not anticipate the full spectrum of employment discrimination that would be directed at the protected categories, it falls to courts to give effect to the broad language that Congress used." The Second Circuit thus sided overwhelmingly with the EEOC and against the DOJ, thoroughly rejecting the Trump administration's arguments, especially the analogy to race and the bathroom issue.[32]

Some judges in the majority were unwilling to endorse the broad approach of Katzmann and the EEOC. Judge Jacobs was critical of Katzmann's opinion, calling the portions that went beyond the discussion of associational discrimination "woke dicta." Judge Sack did not disagree with Katzmann's analysis but thought the associational argument, the "simpler and less fraught theory," would have been sufficient to decide the case. In a preview of Supreme Court justice Neil Gorsuch's approach, Raymond Lohier (an Obama appointee) and José Cabranes (a Clinton appointee) emphasized a narrower textualist approach rather than Katzmann's purposivism. Lohier stated, "I agree with the majority opinion that there is no reasonable way to disentangle sex from sexual orientation in interpreting the plain meaning of the words 'because of . . . sex.'" Sack and Jacobs had been on the three-judge panel that ruled against Zarda and his estate, so it makes sense that their change of position would include a more minimalist approach.[33]

The third member of that initial panel was unwilling to change his approach and wrote a lengthy dissent. Judge Lynch refused to make any legal connection between sex and sexual orientation. He emphasized the Trump administration's arguments about the asserted differences between women and men. He repeatedly emphasized that, in the interest of deferring to majoritarian institutions, only Congress, not the courts, could add sexual orientation–based protections to Title VII. Interestingly, he argued that federal courts could be more innovative in cases involving constitutional interpretation, especially when protecting "liberties enshrined in the Constitution." Most notable for this discussion, Lynch relied on a particular interpretation of early LGB history and its connection to Title VII. In attempting to reinforce the notion that including sexual orientation in "sex" is legally problematic, Lynch provided a brief history of race, gender, sexual orientation, and Title VII, including the role of Pauli Murray, a black, queer, gender nonbinary civil rights attorney and activist (see chapter 2). Though claiming that Title VII was primarily about race, he correctly noted that the inclusion of sex "was not an accident or a stunt." However, he stressed that the movement for sexual minorities had been conducted "through the lens of sexual liberty, rather than equality, grouping the prohibitions of laws against same-sex relations with prohibitions on birth control, abortion, and adultery." This is a cramped understanding of the homophile movement and its stance on equality. Furthermore, for the most part, Lynch ended his historical discussion with the 1960s, neglecting to explore the complicated interactions among sex, gender identity, and sexual orientation in the 1970s and beyond. He briefly noted the rise of antidiscrimination laws at the state and local levels, but this only reinforced his argument that such policies are the proper province of legislative institutions. The larger historical narrative allowed him to create a "law office history" approach that created a wall between sex and sexual orientation. His analysis was designed to separate categories of discrimination rather than draw connections between them. For instance, he offered no discussion of Murray's struggles with gender identity or queerness. Given that Lynch was a Democratic appointee, his dissent would play a central role in efforts to overturn the majority decision on appeal. It would be cited extensively in briefs and oral arguments when Altitude Express appealed the decision to the Supreme Court.[34]

Why was a Democratic appointee so far outside the norm of his colleagues on this issue? In a 2019 speech at NYU Law School, Lynch repeatedly emphasized the importance of judicial restraint. He was concerned about both liberal and conservative judges imposing their policy preferences on the law, noting that the law can be "malleable." He critiqued rulings in favor of same-sex marriage, claiming that support for this policy was driven by the preferences of "elite judges" rather than public opinion. Putting aside the question of public opinion, if Lynch thought marriage equality was mandated by judicial elites, the same critique could be applied to his approach in *Zarda*. Indeed, in his dissent, Lynch noted that he opposed discrimination on the basis of sexual orientation but, as a judge, was not empowered to do anything about it.[35] Thus, ironically, he was arguably the elite judge ruling contrary to public opinion. The reality is that in both cases (marriage equality and Title VII protection), public opinion is strongly in favor of, or rapidly accelerating toward, equal treatment and LGB rights. At the very least, the relationship between judging and public opinion is complicated and not easily reduced to the notion that judicial innovation is nonmajoritarian.

BOSTOCK: LITTLE APPETITE FOR CHANGE IN THE ELEVENTH CIRCUIT

Unfortunately for Gerald Bostock, his discrimination did not occur in a federal circuit where the judges were willing to reevaluate their stance on Title VII and sexual orientation. For instance, the Eleventh Circuit followed the Fifth Circuit precedent of *Blum v. Gulf Oil Co.* (1979), which would prove to be a powerful negative factor in Bostock's case in the lower courts. In addition, during those lower court proceedings, the Eleventh Circuit handed down its decision in *Evans v. Georgia Regional Hospital.* Unlike the Second Circuit, the Eleventh Circuit's en banc panel was unwilling to change its approach, despite a strong plea from an Obama-appointed judge.

Bostock had been a social worker in the Clayton County, Georgia, juvenile court system since 2003. He administered a program designed to support abused and neglected children in the county. In 2013 he joined a gay softball league, the Hotlanta Softball League, and a few months later he was investigated for financial misdeeds. Bostock asserted that this investigation was a pretense for his eventual firing for "conduct unbecoming of a County employee."[36] A *New York Times* profile included Bostock's account: "'When I joined the gay softball league in January of 2013, that's when my life changed,' he said. 'Within months of that, there were negative comments about my sexual orientation.' In particular, he said, he was criticized for recruiting volunteers for the program from the gay community in Atlanta."[37] Bostock filed an EEOC complaint and a lawsuit on his own behalf, claiming discrimination under Title VII on the basis of his sexual orientation. When he hired an attorney, he added a claim of sex stereotyping.

A federal magistrate judge ruled in favor of Clayton County in 2016, and this decision was affirmed by judge Orinda Evans, a Clinton appointee. Magistrate judge Walter Johnson relied on *Blum* in rejecting the sexual orientation claim and found that the sex-stereotyping claim lacked evidence. Johnson described the stereotyping claim as an instance in which the "plaintiff is attempting to avoid dismissal of this case by bootstrapping a conclusory gender stereotyping allegation to his sexual orientation discrimination claim."[38] Judge Evans also emphasized that *Evans* precluded a sexual orientation–based claim, having been decided after, and substantially reinforcing, the magistrate judge's decision.[39] His decision had also been handed down before *Hively*, and Johnson's narrative told the story of a uniform rejection of these claims in federal court, especially appellate courts, and in the bureaucracy, thus minimizing the impact of the EEOC's 2015 *Baldwin* decision. In other words, the EEOC decision was an outlier, and its interpretation of Title VII was not worthy of deference.

In a remarkably brief per curiam opinion, the Eleventh Circuit panel consisting of Kevin Newsom (a Trump appointee), Gerald Tjoflat (a Ford appointee), and Charles Wilson (a Clinton appointee) agreed with Johnson and Evans. In a blunt rejection of cases central to the new approach to Title VII, they declared: "In *Evans*, we specifically rejected the argument that Supreme Court precedent in *Oncale v. Sundowner Offshore Services* and *Price Waterhouse* supported a cause of action for sexual orientation discrimination under Title VII."[40] These judges were not looking for inspiration for a jurisprudential shift. There was no reference to *Hively* or *Zarda* (handed down just a few months earlier) in the short opinion; there was only an inward focus on the Eleventh Circuit's jurisprudence, reinforced by *Evans*. But as we have seen, it is not uncommon for federal judges to reference precedents from other circuits. The appellate panel's myopic approach to these important cases was a purposeful legal tactic. They noted that their hands were tied by precedents, but they expressed no willingness to invite reconsideration by an en banc panel. Their approach was narrow and minimalist.

Although the full Eleventh Circuit refused a rehearing, two Obama appointees dissented in an opinion authored by judge Robin Rosenbaum and joined by judge Jill Pryor. Thus, there were two judges in the Eleventh Circuit who wanted to engage the arguments in favor of a broadened interpretation of Title VII, and their analysis was linked directly to *Hively* and *Zarda*. Recall that Rosenbaum had dissented in *Evans*, and her dissent in *Bostock* was quite vigorous. After noting high rates of discrimination reported by sexual minorities, she wrote:

> Yet rather than address this objectively en-banc-worthy issue, we instead cling to a 39-year-old precedent, *Blum v. Gulf Oil Corp.* that was decided ten years before *Price Waterhouse v. Hopkins*, the Supreme Court precedent that governs the issue and requires us to reach the opposite conclusion of *Blum*. Worse still, *Blum*'s "analysis" of the issue is as conclusory as it gets, consisting of a single sentence that, as relevant to Title VII, states in its entirety, "Discharge for homosexuality is not prohibited by Title VII." And if that's not bad enough, to support this proposition, *Blum* relies solely on *Smith v. Liberty Mutual Insurance Co.*—a case that itself has been necessarily abrogated not only by *Price Waterhouse* but also by our own precedent in the form of *Glenn v. Brumby*. I cannot explain why a majority of our Court is content to rely on the precedential equivalent of an Edsel with a missing engine, when it comes to an issue that affects so many people.[41]

Here, Rosenbaum vividly illustrates judicial selectivity when choosing precedents and how to apply them.

Unlike in the Second Circuit, there was no broad appetite for a reconsideration in the Eleventh. That circuit was more divided ideologically than the Second Circuit, with six judges appointed by Democrats and five by Republicans. Obama had shifted the Eleventh Circuit from a majority-Republican court to an eight-to-three Democratic majority by 2016, but subsequent Trump appointments narrowed that to a six-to-five Democratic majority by 2018. Notably, the two most willing innovators were Obama appointees, but a bipartisan majority of the court was unwilling to follow their lead. The court possessed neither a dominance of Democratic appointees nor the iconoclastic Republican appointees of the Seventh Circuit. Also, unlike in the Second Circuit's reconsideration of *Zarda*, no judges from the original panel changed their positions.

National LGBTQ rights groups did not directly support Gerald Bostock's case. For instance, Lambda Legal did not formally join forces with Bostock's attorneys, represent the plaintiff directly (as it did in *Evans*), or file amicus briefs. *Evans* had been activists' shot in the Eleventh Circuit, and they likely saw no prospect of a change in its approach, especially with more conservative appointees added under President Trump. Ironically, after Bostock's lawyers appealed from the Eleventh Circuit, the Supreme Court took the case, and Bostock's name will forever be associated with this significant change in the interpretation of Title VII. This "orphaned" case also resulted in a circuit split, making Supreme Court review more likely.

The Supreme Court combined the three cases discussed in this chapter and granted certiorari on April 22, 2019. The issue first broached by LGBTQ litigants in the 1970s was now officially before the nation's highest court for a potentially clarifying statement on the proper interpretation of Title VII in the context of discrimination on the basis of gender identity and sexual orientation. Whereas most judges in the Eleventh Circuit had tried to keep gender identity and sexual orientation separate, the Supreme Court significantly undermined that distinction by merging the cases into one.

7. The Supreme Court's Seemingly Minimalist but Remarkably Consequential Decision

The decision in *Bostock v. Clayton County* was unexpected in many quarters, especially the Supreme Court's 6-to-3 vote to include gender identity and sexual orientation under Title VII's protections, but it was also the culmination of the jurisprudential shift ushered in by *Price Waterhouse, Oncale,* Equal Employment Opportunity Commission (EEOC) rulings, and the decisions of (mostly) liberal judges. The division among Republican judges continued, with chief justice John Roberts joining the majority opinion of justice Neil Gorsuch and the court's Democratic appointees. LGBTQ rights activists and their allies effectively framed the litigation as one of textualism, appealing directly to Gorsuch. The three dissenters accused Gorsuch and the majority of employing poor textualist analysis and of engaging in legislating. Remarkably, despite the stronger jurisprudential support for the inclusion of gender identity, the justices struggled with the implications of transgender equality, especially the bathroom question—the focus of conservative opponents of LGBTQ rights. This chapter analyzes the decision, legally and politically; its significant implications for LGBTQ rights in the future; and the conservative opposition to these rights. Ultimately, I argue that the decision was monumental and enormously consequential but legally and politically easy, given the interpretive changes explored in previous chapters and the strong levels of support among elites and the public.

POLITICAL AND LEGAL STRATEGIES

The Trump administration leveraged its control of the Justice Department and the entity responsible for Supreme Court litigation, the Office of the Solicitor General, to neutralize the EEOC's influence, counter any jurisprudential innovation, and build on the most conservative approaches of lower court judges such as Diane Sykes, Gerard Lynch, William Pryor, and James Ho. In October 2017 attorney general Jeff Sessions overturned the Obama

administration's expansive interpretation of Title VII on the question of gender identity. Recall that the Trump administration and the EEOC had argued on opposite sides of the case involving Aimee Stephens, and in the Supreme Court the Trump administration took an even more confrontational stance toward its own agency. It pressured the EEOC to sign on to the administration's brief against Stephens, a move that would have required a new vote by the commissioners and would have changed the EEOC's position established in 2012 and 2015. EEOC officials refused, and the EEOC was absent from the Supreme Court litigation. As journalist Ben Penn described the politics: "Justice Department leadership has ramped up talks with the EEOC's Republican officials in recent weeks, expressing strong interest in having the commission on board in the Stephens case, the sources said. The commission's blessing isn't necessary, but having the EEOC's general counsel named on the brief would allow the Trump administration to present a unified front in a contentious, potentially landmark case." Interestingly, the solicitor general's office urged the Supreme Court not to take the appeal from the Sixth Circuit, despite opposing that decision, likely in recognition of the strong legal case for including gender identity under Title VII, a case bolstered by the actions of the EEOC. Despite losing its majority of Democratic commissioners, including Chai Feldblum, whose reappointment failed during the Trump administration, the agency maintained its position and continued to enforce Title VII according to its inclusive interpretation, despite the political pressure.[1]

In its briefs, the solicitor general offered the typical arguments against LGBTQ inclusion:

- Title VII can be expanded only through legislation, and failed legislative efforts confirm that Congress did not intend to include gender identity and sexual orientation.
- Sex is biological, and any deviation from this approach opens the door to invalidating gender-specific restrooms.
- Sex-stereotyping theory applies to sexual orientation only when there is disparate treatment, not simply discrimination against an individual.
- Associational discrimination analysis does not apply because discrimination based on race is worse and seldom justified.

As one of the briefs noted, "Sex-based distinctions are not invariably invidious because they can reflect physiological differences between men and women, as the lawfulness of sex-specific bathrooms makes clear." Here we see three arguments in rapid succession: no analogy to race, the biological foundation of sex, and the bathroom fear. The government also attempted to cabin *Oncale*, characterizing Justice Scalia's statement that "statutory prohibitions often go beyond the principal evil to cover reasonably comparable evils" as an "unremarkable observation."[2] In his dissent, justice Samuel Alito would describe the precedent as "thoroughly unremarkable."[3]

Not surprisingly, on the question of sexual orientation, the brief liberally cited the dissent of Judge Lynch of the Second Circuit, Judge Ho's concurring opinion in *Whittmer* v. *Phillips 66*, and Judge Sykes's dissenting opinion in *Hively v. Ivy Tech*. In its brief in the Stephens case, the solicitor general limited *Price Waterhouse*, arguing that the decision "did not recognize sex stereotyping as a novel, freestanding category of Title VII liability," in addition to limiting the applicability of *Oncale*.[4] The government argued that transgender plaintiffs could invoke *Price Waterhouse* if they were stereotyped in an employment situation, but "transgender status" was not protected by that case.

Most of the briefs submitted in support of the government's position came from religious right organizations and individuals. Some Republican state attorneys general filed a brief, as did Republican senators and House members. One brief was submitted by Ryan Anderson, the leading anti–transgender rights intellectual in the country and a protégé of natural law scholar Robert George. George was the intellectual godfather of the movement against same-sex marriage, and his disciple is leading the way in opposing transgender rights.[5] Anderson's brief provides a window into conservative thought on transgender rights. Stating that "biology is not bigotry," the brief frequently addressed the issue of bathrooms, asserting that arguments in favor of an inclusive interpretation of Title VII demand "asexuality and androgyny." He denied that Aimee Stephens had any protection under Title VII because "being a woman is not a stereotype," thus rejecting the notion that gender identity is real or legally actionable. His genuine motivation became clear near the end of the brief, when he dramatically stated that ruling in favor of LGBTQ inclusion "would treat disagreement about human embodiment as male and female as sex discrimination. And it would turn our nation's cherished civil rights statutes into swords to persecute people with the wrong beliefs about human sexuality. Antidiscrimination laws should be understood as *shields* to protect citizens from unjust discrimination, *not as swords* imposing a sexual orthodoxy on the nation."[6]

Anderson's brief did not go far enough for Chapman University law professor John Eastman, who filed a brief for the National Organization for Marriage and the Claremont Institute. He invoked arguments about restroom violence, citing reports from mostly conservative news sources and claiming that "these are not isolated incidents, but are happening across the country wherever transgender policies are put in place that allow men claiming to be women to access women's restrooms and showers." Eastman, who was also the chair of a practice group of the Federalist Society at the time, presented a core argument of modern legal conservatism and libertarianism: antidiscrimination laws are a significant limit on freedom and should be opposed or sharply limited to "immutable" characteristics, not "more fluid classifications such as those grounded in claims of sexual orientation or gender identity."[7] Various versions of the bathroom argument have been presented by those opposed to an expansive interpretation of Title VII, so their prominent presence in the Supreme Court oral argument came as no surprise. Notably, however, the approach to LGBTQ rights presented by Anderson and Eastman, especially its rigid biological essentialism and preoccupation with bathrooms, was rejected by the Supreme Court and two of its conservatives. The rejected natural law perspective was also echoed in an amicus brief by, among others, Helen Alvaré, Hadley Arkes, Gerhard Bradley, Patrick Deneen, and Adrian Vermule, who argued that "gender identity and transgender/transitioning status are metaphysical constructs of dubious ideological and political origin."[8]

Another extended discussion in Anderson's brief indicates that conservative opponents of LGBTQ inclusion saw *Oncale* as a significant obstacle, and indeed, that case (which severed the interpretation of Title VII from a consideration of legislative intent) loomed large in Gorsuch's analysis. Anderson argued that *Oncale* is important not for its textualism but for the proposition that Title VII requires comparative analysis of "similarly situated" individuals or "double standards," in contrast to a focus on the harm to an individual without any such comparison. He repeatedly invoked justice Ruth Bader Ginsburg to support this reading of the case. But ultimately, the Supreme Court, including Ginsburg, rejected this view.[9]

The briefs on the side of Stephens, Zarda, and Bostock were carefully calibrated to appeal to Gorsuch and a particular type of textualist argument. As Chase Strangio, one of the American Civil Liberties (ACLU) lawyers representing Stephens, noted, "the arguments that we made completely resonated with Gorsuch, which is who we were targeting."[10] With Anthony Kennedy's retirement from the court in 2018, advocates could no longer rely on his support for lesbian and gay rights and his jurisprudence of dignity.[11] Activists were concerned about how the Supreme Court would deal with transgender issues in particular, as it had never directly addressed that subject. In a profile of Strangio, Masha Gessen is illustrative on this point:

> Strangio describes designing a legal strategy as "a combination of a puzzle and an analytical game, and then having to merge a lot of people's views of those things. It can be brutal. Each sentence gets rewritten fifty times." In the Stephens case, the process was laced with dread. Stephens's lawsuit was originally brought by the Equal Employment Opportunity Commission. By the time it reached the Supreme Court, Trump had been President for more than two years and the federal government was now arguing that employment discrimination against a transgender person was legal. Then Strangio read an article in the *Wake Forest Law Review* by Katie Eyer, a professor at Rutgers Law School. Eyer argued that a truly textualist interpretation of Title VII would leave the Justices no choice but to acknowledge that discriminating against people because they are gay, lesbian, or transgender is to discriminate against them on the basis of sex. "In the briefing room, I said, 'We can win this!'" Strangio said. "Then, after the meeting, I thought, But can we?"[12]

Recall that national LGBTQ rights groups did not directly support the litigation in Bostock's case. And after Kennedy's departure, there was tremendous uncertainty about a more conservative high court.

The ACLU brief reflected this careful and narrow strategy. In the third paragraph, the ACLU outlined the minimalist theory of the case:

> Even if Title VII's reference to "sex" encompasses only one's sex assigned at birth, as Harris Homes asserts, the decision to fire Ms. Stephens was "because of sex." Had Ms. Stephens been assigned a female rather than a male sex at birth, Harris Homes would not have fired her for living openly as a woman. Because Harris Homes would have treated Ms. Stephens differently had her assigned sex at birth been different, its decision to fire Ms. Stephens violated Title VII.

The ACLU also relied on sex-stereotyping analysis and compared gender transition to religious conversion, but its textualist arguments were central. It noted, "A statute's plain text is not limited by speculation about which particular applications of the law Congress or the public may have had in mind at the time of enactment." It told the justices they need not address the bathroom issue to decide the case and maintained that, in fact, the court *could not* address this issue because it was not directly addressed in the litigation. The ACLU concluded with these points, thus bookending its brief with arguments later embraced by Gorsuch.[13]

Other amicus briefs reinforced the same approach. A brief by William Eskridge and Andrew Koppelman emphasized that Justice Scalia abhorred inquiries into legislative intent and urged the justices to stick to the text. As these prominent law professors declared: "The lodestar for interpreting statutes is the ordinary, grammatical meaning of the relevant text, understood in light of the entire statute (as amended) and this Court's precedents interpreting the statute."[14] Another group of law professors that included leading LGBTQ rights scholar Carlos Ball referenced the "plain meaning" of Title VII. Even assuming that sex means biological sex, the statute's plain meaning requires an interpretation that discrimination on the basis of gender identity and sexual orientation is inherently discrimination based on sex. In the most minimalist framing possible, the brief noted, "This conclusion does not, as the Employers in these cases suggest, require the Court to hold that the word 'sex' *means* 'sexual orientation' or 'gender identity.' Rather, individuals who are fired because they are gay or transgender are treated differently because of the[ir] *sex*, as the Employers all acknowledge that term was commonly defined at the time of Title VII's enactment." Lambda Legal called for a "straightforward" interpretation of Title VII, and GLAD argued for a "plain-text straightforward approach."[15]

The opinions by judges Sykes, Ho, and Lynch on the question of sexual orientation were also targeted by amicus briefs on behalf of the employees, in an attempt to undermine and neutralize their arguments. These opinions were the intellectual core of the opposition to LGBTQ inclusion in Title VII and needed to be addressed, especially before a conservative court. Briefs on behalf of the employers cited these decisions frequently, especially to support the argument that sexual orientation and gender identity were not envisioned as part of Title VII in 1964 by either the drafters or the public. Eskridge and Koppelman referenced the "radical implications" of this approach: "If a background belief was so entrenched in the culture at the time of a law's enactment that it was broadly shared, then one can rely on that background belief in order to *subtract* meaning from the plain meaning of the statute, to limit its extension in order to exclude applications that people at the time would not have thought of." This was a direct refutation of the "original public meaning" approach to statutory interpretation. In such arguments, advocates for the employees always had Scalia's ruling in *Oncale* on their side, with its severing of statutory interpretation from the past and from motivations. Eskridge and Koppelman ended their brief with a discussion of Scalia's approach to statutory interpretation, invoking his famous argument that "statutory interpretation ought not be an exercise in looking out over the crowd and picking out your friends."[16]

Thus, while the employees and their allies grounded their analysis in the legacy of *Price Waterhouse, Oncale*, and textualism, the employers stifled these important precedents and grounded their analysis in an "originalist" approach to statutory text—not legislative intent, but a very close relative. In terms of elite opinion, the employees were supported by professional organizations and corporations, while the employers had mostly religious right and conservative organizations, including faith-based businesses, on their side. Mirroring corporate America's approach in litigation in the Second Circuit, one brief in support of the employees was submitted by 206 businesses, and it emphasized the economic benefits of diversity and the harmfulness of anti-LGBTQ discrimination. The American Medical Association, American Psychological Association, and American Psychiatric Association, among other similar groups, were part of the amicus briefs submitted for the employees. It was quite clear to the justices where business and professional elites stood on the question of Title VII interpretation.[17]

Prohibiting employment discrimination on the basis of gender identity and sexual orientation was also overwhelmingly popular among the public. Thus, the justices had no legitimate fear of backlash for a decision expanding the interpretation of Title VII on this basis. Two highly regarded polls from April 2019, just prior to the granting of certiorari, showed high levels of support. In a Quinnipiac University poll, when asked, "Do you think employers should be allowed to fire someone based on their sexual orientation or sexual identity, or don't you think so?" 92 percent of respondents replied "don't think so." Support was lower for, but still strongly supportive of, bans on employment discrimination when combined with protections related to public accommodations; in a Public Religion Research Institute Poll, 71 percent of respondents were in favor of such protections.[18] Public sentiment was more mixed on the question of transgender rights and restroom access. As scholars have noted, "The bathroom issue has become a salient flashpoint in the debate over transgender rights. This issue has been used to oppose or repeal broader nondiscrimination policies for public accommodations." In addition, the transgender community still faces hostility, and "a significant portion of the public finds the concept of transgender identity morally wrong." Thus, litigation is an important tool for transgender individuals and transgender rights advocates, and the victory in the Supreme Court was an impactful one.[19]

ORAL ARGUMENT

The oral argument in the consolidated cases was scheduled to last for two hours, divided between the sexual orientation question (argued first) and the gender identity question. Solicitor general Noel Francisco argued for the Trump administration on both questions. Jeffrey Harris argued on behalf of Altitude Express and Clayton County, and John Bursch, senior counsel for Alliance Defending Freedom (ADF), argued on behalf of the funeral home. Bursch, a Michigan-based appellate attorney and Federalist Society member, represented Michigan and its ban on same-sex marriage in *Obergefell* as the state's solicitor general. According to his Federalist Society biography, Harris clerked for chief justice John Roberts and is an appellate attorney. David Cole of the ACLU argued on behalf of Stephens, and Pamela Karlan argued on behalf of Bostock and Zarda (Bostock's attorney had been denied time by the Supreme Court because only one attorney could argue for the consolidated parties). Karlan, one of the professors and attorneys affiliated with the Supreme Court clinic at Stanford University Law School, had been invited to work on the case by Gregory Antollino. She had been Antollino's professor in law school, and he had followed her career, especially as it pertained to LGBTQ rights litigation. In 2018 Antollino had asked Karlan for help preparing the brief opposing the certiorari petition by Altitude Express. As Karlan described the events, "I had written him to congratulate him about the case, and he contacted me to help out when he realized the other side was going to try and get the Supreme Court to take the case." By this time, the ACLU was also working on Zarda's case.[20]

Even though the issues were divided and the sexual orientation question was argued first, the justices clearly saw them as intertwined. For instance, liberal justice Sonia Sotomayor introduced the bathroom issue early during

Karlan's argument, perhaps sensing that this could be a weak spot in the employees' case. Reflecting the textualist tactic of the briefs supporting the employees, Karlan began with a clear invocation of textualist and *Price Waterhouse*–grounded arguments, and she attempted to downplay the bathroom issue, claiming that it was not directly relevant to the issue of sexual orientation:

> When a[n] employer fires a male employee for dating men but does not fire female employees who date men, he violates Title VII. The employer has, in the words of Section 703(a), discriminated against the man because he treats that man worse than women who want to do the same thing. And that discrimination is because of sex, again in the words of Section 703(a), because the adverse employment action is based on the male employee's failure to conform to a particular expectation about how men should behave; namely, that men should be attracted only to women and not to men. There is no analytic difference between this kind of discrimination and forms of discrimination that have been already recognized by every court to have addressed them. For example, discrimination against men who are . . . effeminate rather than macho. Like the discrimination here, that discrimination is because of non-conformity with an expectation about how men should behave.[21]

Price Waterhouse was the first case mentioned by name in Karlan's argument. In furtherance of this textualist approach, she disparaged the pragmatist approach of judge Richard Posner in *Hively v. Ivy Tech* and distanced the employees' arguments from that approach. When Chief Justice Roberts asked whether her approach to statutory interpretation was similar to Posner's, she emphatically rejected his approach. Later, without prompting, she referred to Posner as a "loose cannon" who argued for judges to "do whatever you feel like."[22]

The bathroom issue eventually evolved into a discussion of appearance and workplace attire, driven by questions from justices Sotomayor and Gorsuch. In particular, Sotomayor referenced the restaurant Hooters and asked, "Is it discriminatory for the restaurant not to hire a transgender man [presumably, Sotomayor meant woman] who wants to wear the uniform?" Karlan replied, "I do want to get to the question of sexual orientation." She then discussed racial discrimination before justice Ruth Bader Ginsburg jumped into the conversation, seemingly to assist Karlan. "Would you say the test is—the injured person," Ginsburg asked. Karlan replied, "Yes, it's a differential based on gender, but most people are not injured by having separate bathrooms. In fact, they—most people would prefer it." This allowed Karlan to dismiss the bathroom issue as a legally minor one that was unlikely to arise as a legitimate Title VII case. It is revealing, however, that this question loomed so large in the argument concerning sexual orientation, and it is consistent with reports that, in their deliberations, the justices struggled most with the bathroom issue. Harris and Francisco would revive the argument during their time at the podium, only to be challenged by Ginsburg, who repeatedly noted the "lack of injury" argument.[23]

Previewing his dissent, justice Samuel Alito challenged Karlan about asking the court to decide "a big policy issue" and act like a legislature, especially in light of congressional inaction. Her response was to cite the two cases at the center of this book: "No more than what you did in *Oncale*. No more than what you did in *Price Waterhouse*."[24] Alito also repeatedly emphasized that he saw a significant and legally controlling distinction between sex and sexual orientation. Among the conservative justices, he was the most oppositional toward Karlan. Clarence Thomas and Brett Kavanaugh were silent during her initial argument, and Roberts asked about religious exemptions to LGBTQ-based antidiscrimination laws.

Harris began his argument by citing Wisconsin's first statute to prohibit sexual orientation–based discrimination, enacted in 1982. Reinforcing Alito's point about policy and legislatures, he noted that "Wisconsin's landmark law actually had little, if any, practical impact because Congress had already banned sexual orientation discrimination nationwide, 18 years earlier in the Civil Rights Act of 1964."[25] He then invoked *Oncale* on behalf of the employers, minimizing its effect and offering the case as a narrow reversal of the blanket exclusion of same-sex sexual harassment, but disregarding Scalia's interpretative approach. This legal sleight of hand—ignoring what *Oncale* was clearly about in the context of this controversy (Scalia's textualist analysis)—reinforced what advocates for the employers already knew: that this giant of conservative statutory interpretation was not on their side. Their attempts at diffusion and distraction were ultimately unsuccessful. *Oncale* continued to stand for the proposition that interpreting statutes should not involve searches for legislative intent.

In his questioning of Harris, Gorsuch's eventual textual approach was vividly apparent. This was reinforced by the liberal wing's leading "conservative whisperer," justice Elena Kagan, during Francisco's argument. Many observers have noted that, due to Kagan's experience as dean of Harvard Law School, she has been able to forge consensus with conservative legal minds, and the court's liberals have increasingly needed to do so, given the three conservative justices added by Donald Trump with the assistance of Senate Republicans.[26] Countering the argument that these cases involved sexual orientation discrimination and had no connection to the word "sex" in the statute, Gorsuch asked, "In what linguistic formulation would one—would one say that sex, biological gender, has nothing to do with what happened in this case." He later continued this line of questioning with Harris: "Let's do truth serum, okay? Wouldn't—wouldn't the employer maybe say it's because this was—this person was a man who liked other men? And isn't that first part sex."[27] Of course, Gorsuch relied on sex or gender essentialism, but this allowed him to reinforce his "linguistic" approach. Channeling Scalia's reasoning in *Oncale*, Kagan attacked the nontextualist approach relied on by Francisco, following Harris's similar approach. After noting that arguments based on legislative history, both contemporaneous and subsequent, "are not ones we typically accept," Kagan launched into an extended discussion of the court's approach to statutory interpretation. For instance, the following statements were seemingly intended to endorse and bolster Gorsuch's textualist analysis: "For many years, the lodestar of this Court's statutory interpretation has been the text of a statute, not the legislative history, and certainly not the subsequent legislative history. . . . We look to laws. We don't look to predictions. We don't look to desires. We don't look to wishes."[28]

Given the prevalence of bathroom and attire arguments in the discussion of sexual orientation, it is no surprise that these topics also dominated the oral argument in support of Stephens in *R. G. & G. R. Harris Funeral Homes*. Cole invoked Ann Hopkins and her case in the second paragraph of his presentation, and he distanced his approach from Posner's. This time, it was Roberts who brought up bathrooms, but Sotomayor again focused on the issue, invoking arguments about the discomfort caused by the presence of transgender persons in such spaces. Unlike Ginsburg, who downplayed the issue, Sotomayor maintained that the question was "inevitable," even though Cole pointed out that it was not directly at issue in the case.[29] When Alito invoked Title IX, Cole replied that Title IX allows for sex-segregated facilities, and he brought up sex stereotyping, noting that "the objection to someone for being transgender is the ultimate stereotype."[30] Cole's argument ended with an extended back-and-forth with Gorsuch. It was during this conversation that Gorsuch referenced the "massive social upheaval" that could result from a decision interpreting Title VII as including gender identity protections. In one of the most powerful statements made during the two hours of argument, Cole responded to Gorsuch's pressing on the bathroom and dress code issues by saying: "Recognizing that transgender people have a right to exist in the workplace and not be turned away because of who they are does not end dress codes or restrooms. There are transgender lawyers in this courtroom today."[31] In a statement that provided LGBTQ rights lawyers and activists with great hope, Gorsuch declared (just before his statement about social upheaval): "I am with you on the textual evidence. It's close, okay? . . . The judge finds it very close."[32]

Justice Stephen Breyer initiated the questioning of Bursch and Francisco, with strong assistance from fellow liberals Ginsburg and Kagan. Their arguments eventually played prominent roles in the majority opinion. Ginsburg and Kagan both made the point that sexual harassment law and its development undermined arguments for legislative intent. The conservative justices seldom came to Bursch's and Francisco's defense. Notably, Breyer attacked Bursch's argument that racial discrimination enjoyed greater protection under Title VII than the other enumerated traits because "there is no nonracist reason why you would fire the [hypothetical] employee in the interracial marriage." Breyer replied, "There isn't? I happen to know people. I won't say who they are, but there are people [laughter] in my life I have heard people say being Jewish is fine, being Catholic is fine, just don't get married."[33] Conservatives made much of this argument in their presentations to the court, but the majority ultimately rejected this hierarchy of discrimination and embraced a more intersectional understanding.

Tragically, after the oral argument, for which she was present, Aimee Stephens died of kidney disease on May 12, 2020, only a few weeks before the Supreme Court handed down its decision in her case.[34] Her decision to pursue the case will stand as one of the most significant acts in the history of transgender rights.

DELIBERATIONS AND OPINIONS

We often do not know what goes on behind the scenes at the Supreme Court until justices release their papers, usually after they die. And even then this knowledge is not guaranteed, depending on how a particular justice chronicled the court's inner workings. In this case, CNN Supreme Court reporter Joan Biskupic was able to gain access to the internal deliberations of the justices. This revealed that, despite the stronger jurisprudential foundation for including gender identity–based protections under Title VII, they were wary of doing so. This fits with their seeming fixation on the bathroom issue during the oral argument, indicating that the court is not always focused on technical matters of law when it decides a prominent case. The justices' hesitancy was more reflective of cultural and political biases. For instance, federal courts have generally been dismissive of privacy concerns related to students' equality rights, but the Supreme Court's excessive attention to the issue may have been related to its greater exposure to public opinion or its anticipation of public reaction. Scholars have demonstrated that judges are more concerned with political considerations when the issues are more salient, but for the Supreme Court, the link is not always direct.[35] In the end, the conservative cultural narrative about transgender rights and privacy, highlighted by conservatives involved in the litigation and designed for the conservative justices, did not undermine the clear jurisprudential trend in this case, although the court left open the possibility of full consideration of the issue.

As chronicled by Biskupic, the justices first, and with less debate, voted to include sexual orientation under Title VII. After a discussion of religious liberty and bathroom concerns, Gorsuch and Roberts joined the four liberals in voting to include gender identity as well. Biskupic speculates that Kagan was persuasive in convincing Roberts, in addition to directing her statements during the oral argument and her private lobbying toward Gorsuch. This coalition held during the months spent drafting the opinion. As Biskupic describes the process, "Nobody was swayed despite forceful argument from the dissenters, according to CNN's reporting." Roberts assigned the majority opinion to Gorsuch, allowing him to define the majority's approach, and the other members of the majority quickly signed on to an early draft.[36]

Although Gorsuch's textualist approach can explain his vote, Roberts's vote was more unexpected and more difficult to square with his conservative approach to LGBTQ rights, especially as defined by his views on marriage. During the oral argument and in conference, he articulated concerns about religious liberty stemming from the protection of LGBTQ rights under Title VII.[37] In *Obergefell*, Roberts wrote a sharp dissent, accusing the majority of extreme judicial activism and even equating the decision with *Lochner v. New*

York (1905), the infamous case involving judicially created economic rights. Here, however, the stakes were lower: the court was not creating a new constitutional right but merely interpreting a statute. This, along with strongly supportive public opinion, Roberts's concern for the court's reputation, and his sympathy for textualist arguments, likely made this position more palatable to him. For instance, during the *Obergefell* oral argument, Roberts offered a formalist and textualist argument, as reported by journalist Robert Barnes: "If Sue loves Joe and Tom loves Joe, Sue can marry him and Tom can't. And the difference is based upon their different sex. Why isn't that a straightforward question of sexual discrimination?"[38]

This, in essence, was the basis of the opinion Roberts joined. Gorsuch's opinion was not simply an exercise in formal textualism, however. It was the culmination of the jurisprudential changes surrounding Title VII and the interpretation of the word "sex" since *Price Waterhouse* and solidified by *Oncale.* The individualized nature of Title VII established in the 1970s and its broad scope, reflected by sexual harassment jurisprudence, also undergirded his analysis. These aspects of Title VII interpretation allowed Gorsuch to reject arguments by the Trump administration, the employers, and judicial conservatives more generally.

Gorsuch and the majority emphatically held that gender and sexual minorities are covered by Title VII and that someone discriminating against LGBTQ individuals can be legally liable, even if this is only part of the discriminatory action. He asserted that "but for" causation is the correct standard to apply, regardless of the employer's motivation. In essence, the decision added gender identity and sexual orientation to the text of Title VII and its employee-protective framework. "At bottom," he declared, "these cases involve no more than the straightforward application of legal terms with plain and settled meanings. For an employer to discriminate against employees for being homosexual or transgender, the employer must intentionally discriminate against individual men and women in part because of sex." According to Gorsuch, and following decades-old LGBTQ legal theory, discrimination on the basis of sexual orientation and gender identity is inherently discrimination because of sex. He did not embrace the fencing off of these categories from one another, as the court had been urged to do by conservatives or by earlier, reluctant judges. As Gorsuch noted, "Homosexuality and transgender status are inextricably bound up with sex. Not because homosexuality or transgender status are related to sex in some vague sense or because discrimination on these bases has some disparate impact on one sex or another, but because to discriminate on these grounds requires an employer to intentionally treat individual employees differently because of their sex."[39]

Price Waterhouse was also central to Gorsuch's analysis, although not for a significant reliance on sex-stereotyping theory. He used the case to emphasize that Title VII addresses discrimination against individuals, not classes or groups, and he cited *Price Waterhouse* directly for the proposition that sex "is not relevant to the selection, evaluation, or compensation of employees." In the preceding paragraph, Gorsuch invoked sex stereotyping as a prohibited form of sex-based discrimination. In doing so, he countered one of the common arguments of opponents of an inclusive interpretation of Title VII: that as long as an employer stereotypes both men and women, there is no Title VII violation. As Gorsuch declared to the contrary:

> This statute works to protect individuals of both sexes from discrimination, and does so equally. So an employer who fires a woman, Hannah, because she is insufficiently feminine and also fires a man, Bob, for being insufficiently masculine may treat men and women as groups more or less equally. But in both cases the employer fires an individual in part because of sex. Instead of avoiding Title VII exposure, this employer doubles it.

It took several decades of careful legal activism, but that statement was the culmination of efforts to use *Price Waterhouse* to protect LGBTQ rights. Gorsuch accepted the analysis advocated by Chai Feldblum, rather than that of his fellow legal conservatives. He completely negated attempts to cabin the effect of that decision, and he was not bothered by leapfrogging. Later in his *Bostock* decision, Gorsuch rejected the employers' similar defense that they fired both lesbians and gay men.[40]

In his dissent, Alito pointed out that Gorsuch did not rely on sex-stereotyping analysis, and he made the typical argument that *Price Waterhouse* was mostly about burden of proof, thus sharply limiting its application as precedent. Indeed, Alito cited Judge Sykes's opinion in *Hively* for the lack of connection between LGBTQ-based discrimination and *Price Waterhouse*.[41] Gorsuch's discussion of gender-based expectations and stereotypes was critical to his argument that discrimination on the basis of gender identity and sexual orientation is inherently discrimination on the basis of sex. Rather than marginalizing *Price Waterhouse*, Gorsuch used its emphasis on gender stereotypes as a strong theme in his opinion, including a discussion of 1950s gender roles.[42] Although the holding in *Bostock* was not explicitly related to sex stereotyping, the analysis from *Price Waterhouse* was deeply embedded in the background and context of Gorsuch's textualism. Alito downplayed the sea change in Title VII interpretation that had created the groundwork for including LGBTQ plaintiffs, reflecting the clear pattern of denial on the part of many conservative judges and conservative legal activists.

Further, as part of the one-two punch of the cases at the heart of this book, Gorsuch used *Oncale* in support of the "unintended results" aspect of Title VII interpretation and for Scalia's rejection of legislative history. He saw the cases as moving in the same direction and mandating the same result; he did not approve of slicing and dicing to keep them from fully protecting LGBTQ employees. For instance, he did not argue that sex-stereotyping theory did not apply because that had been the position of only a plurality in *Price Waterhouse*. And he did not agree with the argument that *Oncale* applied only to sexual harassment, not to other forms of employment discrimination. Gorsuch agreed, however, that the legacy of *Oncale* was to excise a search for legislative intent in statutory interpretation and that Title VII's reach may extend, as he quoted Scalia, "'beyond the principal evil' legislators may have intended or expected to address." For Gorsuch, the case was not "unremarkable," as maintained by the briefs for the employers and by the dissenters. Indeed, he accused the employers of attempting to "unravel" Title VII jurisprudence by ignoring the clear legacy of *Oncale*.[43]

Buttressing his evolutionary understanding, Gorsuch's analysis of the history of Title VII correctly framed the historical evidence linking gender identity and sexual orientation. He did not cite negative precedents to prove that gender and sexual minorities are excluded; rather, he used these lawsuits as evidence of an expectation of their inclusion. As he noted, "Not long after the law's passage, gay and transgender employees began filing Title VII complaints, so at least some people foresaw this potential application. And less than a decade after Title VII's passage, during debates over the Equal Rights Amendment, others counseled that its language—which was strikingly similar to Title VII's—might also protect homosexuals from discrimination." Gorsuch called cynical the argument that this could not have been Congress's expectation because sexual and gender minorities were unpopular, especially given the development of sexual harassment law. He invoked the judicial duty to protect minority rights, thus embracing leapfrogging. Rather than citing the lack of discussion of gender and sexual minorities in 1964 to permanently exclude them from Title VII without explicit legislation, Gorsuch declared: "Certainly nothing in the meager legislative history of this provision suggests it was meant to be read narrowly."[44]

Despite their centrality during the oral argument, bathrooms and dress codes were discussed only briefly at the end of Gorsuch's opinion. He noted that these issues were not directly before the court, potentially leaving them open to future litigation. He downplayed the "parade of horribles," to use Justice Breyer's term, presented by the government and the employers. That was insufficient to undermine what Gorsuch saw as the clear interpretation of the statute. The same was true for the issue that concerned Roberts: religious exemptions. Gorsuch noted that the funeral home had dropped its RFRA claim after losing in the Sixth Circuit but that the "super statute . . . might supersede Title VII's commands in appropriate cases."[45]

Gorsuch's approach to textualism deserves more detailed discussion, given that he was heavily criticized by conservative commentators and explicitly targeted on textualist grounds by supporters of an LGBTQ-inclusive understanding of Title VII. Early in the opinion, he provided his underlying philosophy:

> This Court normally interprets a statute in accord with the ordinary public meaning of its terms at the time of its enactment. After all, only the words on the page constitute the law adopted by Congress and approved by the President. If judges could add to, remodel, update, or detract from old statutory terms inspired only by extratextual sources and our own imaginations, we would risk amending statutes outside the legislative process reserved for the people's representatives. And we would deny the people the right to continue relying on the original meaning of the law they have counted on to settle their rights and obligations.[46]

Gorsuch found that the ordinary public meaning of "sex" was the "biological distinctions between male and female."[47] He then found that gender identity and sexual orientation are inherently part of sex and that it is impossible to discriminate against these identities without discriminating because of sex. This discrimination "has always been prohibited by Title VII's plain terms."[48] Gorsuch believed this was true the day Title VII was signed into law, but it took time to become a tangible legal reality: "Over time, though, the breadth of the statutory language proved too difficult to deny."[49] In addition, for Gorsuch, this understanding of the law was unaffected by subsequent inaction by Congress because there was no way to determine the motivation behind that inaction. Here again, he invoked Scalia: "Arguments based on subsequent legislative history . . . should not be taken seriously, not even in a footnote."[50] Later, he admitted that legislative history could be consulted in cases of unclear statutory language, but he found the text of Title VII to be clear. He accused the employers of making policy by inserting their preferences in place of the clear text. They avoided using the term "legislative intent," but they offered the same analysis compelled by that approach. According to Gorsuch, "However framed, the employer's logic impermissibly seeks to displace the plain meaning of the law in favor of something lying beyond it."[51] In Gorsuch's formulation, broad text such as that in Title VII may achieve unexpected results in the hands of judges, but this was in line with textualism rather than the more subjective search for intent or purpose.

Justice Alito wrote a long and vigorous dissent, joined by Justice Thomas, claiming to apply the true Scalia approach to interpretation, reflecting the conservative approach of judges Sykes, Ho, and Pryor. The dissenters reflected the trend in conservative jurisprudence on the question of statutory interpretation, which increasingly incorporates originalist approaches to textualism. Justice Kavanaugh offered a separate and milder dissent that, interestingly, directly addressed only sexual orientation; he completely, and perhaps conveniently, avoided the issue of gender identity. His position was essentially that of Judge Lynch—that is, reading sexual orientation into Title VII would be an act of judicial policymaking, and only Congress is properly authorized to amend the statute, despite his sympathy for the plight for sexual minorities. Kavanaugh began his dissent with the question, "Who decides?" He accused the majority of acting like Judge Posner by ignoring the "ordinary meaning" of Title VII—a meaning that did not include sexual orientation in 1964. For him, the argument in favor of including sexual orientation was "new theory," and he noted the negative judicial history on the question of sexual orientation. This, of course, overlooks the judicial evolution on the related issue of gender identity, and this omission is curious but, on some level, completely understandable. It is easier to make an argument if you ignore a significant portion of the argument against you. I have made the case in this book that legal arguments in favor of including gender identity are more established and well developed than arguments for including sexual orientation, but the argument for sexual orientation clearly builds on the same foundation. Kavanaugh ignored this reality. He could have signed onto the majority opinion as it applied to Aimee Stephens, but he said nothing about her or her case. Kavanaugh simply erased her and the issue of gender identity and Title VII. He also used LGB history, again erasing transgender people and their history, to argue against sexual minorities and their protection under Title VII. Where Gorsuch saw connections between gender, gender identity, and sexual orientation, Kavanaugh saw bright lines, even walls, of separation: "Seneca Falls was not Stonewall. The women's rights movement was not (and is not) the gay rights movement, although many people obviously support or participate in both. So to think that sexual orientation discrimination is just a form of sex discrimination is not just a mistake of language and psychology, but also a mistake of history and sociology."[52]

In addition to the standard conservative arguments against the inclusion of gender identity and sexual orientation in Title VII, Alito used gender and sexual minorities' own history of oppression against them. For instance, he argued that LGBTQ individuals were considered mentally ill criminals in the 1960s, which obviously excluded them from Title VII's protections. He downplayed *Price Waterhouse* and *Oncale* in typical conservative fashion. Alito asserted that *Oncale* "does not provide the slightest support for what the Court has done today." He played up the bathroom issue, in addition to noting the negative implications for housing and health care policy. He seemed most concerned, however, about the transgender thought police, engaging in an extended discussion of his worries about religious discrimination and free-speech limitations. "Some jurisdictions, such as New York City," he noted, "have ordinances making the failure to use an individual's preferred pronoun a punishable offense, and some colleges have similar rules." This was a sensational misreading of the New York law promoted by conservative and libertarian media outlets. In fact, the intentional and repeated misgendering of a person could lead to civil liability under the law, as it could under gender- and gender identity–based antidiscrimination laws more generally. In a controversial speech to the Federalist Society a few months later, Alito emphasized a similar theme, noting his perception that the First Amendment rights of those who opposed same-sex marriage were increasingly limited. To his dissent, he attached extensive appendices of dictionary definitions, lists of statutes, and the US armed services application form—all presumably designed to illustrate the differences between sex, gender identity, and sexual orientation.[53] Overall, Alito's dissent was more of a conservative screed than a thoughtful opinion.

In their dissents, both Alito and Kavanaugh embraced originalism-influenced textualism, focusing on how statutory language would have been generally understood at the time of its enactment, rather than Gorsuch's method of reading the language literally without an inquiry into historical understanding. Alito claimed to be following Scalia's approach to statutory interpretation and accused Gorsuch of engaging in Posner-like updating. He wrote:

> The Court attempts to pass off its decision as the inevitable product of the textualist school of statutory interpretation championed by our late colleague Justice Scalia, but no one should be fooled. The Court's opinion is like a pirate ship. It sails under a textualist flag, but what it actually represents is a theory of statutory interpretation that Justice Scalia excoriated—the theory that courts should "update" old statutes so that they better reflect the current values of society.[54]

Of course, the problem with this assertation is that Scalia included same-sex sexual harassment in Title VII, despite any evidence that this was the original intention of the statute. Rather than Gorsuch's more literal approach to the text, Alito focused on the original understanding of Title VII, reinforced by decades of congressional inaction, despite Scalia's admonition not to use subsequent legislative history as a guide. Kavanaugh objected to what he described as Gorsuch's mechanical approach to interpretation, which can lead to undemocratic results. "A literalist approach to interpreting phrases disrespects ordinary meaning and deprives the citizenry of fair notice of what the law is. It destabilizes the rule of law and thwarts democratic accountability," he asserted.[55] Both Kavanaugh and Alito created a legal narrative in which gender identity and sexual orientation have virtually no connection to their understanding of sex in Title VII. Under this approach, *Oncale* cannot exist and must be ignored or marginalized. Scalia's textualism in that case must be abandoned for an originalist textualism that is increasingly favored by conservative judges and conservative legal activists.

Ultimately, the conservative dissenters were unable to counter the more sophisticated approach to gender represented by *Price Waterhouse* and its progeny and by Scalia's severing of Title VII interpretation from legislative or public intent in *Oncale*. These legal paths were quite durable.

REACTIONS AND IMPLICATIONS

Progressives and LGBTQ advocates were, of course, delighted and surprised by the decision, especially by the presence of Roberts in the majority. Judicial conservatives were nearly uniformly critical and outraged, often utilizing hyperbolic language to describe the decision. One commentator, Varad Mehta, called it "the end of the Federalist Society judicial project." Carrie Severino of the Judicial Crisis Network asserted that Gorsuch made his decision "for the sake of appealing to college campuses and editorial boards" and referred to it as "a brute force attack on our constitutional system." Severino is one of the leading activists behind the campaign to fill the federal judiciary with conservative and Federalist Society judges. Not surprisingly, Robert George was also a strong critic:

> The *Bostock* ruling (further) politicizes the judiciary and undermines the very thing courts exist to uphold: the Rule of Law. It will destroy what faith remains in the moral and intellectual integrity of our courts. It also vindicates Adrian Vermeule's warning to conservatives that trying to combat the longstanding "progressive" strategy of imposing a substantive moral-political agenda through the courts by appointing "originalist" and "textualist" judges is hopeless. Conservatives, Professor Vermeule famously argued, need to shift to their own version of liberal legal theorist Ronald Dworkin's "moral reading" of the Constitution and laws to advance a socially conservative moral and political vision. Who is to gainsay him now?

For George, only explicitly Christian nationalist courts, sharing his moral vision, can be the solution. Gorsuch clearly struck a nerve with his fellow conservatives and was accused of being a traitor to the conservative judicial project.[56]

The depth of conservatives' hostility to the decision, and progressives' support for it, stems in large part from its potential implications for other areas of federal law, especially statutes that use the term "sex." As GLAD's Jennifer Levi, one of the architects of the legal project to expand Title VII interpretation, notes, the decision will have "broad implications," including in the areas of "housing, education, credit, health care and beyond that as well." For instance, *Bostock* will reinforce the already strong federal legal consensus about the rights of transgender students under Title IX.[57]

The decision also affects legal interpretations in states where gender identity and sexual orientation are not protected categories, especially those with a jurisprudential tradition of following federal legal approaches. A case from Michigan demonstrates this and reflects the interpretive gymnastics judges utilize when their ideology conflicts with clear legal mandates. Court of claims judge Christopher Murray ruled that *Bostock* can be applied to gender identity–based discrimination under the state law prohibiting sex discrimination in public accommodations but not to sexual orientation–based discrimination. In excluding sexual orientation, he cited a 1993 state appeals court precedent and claimed he could not use the "persuasive authority" of *Bostock* to change this interpretation; only that higher state court could do so. However, he applied the authority of *Bostock* to gender identity. Arguably, he could have found that *Bostock* overturned or significantly weakened the 1993 precedent, but he chose not to do so. Murray is a graduate of ultraconservative Hillsdale College and is a member of the Federalist Society. Like Sean Cox, his Michigan colleague who cited an RFRA exemption in Aimee Stephens's case, Murray found a way to not apply the law in a way that protected LGB rights. Some conservative judges will likely continue to play these legal games to deny the applicability of *Bostock* in a variety of contexts, especially if they can find some kind of legal loophole. Even before *Bostock,* the Michigan Department of Civil Rights, like the EEOC, found that discrimination based on sexual orientation and gender identity is prohibited by the state's ban on sex discrimination, but it placed sexual orientation–based complaints in abeyance in the wake of Judge Murray's decision. Thus, Murray's decision moved civil rights policy in a conservative direction.[58]

The main path for the conservative attack on the Supreme Court's protection of LGBTQ rights will be to expand religious liberty objections, led by organizations such as the Alliance Defending Freedom. Indeed, the Supreme Court seems poised to create significant protections for religious entities in the application of antidiscrimination law, as evidenced by a case argued in the 2020–2021 term, *Fulton v. City of Philadelphia.*[59] As Aaron Belkin notes, "An expansion of the religious liberty to discriminate could eat away at *Bostock.*"[60] Fortunately for LGBTQ rights, *Fulton* was decided narrowly, but it could be used to bolster the conservative project to create broad religious-based objections in future cases. The Supreme Court also undermined efforts to restrict the rights of transgender students when it refused an appeal in Gavin Grimm's case, thereby allowing the powerful Fourth Circuit precedent to stand. Alito and Thomas disagreed with the denial of certiorari, but Roberts and Gorsuch did not.[61] This is an early signal of the enduring power of *Bostock*, especially since a majority of the court could have used *Grimm* to address the question of restroom access and narrow the application of *Bostock*.

Reflecting the power of conservative and Republican opposition to *Bostock* in the political arena, the Justice Department issued a memorandum sharply limiting its impact in the waning days of the Trump administration. As described by the *Wall Street Journal*, "The new memo, dated Sunday [January 17, 2021] and sent by the acting head of the Justice Department's civil rights division, acknowledges the court's ruling was sweeping, but says the department should not extend it further to areas such as housing and education, where longstanding gender-based policies on bathrooms and sports teams could come into play." The memo by acting assistant attorney general John Daukas echoed the failed conservative arguments in *Bostock*: "We must hesitate to apply the reasoning of Bostock to different texts, adopted at different times, in different contexts. . . . Unlike racial discrimination, the Supreme Court has never held that a religious employer's decision not to hire homosexual or transgender persons 'violates deeply and widely accepted views of elementary justice' or that the government has a 'compelling' interest in the eradication of such conduct." Of course, this memo was withdrawn by the Biden administration, and an expansive view of *Bostock* is guiding that administration's efforts on LGBTQ rights. One of President Biden's first official acts was to sign an executive order protecting LGBTQ rights under the framework of *Bostock*.[62]

The positive reaction from LGBTQ rights activists stems from the fact that the ramifications of *Bostock* extend far beyond employment discrimination, as reflected in Biden's executive order. He directed all federal agencies to include gender identity and sexual orientation under federal statutes that use "sex" as a basis for protection.[63] The Biden administration and the federal courts will increasingly apply *Bostock* to gender- and sex-based discrimination in other areas of federal law. Thus, much of the work of the proposed Equality Act was accomplished by the Supreme Court in *Bostock*. Even so, that bill faces an uphill climb, despite Democratic control of Congress and the White House in 2021, largely because of the filibuster and continued Republican opposition. In addition, Title VII does not apply to public accommodations, and the Equality Act would extend coverage to such entities. It would also guarantee that other areas of federal law would explicitly ban LGBTQ discrimination and not rely on a potentially shifting administrative interpretation.

LGBTQ rights in the states, especially transgender rights, face a more uncertain future. The ADF has been spearheading efforts to restrict the rights of transgender youth. In particular, opposition to transgender athletes participating in school sports based on their gender identity is being mobilized to enact restrictive policies in conservative and Republican-controlled states. Conservative activists are also working to ban transition-related health care for transgender youth. This opposition is also being used to undermine efforts to pass the Equality Act. *Bostock* and the strongly protective Title IX jurisprudence discussed in chapter 4 should be valuable resources for legal activists challenging these restrictive policies, but Trump appointees could complicate these efforts.[64]

Consequently, the disconnect between jurisprudential protections for transgender rights and political support for such protections continues. But the strategy to achieve an expanded interpretation of Title VII was wildly successful, after recalibrating in the wake of Justice Kennedy's retirement and his replacement by Gorsuch. Ann Hopkins could not have envisioned this trajectory for her case, but the result was not accidental. It was envisioned by scholars and activists as a way to leverage the law to protect LGBTQ victims of discrimination.

THE LIMITATIONS AND POTENTIAL OF RIGHTS-BASED APPROACHES

The Supreme Court's decision in *Bostock* fundamentally changed the relationship between LGBTQ rights and federal law and policy, but it should not be seen as a complete victory. Conservative activists will continue to invoke religious freedom arguments and push for the enactment of antitransgender policies at state and local levels. Despite the stronger legal foundation for transgender rights in federal law, the politics of transgender rights will remain unsettled for the foreseeable future. Although conservative arguments have been undermined by court decisions, they have not gone away, and conservatives will continue to advocate for a rigid gender binary in law and policy. However, *Bostock* illustrates the continuing and critical role played by litigation for LGBTQ rights. Here, a case not planned by LGBTQ activists, *Price Waterhouse v. Hopkins*, formed the foundation for a significant legal reevaluation of Title VII's protections by legal theorists, legal activists, plaintiffs, and judges. These events represent an important case study of litigation's role in the politics of marginalized communities in the United States. This study also confirms that judicial ideology can play an important role in civil rights policymaking and illustrates that judges can both facilitate and constrain such policymaking through the interpretative choices they make.

Despite these successes, rights-based litigation campaigns are disparaged by critics of judicial policymaking and scholars who question the efficacy and wisdom of rights-based politics. The evidence provided in this book illustrates that these criticisms are driven by normative desires as much as by empirical insights. The reality is that judicial policymaking is deeply embedded in the US system; it is often messy, slow, and unpredictable. At the same time, however, activists can carefully leverage the judicial process to achieve their goals, using the resources of a dynamic and evolving legal system.

Courtenay Daum's book *The Politics of Right Sex* offers a powerful critique of rights-based politics in the context of transgender rights. Daum argues that such politics are both illusory and harmful for transgender politics and the goal of equality and dignity for transgender individuals. She states, "The politics of rights are of limited utility for marginalized communities because they are unable to reach the myriad forces of governmentality that work as a type of infra law—the informal and implicit norms and regulations that operate below the surface—to mark and discipline transgressive individuals in order to maintain extant hierarchies."[65] This is an important reminder of the complexity of power and the limits of traditional legal reform; it also leads to a discounting of litigation as a tool for marginalized groups to achieve real change. As scholars of LGBTQ rights and judicial policymaking continue this debate, it is important to consider both the limits and the opportunities presented by litigation. Daum's book is part of a body of work from rights-skeptic scholars of transgender politics, but this scholarship often overlooks the real, yet sometimes slow and gradual, change that can result from litigation strategies.[66] We need to continue to interrogate the limits of rights-based litigation, but we also need to understand its unique and potentially transformative place in the US political system. This also applies to critics such as R. Shep Melnick, who oppose this litigation and similar policymaking in the bureaucracy for being antimajoritarian, similar to the critiques of Robert Kagan and Gerald Rosenberg.

This book offers a counter to rights-critical scholarship. Ann Hopkins did not know she was starting a legal revolution, but victims of discrimination, scholars of gender, LGBTQ activists, and judges transformed her case into a powerful tool to combat discrimination. Given the deeply embedded nature of judicial policymaking in the United States, activists have successfully used litigation to blaze paths to change, in this case resulting in a profound legal shift in civil rights protections for LGBTQ individuals. By the late 1990s, and with an assist from Justice Scalia, transgender rights litigators saw an opportunity to include gender identity–based protections in Title VII. They were eventually aided by mostly liberal judges serving as legal innovators, spurring and furthering the intentional shift in Title VII interpretation in the EEOC. Conservative judges, especially those connected to the powerful and effective conservative legal movement through the Federalist Society, will likely continue to find ways to undermine and limit *Bostock*, but that decision undermined many of the movement's legal narratives about Title VII and LGBTQ rights. The deeply negative legal landscape for LGBTQ rights and the lack of faith in Title VII were indirectly but powerfully altered by *Price Waterhouse* and *Oncale*. Despite the best efforts of some conservative activists and judges, the Supreme Court affirmed this new path for Title VII just two decades after the first federal judges began to apply the new approach.

Notes

1. LGBTQ RIGHTS, STATUTORY INTERPRETATION, AND JUDICIAL POLICYMAKING

1. Bostock v. Clayton County, 140 S. Ct. 1731 (2020).

2. *R. G. & G. R. Harris Funeral Homes*, Oral Argument, October 8, 2019, https://www.supremecourt.gov/oral_arguments/argument_transcripts/2019/18-107_c18e.pdf, 25; Joan Biskupic, "Anger, Leaks and Tensions at the Supreme Court during the LGBTQ Rights Case," CNN, July 28, 2020, https://www.cnn.com/2020/07/28/politics/neil-gorsuch-supreme-court-lgbtq-civil-rights-act-alito/index.html.

3. Price Waterhouse v. Hopkins, 490 U.S. 228 (1989), 251.

4. Gordon Silverstein, *Law's Allure: How Law Shapes, Constrains, Saves, and Kills Politics* (New York: Cambridge University Press, 2009).

5. Jami K. Taylor, Donald P. Haider-Markel, Daniel C. Lewis, and Jason Pierceson, "Transgender Rights and the Judiciary," in *The Remarkable Rise of Transgender Rights*, ed. Jami K. Taylor, Donald P. Haider-Markel, and Daniel C. Lewis (Ann Arbor: University of Michigan Press, 2018), 136–160.

6. For an overview of these dynamics, see Jason Pierceson, "Theoretical Perspectives on Subnational Public Policy and LGBT Law," in *Oxford Research Encyclopedia of Politics*, May 2019, https://doi.org/10.1093/acrefore/9780190228637.013.1227.

7. Silverstein, *Law's Allure*, 29.

8. See, for example, Thomas F. Burke, *Lawyers, Lawsuits, and Legal Rights: The Battle over Litigation in American Society* (Berkeley: University of California Press, 2002); Sean Farhang, *The Litigation State: Public Regulation and Private Lawsuits in the U.S.* (Princeton, NJ: Princeton University Press, 2010).

9. Burke, *Lawyers, Lawsuits, and Legal Rights*, 15.

10. Jeremiah J. Garretson, *The Path to Gay Rights: How Activism and Coming out Changed Public Opinion* (New York: NYU Press, 2018), 185. On federalism, see Pierceson, "Theoretical Perspectives."

11. EEOC v. R. G. & G. R. Harris Funeral Homes, Inc., 201 F. Supp. 3d 837 (E.D. Mich. 2016).

12. R. Shep Melnick, *The Transformation of Title IX: Regulating Gender Equality in Education* (Washington, DC: Brookings Institution Press, 2018), 226, 21–22, 247. As discussed later, Melnick appears to be skeptical of even a category for a transgender person that is not subjective and not legally separable from sex assigned at birth.

13. See Robert A. Kagan, *Adversarial Legalism: The American Way of Law*, 2nd ed. (Cambridge, MA: Harvard University Press, 2019); Gerald N. Rosenberg, *The Hollow*

Hope: Can Courts Bring about Social Change? 2nd ed. (Chicago: University of Chicago Press, 2008).

14. Michael McCann and William Haltom, "Seeing through the Smoke: Adversarial Legalism and U.S. Tobacco Politics," in *Varieties of Legal Order: The Politics of Adversarial and Bureaucratic Legalism,* ed. Thomas F. Burke and Jeb Barnes (New York: Routledge, 2018), 63.

15. See Benjamin G. Bishin, Thomas J. Hayes, Matthew B. Incantalupo, and Charles Anthony Smith, "Opinion Backlash and Public Attitudes: Are Political Advances in Gay Rights Counterproductive?" *American Journal of Political Science* 60, 3 (July 2016): 625–648; Robert M. Howard and Amy Steigerwalt, *Judging Law and Policy: Courts and Policymaking in the American Political System* (New York: Routledge, 2012); Thomas A. Keck, "Beyond Backlash: Assessing the Impact of Judicial Decisions on LGBT Rights," *Law & Society Review* 43, 1 (2009): 151–185. Also see the works cited in note 17.

16. See John D. Skrentny, *The Minority Rights Revolution* (Cambridge, MA: Belknap Press, 2002).

17. See, for example, Ellen Ann Andersen, *Out of the Closets & into the Courts: Legal Opportunity Structure and Gay Rights Litigation* (Ann Arbor: University of Michigan Press, 2005); Carlos A. Ball, *From the Closet to the Courtroom: Five LGBT Rights Lawsuits that Have Changed Our Nation* (Boston: Beacon Press, 2010); Alison L. Gash, *Below the Radar: How Silence Can Save Civil Rights* (New York: Oxford University Press, 2015); Susan Gluck Mezey, *Queers in Court: Gay Rights Law and Public Policy* (Lanham, MD: Rowman & Littlefield, 2007); Jason Pierceson, *Court, Liberalism, and Rights: Gay Law and Politics in the United States and Canada* (Philadelphia: Temple University Press, 2005); Jason Pierceson, *Same-Sex Marriage in the United States: The Road to the Supreme Court* (Lanham, MD: Rowman & Littlefield, 2013).

18. For a description of the ideological movement to create this new interpretation, see Amanda Hollis-Brusky, *Ideas with Consequences: The Federalist Society and the Conservative Counterrevolution* (New York: Oxford University Press, 2015).

19. Howard and Steigerwalt, *Judging Law and Policy,* 5.

20. Howard and Steigerwalt; Pierceson, *Same-Sex Marriage.*

21. Hollis-Brusky, *Ideas with Consequences,* 10, 13, 21.

22. Lawrence Baum, *Judges and Their Audiences: A Perspective on Judicial Behavior* (Princeton, NJ: Princeton University Press, 2006).

23. Cass R. Sunstein, David Schkade, Lisa M. Ellman, and Andres Sawicki, *Are Judges Political? An Empirical Analysis of the Federal Judiciary* (Washington, DC: Brookings Institution Press, 2006), 30, 130.

24. William D. Popkin, *Statutes in Court: The History and Theory of Statutory Interpretation* (Durham, NC: Duke University Press, 1999), 152.

25. Leif H. Carter and Thomas F. Burke, *Reason in Law,* 9th ed. (Chicago: University of Chicago Press, 2016), 127.

26. William N. Eskridge Jr., *Dynamic Statutory Interpretation* (Cambridge, MA: Harvard University Press, 1994), 48.

27. Frank B. Cross, *The Theory and Practice of Statutory Interpretation* (Stanford, CA: Stanford University Press, 2009), 29. For more on Scalia's textualism, see Richard L. Hasen, *The Justice of Contradictions: Antonin Scalia and the Politics of Disruption* (New Haven, CT: Yale University Press, 2018).

28. Cross, *Theory and Practice of Statutory Interpretation*, 139.

29. Goluszek v. Smith, 697 F. Supp. 1452 (N.D. Ill. 1988), 1456.

30. Hively v. Ivy Tech Community College, 853 F.3d 339 (7th Cir. 2017).

31. Oncale v. Sundowner Offshore Services, 523 U.S. 75 (1998), 79; emphasis added.

32. Harris v. Forklift Systems, 510 U.S. 17 (1993), 25.

33. *Hively*, 345, 350–351.

34. *Hively*, 355.

35. Richard A. Posner, *Sex and Reason* (Cambridge, MA: Harvard University Press, 1992). For a contemporaneous critical review, see Robin West, "Sex, Reason, and a Taste for the Absurd," *Georgetown Law Journal* 81 (1993): 2413–2456.

36. *Hively*, 360.

37. Hasen, *Justice of Contradictions*, 37–38.

38. David Lat, "A Federal Judge's Rather Rude Joke about Lesbians," Above the Law, December 2, 2016, https://abovethelaw.com/2016/12/a-federal-judges-rather -rude-joke-about-lesbians/.

39. Katie R. Eyer, "Statutory Originalism and LGBT Rights," *Wake Forest Law Review* 54, 1 (2019): 63–104, 65, 96, 67. For more on the shift in constitutional originalism, see Eric Segall, *Originalism as Faith* (New York: Cambridge University Press, 2018).

40. Ball, *From the Closet to the Courtroom*, 36.

41. Ball, 56–57.

42. Farhang, *Litigation State*, 172–173.

43. DeSantis v. Pacific Telephone & Telegraph Co., 608 F.2d 327 (9th Cir. 1979).

44. For an overview of these developments, see Howard and Steigerwalt, *Judging Law and Policy*, 56–74.

45. *Hively*, 348, 349.

46. Bostock v. Clayton County, 2016 U.S. Dist. LEXIS 192898 (N.D. Ga. 2016), 16.

2. THE HISTORY OF LGBTQ RIGHTS, SEX, AND TITLE VII

1. R. Shep Melnick, *The Transformation of Title IX: Regulating Gender Equality in Education* (Washington, DC: Brookings Institution Press, 2018), 263.

2. See David K. Johnson, *The Lavender Scare: The Cold War Persecution of Gays and Lesbians in the Federal Government* (Chicago: University of Chicago Press, 2004).

3. Executive Order 10450—Security Requirements for Government Employment, https://www.archives.gov/federal-register/codification/executive-order/10450.html.

4. *Employment of Homosexual and Other Sex Perverts in Government*, Interim

Report (pursuant to S. Res. 280, 81st Congress, 2nd session), Made to the Committee on Expenditures in Executive Departments by Its Subcommittee on Investigations, Document No. 241 (Washington, DC: Government Printing Office, 1950), 3.

5. See Jason Pierceson, *Sexual Minorities and Politics: An Introduction* (Lanham, MD: Rowman & Littlefield, 2016).

6. Joyce Murdoch and Deb Price, *Courting Justice: Gay Men and Lesbians v. the Supreme Court* (New York: Basic Books: 2001), 59. For Kameny's petition, see Charles Francis, ed., "Petition Denied. Revolution Begun. The 50th Anniversary of Kameny at the Court: Frank Kameny's Petition to the U.S. Supreme Court," Kameny Papers Project, Library of Congress.

7. Rick Valelly, "How Gay Rights Activists Remade the Federal Government," *Washington Post,* October 1, 2018, https://www.washingtonpost.com/outlook/2018/10/01/how-gay-rights-activists-remade-federal-government/; Marc Stein, *Sexual Injustice: Supreme Court Decisions from* Griswold *to* Roe (Chapel Hill: University of North Carolina Press, 2010), 141–142.

8. Lillian Faderman, *The Gay Revolution: The Story of the Struggle* (New York: Simon & Schuster, 2015), 146–148; Johnson, *Lavender Scare,* 192.

9. William N. Eskridge, *Gaylaw: Challenging the Apartheid of the Closet* (Cambridge, MA: Harvard University Press, 1999), 125.

10. Franklin E. Kameny, "Civil Liberties: A Progress Report," *New York Mattachine Newsletter,* July 1965, 1–22, copy on file with the author. The article is the text of a July 22, 1964, speech.

11. Eric Marcus, "Ernestine Eckstein," Making Gay History: The Podcast, https://makinggayhistory.com/podcast/ernestine-eckstein/. See also the interview with Eckstein in *Ladder* 10, 9 (June 1966), https://digitalassets.lib.berkeley.edu/sfbagals/The_Ladder/1966_Ladder_Vol10_No09_Jun.pdf.

12. Marilyn Berger, "David Bazelon Dies at 83; Jurist Had Wide Influence," *New York Times,* February 21, 1993, 38.

13. Bowers v. Hardwick, 478 U.S. 186 (1986), 197. For the lobbying, see Jason Pierceson, *Courts, Liberalism, and Rights: Gay Law and Politics in the United States and Canada* (Philadelphia: Temple University Press, 2005), 24–25.

14. Scott v. Macy, 349 F.2d 182 (D.C. Cir. 1965), 189.

15. Stein, *Sexual Injustice.*

16. Rhonda R. Rivera, "Our Straight-laced Judges: The Legal Position of Homosexual Persons in the United States," *Hastings Law Journal* 30, 4 (March 1979): 799–956, 820.

17. Norton v. Macy, 417 F.2d 1161 (D.C. Cir. 1969), 1165.

18. Gregory B. Lewis, "Lifting the Ban on Gays in the Civil Service: Federal Policy toward Gay and Lesbian Employees since the Cold War," *Public Administration Review* 57, 5 (September–October 1997): 387–395, 392.

19. Society for Individual Rights v. Hampton, 63 F.R.D. 399 (N.D. Cal. 1973).

20. Jason Pierceson, *Same-Sex Marriage in the United States: The Road to the Supreme Court* (Lanham, MD: Rowman & Littlefield, 2013), 29; Eli Sanders, "Meet

Faygele Ben Miriam, the Radical Activist Who Pioneered the Fight for Same-Sex Marriage in Washington State," Tabletmag.com, June 6, 2012, https://www.tabletmag .com/jewish-news-and-politics/101628/gay-marriages-jewish-pioneer.

21. Sanders, "Meet Faygele Ben Miriam."

22. Rivera, "Our Straight-laced Judges," 823.

23. Singer v. United States Civil Service Commission, 530 F.2d 247 (1976), 250.

24. *Singer*, 255.

25. Sanders, "Meet Faygele Ben Miriam."

26. See Fred Fejes, *Gay Rights and Moral Panic: The Origins of America's Debate on Homosexuality* (New York: Palgrave Macmillan, 2008); Tina Fetner, *How the Religious Right Shaped Lesbian and Gay Activism* (Minneapolis: University of Minnesota Press, 2008).

27. James W. Button et al., "The Politics of Gay Rights at the Local and State Level," in *The Politics of Gay Rights*, ed. Craig A. Rimmerman et al. (Chicago: University of Chicago Press, 2000), 269–289.

28. Amy L. Stone, *Gay Rights at the Ballot Box* (Minneapolis: University of Minnesota Press, 2012), xv; Pierceson, *Sexual Minorities and Politics*, 109; "Employment Non-discrimination," Movement Advancement Project, https://www.lgbtmap.org/equality -maps/employment_non_discrimination_laws.

29. Jo Freeman, *We Will Be Heard: Women's Struggles for Political Power in the United States* (Lanham, MD: Rowman & Littlefield, 2008), 171.

30. See Cynthia Harrison, *On Account of Sex: The Politics of Women's Issues, 1945– 1968* (Berkeley: University of California Press, 1988); Hugh Davis Graham, *The Civil Rights Era: Origins and Development of National Policy, 1960–1972* (New York: Oxford University Press, 1990), 136–137.

31. Harrison, *On Account of Sex*, 16.

32. Harrison, 22.

33. Harrison, 38.

34. Graham, *Civil Rights Era*, 206.

35. Harrison, *On Account of Sex*, 172.

36. Freeman, *We Will Be Heard*, 177, 185.

37. *Congressional Record—House*, February 9, 1964, 2577–2578.

38. *Congressional Record—House*, February 9, 1964, 2578.

39. Pauli Murray and Mary Eastwood, "Jane Crow and the Law: Sex Discrimination and Title VII," *George Washington Law Review* 34, 2 (December 1965): 232–256, 243.

40. *Congressional Record—House*, February 9, 1964, 2580.

41. *Congressional Record—House*, February 9, 1964, 2581.

42. *Congressional Record—House*, February 9, 1964, 2581–2582.

43. Freeman, *We Will Be Heard*, 184.

44. Freeman, 182.

45. Serena Mayeri, *Reasoning from Race: Feminism, Law, and the Civil Rights Revolution* (Cambridge, MA: Harvard University Press, 2011), 14.

46. Pauli Murray, "A Proposal to Reexamine the Applicability of the Fourteenth Amendment to State Laws and Practices which Discriminate on the Basis of Sex per Se," December 1, 1962, box 8, folder 62, President's Commission on the Status of Women Records, 1961–1963, Schlesinger Library, Radcliffe Institute for Advanced Study, Harvard University, https://documents.alexanderstreet.com/d/1000681163.

47. Pauli Murray, "Memorandum in Support of Retaining the Amendment to H.R. 7152, Title VII (Equal Employment Opportunity) to Prohibit Discrimination in Employment Because of Sex," April 14, 1964, Pauli Murray Papers, series II, 1935–1984, box 85, folder 1485, Schlesinger Library, Radcliffe Institute for Advanced Study, Harvard University, 9, https://documents.alexanderstreet.com/d/1000680941.

48. Nancy MacLean, *Freedom Is Not Enough: The Opening of the American Workplace* (New York: Russell Sage Foundation, 2006), 121.

49. Rosalind Rosenberg, "The Conjunction of Race and Gender," *Journal of Women's History* 14, 2 (2002): 68–73, 70.

50. Murray, "Proposal to Reexamine the Applicability of the Fourteenth Amendment," 34.

51. MacLean, *Freedom Is Not Enough*, 123.

52. Peggy Pascoe, "Sex, Gender, and Same-Sex Marriage," in *Is Academic Feminism Dead? Theory in Practice*, ed. Social Justice Group at the Center for Advanced Feminist Studies (New York: New York University Press, 2000), 91.

53. Jones v. Hallahan, 501 S.W.2d 588 (Ky. 1973); Jeff Lyon, "Lesbians Protest at Marriage Office," *Chicago Tribune*, October 21, 1975.

54. Pierceson, *Same-Sex Marriage in the United States*, 34–35.

55. Jason Pierceson, "Elaine Noble," in *LGBTQ Americans in the U.S. Political System: An Encyclopedia of Activists, Voters, Candidates, and Officeholders*, ed. Jason Pierceson (Santa Barbara, CA: ABC-CLIO, 2020), 305–307.

56. "Advocates; Should Marriage between Homosexuals Be Permitted?" May 2, 1974, WGBH Media Library and Archives, http://openvault.wgbh.org/catalog/V_57993D38129A433AAD10C7B04D019EF6.

57. For a discussion of the Dixon bill, see Pierceson, *Same-Sex Marriage in the United States*, 35–40. For Freund's role in the 1973 law, see "Freund, Howell Discuss History of Title 34, Gay-Inclusive 1973 D.C. Non-discrimination Law," April 15, 2004, http://www.glaa.org/archive/2004/title34history0415.shtml; Samantha Schmidt, "Gay Rights or Women's Rights? This Pioneering Lesbian Activist Refused to Take a Side," *Washington Post*, June 26, 2019, https://www.washingtonpost.com/local/social-issues/gay-rights-or-womens-rights-this-pioneering-lesbian-activist-refused-to-take-a-side/2019/06/26/bbc79930-977b-11e9-8d0a-5edd7e2025b1_story.html. For Freund's statement, see "Statement of Eva Freund, NCAC Board Member on Behalf of the National Capital Area Chapter, National Organization for Women, before the Committee on Economic Development, Manpower, and Labor of the Council of the District of Columbia," June 7, 1973, Eva Freund Papers, 1961–1974, Rainbow History Project Digital Collections, https://archives.rainbowhistory.org/items/show/736.

58. Pascoe, "Sex, Gender, and Same-Sex Marriage," 101.

59. Pascoe, 103. For Wolfson's approach, see Nathaniel Frank, *Awakening: How Gays and Lesbians Brought Marriage Equality to America* (Cambridge, MA: Belknap Press, 2017).

60. "Plaintiff's Post-Hearing Submission," Papers of Franklin Kameny, Library of Congress, 16, copy on file with the author. This document was submitted during the trial proceedings. See note 17 in Dean v. District of Columbia, 653 A.2d 307 (D.C. App. 1995). The copy in Kameny's possession could have been a draft, but I assume the actual submission is similar.

61. William N. Eskridge Jr., "A History of Same-Sex Marriage," *Virginia Law Review 79*, 7 (1993): 1419–1513, 1425; Andrew Koppelman, "Why Discrimination against Gays Is Sex Discrimination," *New York University Law Review 69*, 2 (1994): 197–287.

62. Franklin E. Kamey to Craig R. Dean, July 29, 1991, Kameny Papers, Library of Congress, copy on file with the author.

63. Franklin E. Kamey to William N. Eskridge Jr., February 12, 1992, Kameny Papers, Library of Congress, copy on file with the author.

64. *Dean*, 336.

65. See Pierceson, *Courts, Liberalism, and Rights*, 121–122; Baehr v. Lewin, 852 P.2d 44 (Haw. 1993).

66. Baker v. State of Vermont, 744 A.2d 864 (Vt. 1999). For a discussion of the court's approach, see Pierceson, *Courts, Liberalism, and Rights*, 132–135. For a discussion of the Maryland case, see Pierceson, *Same-Sex Marriage in the United States*, 168–170.

67. Abigail C. Saguy, *What Is Sexual Harassment? From Capitol Hill to the Sorbonne* (Berkeley: University of California Press, 2003); Kathrin S. Zippel, *The Politics of Sexual Harassment: A Comparative Study of the United States, the European Union, and Germany* (New York: Cambridge University Press, 2006).

68. Melnick, *Transformation of Title IX*, 15.

69. Anna-Maria Marshall, "Closing the Gaps: Plaintiffs in Pivotal Sexual Harassment Cases," *Law & Social Inquiry* 23, 4 (1998): 761–793, 784.

70. Saguy, *What Is Sexual Harassment*, 10.

71. Meritor Savings Bank v. Vinson, 477 U.S. 57 (1986). For a discussion of the 1970s cases, see Zippel, *Politics of Sexual Harassment*, 44–50.

72. Zippel, *Politics of Sexual Harassment*, 58.

73. *Meritor*, 66.

74. Ellen Ann Andersen, *Out of the Closets & into the Courts: Legal Opportunity Structure and Gay Rights Litigation* (Ann Arbor: University of Michigan Press, 2005), 29.

75. See Murdoch and Price, *Courting Justice*, 61–62.

76. Katherine Turk, *Equality on Trial: Gender and Rights in the Modern American Workplace* (Philadelphia: University of Pennsylvania Press, 2016), 169.

77. Jessica A. Clarke, "Past Cases Have Labeled LGBTQ People as Deviants. Will the Supreme Court Move beyond that Now?" *Los Angeles Times*, October 7, 2019, https://www.latimes.com/opinion/story/2019-10-07/supreme-court-lgbtq-case-oral-arguments.

78. Smith v. Liberty Mutual Insurance Co., 395 F. Supp. 1098 (N.D. Ga. 1975), 1099.

79. Smith v. Liberty Mutual Insurance Co., 569 F.2d 325 (5th Cir. 1978).

80. Willingham v. Macon Telegraph Publishing Co., 507 F.2d 1084 (5th Cir. 1974), 1087.

81. Willingham v. Macon Telegraph Publishing Co., 482 F.2d 535 (5th Cir. 1973), 538.

82. *Willingham* (5th Cir. 1974), 1091.

83. Gary Siniscalso, "Homosexual Discrimination in Employment," *Santa Clara Law Review* 16, 3 (1976): 495–512, 503–504. Siniscalso was a regional counsel for the EEOC in San Francisco.

84. EEOC Decision 76-75 (CCH) ¶6495 (1976), quoted in Avi Sinesky, "Not That There Is Anything Wrong with That: The Practical and Legal Implications of a Homosexual Professional Athlete," *University of Pennsylvania Journal of Business and Employment Law* 10, 4 (2008): 1009–1027, 1013n27.

85. *Smith* (5th Cir. 1978), 327n1.

86. Voyles v. Ralph K. Davies Medical Center, 403 F. Supp. 456 (N.D. Ca. 1975), 456.

87. *Voyles*, 457.

88. In re Grossman, 127 N.J. Super. 13 (1974).

89. *In re Grossman*, 20.

90. *Grossman v. Bernards Township Board of Education*, 1975 U.S. Dist. LEXIS 16261 (D.N.J. 1975), 3, 10; EEOC Decision 75-030 (CCH) ¶6499 (September 24, 1974).

91. Andersen, *Out of the Closets*, 28–30.

92. Holloway v. Arthur Andersen & Co., 566 F.2d 659 (9th Cir. 1977), 663. The footnotes referenced are 1, 6, and 7.

93. *Holloway*, 664.

94. *Ulane v. Eastern Airlines*, 1982 U.S. Dist. LEXIS 13049 (N.D. Ill. 1982), 3–4.

95. Ulane v. Eastern Airlines, 581 F. Supp. 821 (N.D. Ill. 1983), 825.

96. Ulane v. Eastern Airlines, 742 F.2d 1081 (7th Cir. 1984), 1087.

97. Megan Graydon, "Federal Judge John Grady, Who Oversaw Landmark AT&T Antitrust and Marquette 10 Police Corruption Trials, Dies at 90," *Chicago Tribune*, December 9, 2019.

98. Zbaraz v. Quern, 469 F. Supp. 1212 (N.D. Ill. 1979).

99. See Amanda Hollis-Brusky, *Ideas with Consequences: The Federalist Society and the Conservative Counterrevolution* (New York: Oxford University Press, 2015).

100. Sommers v. Budget Marketing, 667 F.2d 748 (8th Cir. 1082), 748, 750.

101. Katherine Turk, "'Our Militancy Is in Our Openness': Gay Employment Rights Activism in California and the Question of Sexual Orientation in Sex Equality Law," *Law and History Review* 31, 2 (2013): 423–469, 453.

102. Carlos A. Ball, *The Queering of Corporate America: How Big Business Went from LGBTQ Adversary to Ally* (Boston: Beacon Press, 2019), 36.

103. Griggs v. Duke Power Company, 401 U.S. 424 (1971).

104. Turk, "'Our Militancy Is in Our Openness,'" 455.

105. Turk, *Equality on Trial*, 152.
106. DeSantis v. Pacific Telephone & Telegraph Co., 608 F.2d 327 (9th Cir. 1979), 329–330.
107. Chai R. Feldblum, "Law and Culture in the Making of *Macy v. Holder*," in *Gender Identity and Sexual Orientation in the Workplace: A Practical Guide*, ed. Christine Michelle Duffy and Denise M. Visconti (Arlington, VA: Bloomberg BNA, 2014), 39-1–39-22, 39-6.

3. *PRICE WATERHOUSE V. HOPKINS* AND THE SHIFT IN
TITLE VII INTERPRETATION

1. Meritor Savings Bank v. Vinson, 477 U.S. 57 (1986); Susan Gluck Mezey, *Beyond Marriage: Continuing Battles for LGBT Rights* (Lanham, MD: Rowman & Littlefield, 2017), 26.
2. Ann Branigar Hopkins, *So Ordered: Making Partner the Hard Way* (Amherst: University of Massachusetts Press, 1996), 9.
3. Gillian Thomas, *Because of Sex: One Law, Ten Cases, and Fifty Years that Changed American Women's Lives at Work* (New York: St. Martin's Press, 2016), 128.
4. Hopkins, *So Ordered*, 154.
5. Hopkins v. Price Waterhouse, 618 F. Supp. 1109 (D.D.C. 1985), 1112–1113; Hopkins, *So Ordered*, 120–121.
6. Hopkins, *So Ordered*, 151.
7. Thomas, *Because of Sex*, 130.
8. Hishon v. King & Spaulding, 467 U.S. 69 (1984).
9. Cynthia Estlund, "The Story of *Price Waterhouse v. Hopkins*," in *Employment Discrimination Stories*, ed. Joel Wm. Friedman (St. Paul: Foundation Press, 2006), 72.
10. Hopkins, *So Ordered*, 193.
11. Hopkins, 194.
12. Estlund, "Story of *Price Waterhouse v. Hopkins*," 74.
13. Estlund, 70.
14. *Hopkins* (D.D.C. 1985), 1116–1117.
15. Estlund, "Story of *Price Waterhouse v. Hopkins*," 75.
16. Bruce Lambert, "Judge Gerhard Gesell Dies at 82; Oversaw Big Cases," *New York Times*, February 21, 1993, https://www.nytimes.com/1993/02/21/us/judge-gerhard-gesell-dies-at-82-oversaw-big-cases.html.
17. *Matlovich v. Secretary of Air Force*, 1976 U.S. Dist. LEXIS 13491 (D.D.C. 1976), 9–10.
18. Hopkins, *So Ordered*, 229.
19. Fiske's testimony is summarized and quoted from Hopkins, 233–239.
20. *Hopkins* (D.D.C. 1985), 1117–1118.
21. *Hopkins* (D.D.C. 1985), 1119.
22. *Hopkins* (D.D.C. 1985), 1119–1120.

23. Nadine Taub, "Keeping Women in Their Place: Stereotyping per se as a Form of Employment Discrimination," *Boston College Law Review* 21, 2 (January 1980): 345–417. For Judge Gesell's citation of Taub on the question of employer liability, see *Hopkins* (D.D.C. 1985), 1120.

24. Hopkins, *So Ordered*, 263–264.

25. Hopkins v. Price Waterhouse, 825 F.2d 458 (D.C. Cir. 1987), 468.

26. *Hopkins* (D.C. Cir. 1987), 469.

27. *Hopkins* (D.C. Cir. 1987), 473.

28. *Hopkins* (D.C. Cir. 1987), 471.

29. *Hopkins* (D.C. Cir. 1987), 473, 475.

30. *Hopkins* (D.C. Cir. 1987), 475–476.

31. *Hopkins* (D.C. Cir. 1987), 475.

32. *Hopkins* (D.C. Cir. 1987), 477.

33. *Hopkins* (D.C. Cir. 1987), 477.

34. Augustus B. Cochran III, *Sexual Harassment and the Law: The Mechelle Vinson Case* (Lawrence: University Press of Kansas, 2004).

35. *Hopkins* (D.C. Cir. 1987), 473–474.

36. Hopkins So Ordered, 283.

37. Thomas, *Because of Sex*, 140.

38. Thomas, 140.

39. Amicus Brief of NOW Legal Defense and Education Fund and other organizations, *Price Waterhouse v. Hopkins*, 1988 U.S. S. Ct. Briefs LEXIS 1249.

40. Amicus Brief of NOW, 29–31.

41. Amicus Brief of the American Psychological Association, *Price Waterhouse v. Hopkins*, 1988 U.S. S. Ct. Briefs LEXIS 1254, 14–16.

42. Brief for the United States as Amicus Curiae, *Price Waterhouse v. Hopkins*, 1988 U.S. S. Ct. Briefs LEXIS 1256, 46.

43. See, for example, Stephen B. Burbank and Sean Farhang, *Rights and Retrenchment: The Counterrevolution against Federal Litigation* (New York: Cambridge University Press, 2017); Sean Farhang, *The Litigation State: Public Regulation and Private Lawsuits in the U.S.* (Princeton, NJ: Princeton University Press, 2010).

44. Oral argument, *Price Waterhouse v. Hopkins*, Oyez, https://www.oyez.org/cases/1988/87-1167.

45. Thomas, *Because of Sex*, 142–143.

46. Price Waterhouse v. Hopkins, 490 U.S. 228 (1989), 250–251.

47. *Price Waterhouse*, 251.

48. *Price Waterhouse*, 256.

49. *Price Waterhouse*, 277.

50. Thomas, *Because of Sex*, 144.

51. *Price Waterhouse*, 291.

52. *Price Waterhouse*, 294.

53. Hopkins v. Price Waterhouse, 737 F. Supp. 1202 (D.D.C. 1990), 1203.

54. *Hopkins* (D.D.C. 1990), 1217; Hopkins, *So Ordered*, 384.

55. Hopkins, *So Ordered*, 385; Tamar Lewin, "Winner of Sex Bias Suit Set to Enter Next Arena," *New York Times*, May 19, 1990, 7; Brooks Barnes, "Ann Hopkins, Who Struck an Early Blow to the Glass Ceiling, Dies at 74," *New York Times*, July 17, 2018, https://www.nytimes.com/2018/07/17/obituaries/ann-hopkins-winner-of-a-workplace-bias-fight-dies-at-74.html.

56. Farhang, *Litigation State*, 172.

57. Farhang, 189.

58. Philip McGough, "Same-Sex Harassment: Do Either *Price Waterhouse* or *Oncale* Support the Ninth Circuit's Holding in *Nichols v. Azteca Restaurant Enterprises, Inc.* that Same-Sex Harassment Based on Failure to Conform to Gender Stereotypes Is Actionable," *Hofstra Labor & Employment Law Journal* 22, 1 (Fall 2004): 206–234, 215. The relevant language from the statute allows liability "on a claim in which an individual proves a violation . . . and a respondent demonstrates that the respondent would have taken the same action in the absence of the impermissible motivating factor." https://www.eeoc.gov/civil-rights-act-1991-original-text.

59. McGough, "Same-Sex Harassment," 211.

60. R. Shep Melnick, *The Transformation of Title IX: Regulating Gender Equality in Education* (Washington, DC: Brookings Institution Press, 2018), 227.

61. Romer v. Evans, 517 U.S. 620 (1996), 653.

62. Melnick, *Transformation of Title IX*, 244, emphasis added.

63. Melnick, 224, 240.

64. For a discussion and critique of this approach, see Estlund, "Story of *Price Waterhouse v. Hopkins*," 91–95.

65. Mary Anne Case, "Legal Protections for the Personal Best of Each Employee: Title VII's Prohibition on Sex Discrimination, the Legacy of *Price Waterhouse v. Hopkins*, and the Prospect of ENDA," *Stanford Law Review* 66 (2014): 1333–1380, 1342.

66. Amicus Brief of National Organization on Male Sexual Victimization, Inc., et al., *Oncale v. Sundowner Offshore Services*, 1997 U.S. S. Ct. Briefs LEXIS 514, 7.

67. See Leif H. Carter and Thomas F. Burke, *Reason in Law*, 9th ed. (Chicago: University of Chicago Press, 2016).

68. Brief for Respondents, *Oncale v. Sundowner Offshore Services*, 1997 U.S. S. Ct. Briefs LEXIS 628, 7.

69. Brief for Petitioner, *Oncale v. Sundowner Offshore Services*, 1996 U.S. S. Ct. Briefs LEXIS 1342, 45.

70. Goluszek v. Smith, 697 F. Supp. 1452 (N.D. Ill. 1988), 1456.

71. Oncale v. Sundowner, 83 F.3d 119 (5th Cir. 1996).

72. Doe v. City of Belleville, 119 F.3d 563 (7th Cir. 1997), 573.

73. Amicus Brief of Law Professors, *Oncale v. Sundowner Offshore Services*, 1997 U.S. S. Ct. Briefs LEXIS 470, 31. The signatories to the brief were a who's who of prominent feminist and LGBTQ law professors.

74. Amicus Brief of National Organization on Male Sexual Victimization, 50.

75. Amicus Brief of the United States and the Equal Employment Opportunity Commission, *Oncale v. Sundowner Offshore Services*, 1997 U.S. S. Ct. Briefs LEXIS 546, 9.

76. Amicus Brief of the Texas Association of Businesses & Chambers of Commerce, *Oncale v. Sundowner Offshore Services*, 1997 U.S. S. Ct. Briefs LEXIS 653, 8.

77. Oral argument, *Oncale v. Sundowner Offshore Services, Inc.*, Oyez, https://www.oyez.org/cases/1997/96-568.

78. Oral argument, *Oncale v. Sundowner Offshore Services*.

79. Oral argument, *Oncale v. Sundowner Offshore Services*.

80. Oncale v. Sundowner Offshore Services, Inc., 523 U.S. 75 (1998), 79.

81. *Oncale*, 79.

82. *Oncale*, 81.

4. TRANSGENDER RIGHTS AND *PRICE WATERHOUSE*

1. Jami K. Taylor, Daniel C. Lewis, and Donald P. Haider-Markel, eds., *The Remarkable Rise of Transgender Rights* (Ann Arbor: University of Michigan Press, 2018), 15.

2. Marc Stein, *City of Sisterly and Brotherly Loves: Lesbian and Gay Philadelphia, 1945–1972* (Philadelphia: Temple University Press, 2004), 246.

3. Susan Stryker, *Transgender History: The Roots of Today's Revolution*, 2nd ed. (New York: Seal Press, 2017), 97–98.

4. Stryker, 151.

5. Taylor, Lewis, and Haider-Markel, *Remarkable Rise of Transgender Rights*, 17–18.

6. See Jami K. Taylor, Daniel C. Lewis, and Donald P. Haider-Markel, "The Rise of the Transgender Rights Movement and LGBT Rights," in Taylor, Lewis, and Haider-Markel, *Remarkable Rise of Transgender Rights*, 26–57; Zein Murib, "Transgender: Examining an Emerging Political Identity Using Three Political Processes," *Politics, Groups, and Identities* 3, 3 (2015): 381–397.

7. Jami K. Taylor, Daniel C. Lewis, Donald P. Haider-Markel, and Jason Pierceson, "Transgender Rights and the Judiciary," in Taylor, Lewis, and Haider-Markel, *Remarkable Rise of Transgender Rights*, 139, 141.

8. Jess Braverman and Christy Hall, "The Groundbreaking Minnesota Human Rights Act in Need of Renovation," n.d., Hennepin County Bar Association, https://www.mnbar.org/hennepin-county-bar-association/resources/hennepin-lawyer/articles/2020/03/04/the-groundbreaking-minnesota-human-rights-act-in-need-of-renovation.

9. Phyllis Randolph Frye, "History of the International Conference on Transgender Law and Employment Policy, Inc.," n.d., Digital Transgender Archive, https://www.digitaltransgenderarchive.net/files/wd375w32h.

10. Stryker, *Transgender History*, 177.

11. Phyllis Randolph Frye, "The International Bill of Gender Rights vs. the Cider House Rules: Transgenders Struggle with the Courts over What Clothing They Are Allowed to Wear on the Job, Which Restroom They Are Allowed to Use on the Job, Their Right to Marry, and the Very Definition of Their Sex," *William & Mary Journal of Women and the Law* 7, 1 (2000): 133–216, 151–152.

12. Phyllis Randolph Frye, "Repeal of the Houston Crossdressing Ordinance," 107, First Annual International Conference on Transgender Law and Employment Policy, 1992, Digital Transgender Archive, https://www.digitaltransgenderarchive.net/files/b2773v78r.

13. "International Bill of Gender Rights," in *Transgender Rights*, ed. Paisley Currah, Richard M. Juang, and Shannon Price Minter (Minneapolis: University of Minnesota Press, 2006). For a critique of a rights-based approach, see Dean Spade, *Normal Life: Administrative Violence, Critical Trans Politics, & the Limits of the Law*, 2nd ed. (Durham, NC: Duke University Press, 2015).

14. Taylor, Lewis, and Haider-Markel, "Rise of the Transgender Rights Movement and LGBT Rights," 27.

15. Alice Oliver-Parrott, "Cherish the Lawyers Who Protect Your Freedom," First Annual International Conference on Transgender Law and Employment Policy, 1992, Digital Transgender Archive, https://www.digitaltransgenderarchive.net/downloads/tq57nr067.

16. Laura E. Skaer, "Report from the Employment Law Project," 122, Employment Law Luncheon, Second Annual International Conference on Transgender Law and Employment Policy, 1993, Digital Transgender Archive, https://www.digitaltransgenderarchive.net/downloads/1j92g755s.

17. Skaer, 120.

18. Helen Cassidy, "Anti-Discrimination Law Project," 278, First Annual International Conference on Transgender Law and Employment Policy, 1992, Digital Transgender Archive, https://www.digitaltransgenderarchive.net/files/v979v313f.

19. Phyllis Frye, "Employment Law and Policy Project," 190, First Annual International Conference on Transgender Law and Employment Policy, 1992, Digital Transgender Archive, https://www.digitaltransgenderarchive.net/files/5x21tf45j.

20. "Transgender Law and Employment Policy," appendix 6, Second Annual International Conference on Transgender Law and Employment Policy, 1993, Digital Transgender Archive, https://www.digitaltransgenderarchive.net/files/fn106z01z.

21. Jim Sacher, "Equal Employment Opportunity Commission," 175, Closing Remarks Dinner, Second Annual International Conference on Transgender Law and Employment Policy, 1993, Digital Transgender Archive, https://www.digitaltransgenderarchive.net/files/5d86p030t.

22. Sharon F. Kahn, "Report from the Education in Transgender Issues Project," 87, Second Annual International Conference on Transgender Law and Employment Policy, 1993, Digital Transgender Archive, https://www.digitaltransgenderarchive.net/downloads/xk81jk434.

23. Sharon F. Kahn, "Gender Non-Conformity and the Law: A 'Crying Game' in More Ways than One," appendix 3, Second Annual International Conference on Transgender Law and Employment Policy, 1993, Digital Transgender Archive, https://www.digitaltransgenderarchive.net/downloads/9306sz356.

24. JoAnna McNamara, "Employment Discrimination and the Transsexual," appendix E, Fourth Annual International Conference on Transgender Law and

Employment Policy, 1995, Digital Transgender Archive, https://www.digitaltransgen derarchive.net/downloads/cn69m420z.

25. See Jennifer L. Levi and Bennett H. Klein, "Pursuing Protection for Transgender People through Disability Laws," in Currah, Juang, and Minter, *Transgender Rights*, 74–92.

26. Phyllis Randolph Frye, "Facing Discrimination, Organizing for Freedom: The Transgender Community," in *Creating Change: Sexuality, Public Policy, and Civil Rights*, ed. John D'Emilio, William B. Turner, and Urvashi Vaid (New York: St. Martin's Press, 2000), 462. For exclusion from the marches, see Frye, 459–460. For Feldblum's early position supporting a trans-exclusive ENDA, see Frye, 464. For a discussion of the opposition to trans inclusion, see Phyllis Randolph Frye and Jason Pierceson, *Sexual Minorities in Politics: An Introduction* (Lanham, MD: Rowman & Littlefield, 2016), 106–107.

27. Frye, "Facing Discrimination," 466.

28. Jennifer L. Levi, "Paving the Road: A Charles Hamilton Houston Approach to Securing Trans Rights," *Willian & Mary Journal of Women and the Law* 7 (2000): 5–35, 21.

29. Katherine M. Franke, "The Central Mistake of Sex Discrimination Law: The Disaggregation of Sex from Gender," *University of Pennsylvania Law Review* 144, 1 (1995): 1–99, 95.

30. Mary Anne C. Case, "Disaggregating Gender from Sex and Sexual Orientation: The Effeminate Man in the Law and Feminist Jurisprudence," *Yale Law Journal* 105, 1 (1995): 1–105, 4.

31. Rosa v. Park West Bank & Trust Company, 214 F.3d 213 (1st Cir. 2000), 214.

32. Leandra Ruth Zarnow, *Battling Bella: The Protest Politics of Bella Abzug* (Cambridge, MA: Harvard University Press, 2019), 256.

33. Gordene O. MacKenzie and Nancy R. Nangaroni, "Jennifer Levi: Attorney for Gender Justice," *Transgender Tapestry* 98 (Summer 2002): 29, Digital Transgender Archive, https://www.digitaltransgenderarchive.net/files/6q182k17w.

34. GLBTQ Advocates and Defenders, "What Men and Women Should Look Like: *Rosa v. Park West Bank*," podcast, https://soundcloud.com/gladlaw/rosa.

35. *Rosa*, 214. The quote is from the First Circuit's discussion of Freedman's decision.

36. Jennifer L. Levi and Mary L. Bonauto, "Brief for the Plaintiff-Appellant Lucas Rosa," *Michigan Journal of Gender & Law* 7 (2001): 147–161, 152.

37. Katherine M. Franke, "Amicus Curiae Brief of NOW Legal Defense and Education Fund and Equal Rights Advocates in Support of Plaintiff-Appellant and in Support of Reversal," *Michigan Journal of Gender & Law* 7 (2001): 163–177, 168.

38. Katherine M. Franke, "*Rosa v. Park West Bank*: Do Clothes Really Make the Man?" *Michigan Journal of Gender & Law* 7 (2001): 143–146, 145.

39. Sharon M. McGowan, "Special Project: Working with Clients to Develop Compatible Visions of What It Means to 'Win' a Case: Reflections on *Schroer v. Billington*," *Harvard Civil Rights & Civil Liberties Law Review* 45 (Winter 2010): 205–245, 212.

40. *Rosa,* 215.

41. Schwenk v. Hartford, 204 F.3d 1187 (9th Cir. 2000), 1200–1202.

42. Frye, "International Bill of Gender Rights," 192.

43. Susan Gluck Mezey, *Beyond Marriage: Continuing Battles for LGBT Rights* (Lanham, MD: Rowman & Littlefield, 2017), 28.

44. *Oiler v. Winn-Dixie Louisiana, Inc.,* 2002 U.S. Dist. LEXIS 17417 (E.D. La. 2002), 28.

45. *Oiler,* 32.

46. *Oiler,* 30.

47. *Smith v. City of Salem,* 2003 U.S. Dist. LEXIS 26301 (N.D. Ohio 2003), 9.

48. Smith v. City of Salem, 378 F.3d 566 (6th Cir. 2004), 573.

49. McGowan, "Special Project," 211.

50. Schroer v. Billington, 577 F. Supp. 2d 293 (D.D.C. 2008), 302.

51. *Schroer,* 304.

52. *Schroer,* 306–307.

53. *Schroer v. Billington,* 2009 U.S. Dist. LEXIS 43903 (D.D.C. 2009).

54. Christine Michelle Duffy, Robyn B. Gigl, and CJ Griffin, "Title VII of the Civil Rights Act of 1964," in *Gender Identity and Sexual Orientation Discrimination in the Workplace: A Practical Guide,* ed. Christine Michelle Duffy and Denise M. Visconti (Arlington, VA: Bloomberg BNA, 2014), 52–53.

55. *Etsitty v. Utah Transit Authority,* 2005 U.S. Dist. LEXIS 12645 (D. Utah 2005), 8, 15.

56. Etsitty v. Utah Transit Authority, 502 F.3d 1215 (10th Cir. 2007), 1224.

57. Brief of Amicus Curiae, American Civil Liberties Union, American Civil Liberties Union of Utah, Lambda Legal Defense & Education Fund, Inc., and National Center for Lesbian Rights, *Etsitty v. Utah Transit Authority,* No. 05-4193, October 5, 2005, https://www.acluutah.org/images/etsittybrief.pdf.

58. Lopez v. River Oaks Imaging, Inc., 542 F. Supp. 2d 653 (S.D. Tex. 2008).

59. *Trevino v. Center for Health Care Services,* 2009 U.S. Dist. LEXIS 68793 (W.D. Tex. 2009).

60. Glenn v. Brumby, 632 F. Supp. 2d 1308 (N.D. Ga. 2009).

61. Duffy, Gigl, and Griffin, "Title VII," 54.

62. Vandy Beth Glenn, "*Glenn v. Brumby:* Forty Years after *Grossman,*" in Duffy and Visconti, *Gender Identity and Sexual Orientation Discrimination,* 2.

63. Glenn v. Brumby, 663 F.3d 1312 (11th Cir. 2011), 1314.

64. Glenn, "*Glenn v. Brumby,*" 7.

65. *Glenn* (11th Cir. 2011), 1319.

66. *Glenn* (11th Cir. 2011), 1317; Ilona M. Turner, "Sex Stereotyping per se: Transgender Employees and Title VII," *California Law Review* 95 (2007): 561–596.

67. Ilona Turner, "Passing the Torch," Transgender Law Center, June 30, 2017, https://transgenderlawcenter.org/archives/13942.

68. *Glenn* (11th Cir. 2011), 1321.

69. "EEOC Informal Discussion Letter: Title VII: Sex Discrimination/Coverage

of Transgendered," US Equal Employment Opportunity Commission, May 25, 2007, https://www.eeoc.gov/foia/eeoc-informal-discussion-letter-183.

70. Duffy, Gigl, and Griffin, "Title VII," 56–57.

71. Braden Campbell, "Decade of Work Pays off in Landmark LGBTQ Rights Ruling," Law360, June 15, 2020, https://www.law360.com/articles/1283136/decade-of -work-pays-off-in-landmark-lgbtq-rights-ruling.

72. Chai R. Feldblum, "Law and Culture in the Making of *Macy v. Holder*," in Duffy and Visconti, *Gender Identity and Sexual Orientation Discrimination*, 18.

73. David Lopez, "Title VII: A Magna Carta of Human Rights," Harvard Law School, November 3, 2016, https://www.youtube.com/watch?v=RXZ8R1-do6c.

74. *Macy v. Holder,* Appeal No. 0120120821, US Equal Employment Opportunity Commission, April 20, 2012, 14.

75. *Macy,* 13.

76. Alissa Wickham, "EEOC Files Historic Sex Bias Suits for Transgender Workers," Law360, September 25, 2014, https://www.law360.com/articles/581182/eeoc-files -historic -sex-bias-suits-for-transgender-workers.

77. This assessment is based on an examination of cases archived by the National Center for Transgender Equality, https://transequality.org/federal-case-law-on -transgender-people-and-discrimination.

78. Evans v. Georgia Regional Hospital, 850 F.3d 1248 (11th Cir. 2017).

79. Complaint, *USA v. Southeastern Oklahoma State University*, Case No. 5:15-cv-00324 (W.D. Okla. March 30, 2015), 5.

80. Slip opinion, *USA/Tudor v. Southeastern Oklahoma State University*, Case No. 5:15-cv-00324 (W.D. Okla. July 10, 2015), 5.

81. Erica L. Green, "Dormant Transgender Rights Cases See New Life in Supreme Court Ruling," *New York Times,* June 17, 2020, https://www.nytimes.com/2020/06/17/us /politics/transgender-rights-cases-supreme-court.html; *Tudor v. Southeastern Oklahoma State University,* 2021 U.S. App. LEXIS 27404 (10th Cir. 2021).

82. Blum v. Gulf Oil Corporation, 597 F.3d 936 (5th Cir. 1979); Wittmer v. Phillips 66 Company, 915 F.3d. 328 (5th Cir. 2019); Amy Howe, "Trump Releases New List of Potential Supreme Court Nominees," SCOTUSBlog, September 9, 2020, https://www.scotus blog.com/2020/09/trump-releases-new-list-of-potential-supreme-court-nominees/.

83. Dodds v. U.S. Dept. of Education, 845 F.3d 217 (6th Cir. 2016); Whitaker v. Kenosha Unified School District, 858 F.3d 1034 (7th Cir. 2017); Flack v. Wisconsin Department of Health Services, 395 F. Supp. 3d 1001 (W.D. Wis. 2019); Grimm v. Gloucester County School Board, 972 F.3d 586 (4th Cir. 2020). The text of Title IX can be found at https://www.justice.gov/crt/title-ix-education-amendments-1972.

84. *Adams v. School Board of St. Johns County,* 2020 U.S. App. LEXIS 24968 (11th Cir. 2020), 52, 39, 47.

85. Taylor, Lewis, Haider-Markel, and Pierceson, "Transgender Rights and the Judiciary," 153–154.

86. *Adams,* 56n9.

87. *Adams,* 59–61.

88. Mark Joseph Stern, "The Trump Bench: Kyle Duncan," Slate.com, January 22, 2020, https://slate.com/news-and-politics/2020/01/the-trump-bench-kyle-duncan-the-fifth-circuit.html.

89. Adams v. School Board of St. Johns County, 318 F. Supp. 3d 1293 (M.D. Fla. 2018), 1313, 1324.

90. Jo Yurcaba, "Supreme Court Could Hear Transgender Student Bathroom Case, Experts Say," NBC News, August 27, 2021, https://www.nbcnews.com/nbc-out/out-news/supreme-court-hear-transgender-student-bathroom-case-experts-say-rcna1797.

91. Taylor, Lewis, Haider-Markel, and Pierceson, "Transgender Rights and the Judiciary," 154–155.

92. *Grimm*, 593, 626, 634.

93. See *Parents for Privacy v. Barr*, No. 18-35708 (9th Cir. Feb. 12, 2020); Doe v. Boyertown Area School District, 897 F.3d 518 (3rd Cir. 2018).

94. Emma Platoff, "By Gutting Obamacare, Judge Reed O'Connor Handed Texas a Win. It Wasn't the First Time," *Texas Tribune*, December 19, 2018, https://www.texas tribune.org/2018/12/19/reed-oconnor-federal-judge-texas-obamacare-forum-shop ping-ken-paxton/.

95. Texas v. United States, 201 F. Supp. 3d 810 (N.D. Tex. 2016), 832–833.

96. The statute reads:

> Except as otherwise provided for in this title (or an amendment made by this title), an individual shall not, on the ground prohibited under title VI of the Civil Rights Act of 1964 (42 U.S.C. 2000d et seq.), title IX of the Education Amendments of 1972 (20 U.S.C. 1681 et seq.), the Age Discrimination Act of 1975 (42 U.S.C. 6101 et seq.), or section 794 of title 29, be excluded from participation in, be denied the benefits of, or be subjected to discrimination under, any health program or activity, any part of which is receiving Federal financial assistance, including credits, subsidies, or contracts of insurance, or under any program or activity that is administered by an Executive Agency or any entity established under this title [1] (or amendments).

Pub. L. 111-148, title I, §1557, March 23, 2010, 124 Stat. 260.

97. Boyden v. Conlin, 341 F. Supp. 3d 979 (W.D. Wis. 2018); Flack v. Wisconsin Department of Health Services, 395 F. Supp. 3d 1001 (W.D. Wis. 2019); *Toomey v. Arizona*, 2019 U.S. Dist. LEXIS 219781 (D. Ariz. 2019); Kadel v. Folwell, 446 F. Supp. 3d 1 (M.D. N.C. 2020). O'Connor's decision was Franciscan Alliance, Inc. v. Azar, 414 F. Supp. 3d 928 (N.D. Tex. 2018).

5. SEXUAL ORIENTATION, *PRICE WATERHOUSE*, AND *ONCALE*

1. Susan Gluck Mezey, *Beyond Marriage: Continuing Battles for LGBT Rights* (Lanham, MD: Rowman & Littlefield, 2017), 35–36. For jurisprudence in the 2000s and

2010s, see Zachary R. Herz, "Price's Progress: Sex Stereotyping and Its Potential for Antidiscrimination Law," *Yale Law Journal* 124 (2014): 396–446.

2. For the early years of the Obama administration, see Kerry Eleveld, *Don't Tell Me to Wait: How the Fight for Gay Rights Changed America and Transformed Obama's Presidency* (New York: Basic Books, 2015).

3. Jeremy W. Peters, "Senate Approves Ban on Antigay Bias in Workplace," *New York Times*, November 7, 2013, https://www.nytimes.com/2013/11/08/us/politics/senate -moves-to-final-vote-on-workplace-gay-bias-ban.html.

4. Colby Itkowitz, "House Passes Bill to Ban Discrimination Based on Sexual Orientation and Gender Identity," *Washington Post*, May 17, 2019, https://www.washing tonpost.com/politics/house-passes-bill-to-ban-discrimination-based-on-sexual-ori entation-and-gender-identity/2019/05/17/aed18a16-78a3-11e9-b3f5-5673edf2d127_story .html; Catie Edmonson, "House Passes Sweeping Gay and Transgender Equality Legislation," *New York Times*, February 25, 2021, https://www.nytimes.com/2021/02/25/us /politics/house-equality-act-gay-rights.html.

5. Jeremiah J. Garretson, *The Path to Gay Rights: How Activism and Coming out Changed Public Opinion* (New York: New York University Press, 2018), 11; "LGBT," PollingReport.com, http://pollingreport.com/lgbt.htm; Jami K. Taylor, Donald P. Haider-Markel, and Daniel C. Lewis, *The Remarkable Rise of Transgender Rights* (Ann Arbor: University of Michigan Press, 2018), 74.

6. Neal Devins, "Is Judicial Policymaking Countermajoritarian?" in *Making Policy, Making Law: An Interbranch Perspective*, ed. Mark Miller and Jeb Barnes (Washington, DC: Georgetown University Press, 2004), 191–192.

7. Jason Pierceson, "From Kameny to Kennedy: The Road to the Positive Rights Protection of Marriage Equality in *Obergefell v. Hodges*," *Politics, Groups, and Identities* 3, 4 (2005): 703–710. For more on the Supreme Court's hostility toward LGB plaintiffs, see Joyce Murdoch and Deb Price, *Courting Justice: Gay Men and Lesbians and the Supreme Court* (New York: Basic Books, 2001).

8. Romer v. Evans, 517 U.S. 620 (1996), 635, 633.

9. Masterpiece Cakeshop v. Colorado Civil Rights Commission, 138 S. Ct. 1719 (2018), 1727.

10. Lawrence v. Texas, 539 U.S. 558 (2003), 578.

11. United States v. Windsor, 570 U.S. 744 (2013), 770, 772.

12. Obergefell v. Hodges, 576 U.S. 644 (2015), 667, 669.

13. Jason Pierceson, *Same-Sex Marriage in the United States: The Road to the Supreme Court and Beyond* (Lanham, MD: Rowman & Littlefield, 2014), 247–255.

14. Jason Pierceson, *Sexual Minorities and Politics: An Introduction* (Lanham, MD: Rowman & Littlefield, 2016), 72.

15. Christine Michelle Duffy, Robyn B. Gigl, and CJ Griffin, "Title VII of the Civil Rights Act of 1964," in *Gender Identity and Sexual Orientation Discrimination in the Workplace: A Practical Guide*, ed. Christine Michelle Duffy and Denise M. Visconti (Arlington, VA: Bloomberg BNA, 2014), 78n356.

16. Higgins v. New Balance Athletic Shoe, Inc., 194 F.3d 252 (1st Cir. 1999), 258–259.

17. *Higgins*, 261. This framing helps explain the post-*Oncale* strategy of identifying gender nonconforming plaintiffs as men.

18. Simonton v. Runyon, 225 F.3d 122 (2nd Cir. 2000), 124.

19. *Simonton*, 126.

20. *Simonton*, 127.

21. Nichols v. Azteca Restaurant Enterprises, 256 F.3d 864 (9th Cir. 2001), 875.

22. Mezey, *Beyond Marriage*, 39.

23. Eliana Johnson and Shane Goldmacher, "Trump's Down to 3 in Supreme Court Search," Politico, January 24, 2017, https://www.politico.com/story/2017/01/trump-supreme-court-senators-234102.

24. Prowel v. Wise Business Forms, 579 F.3d 285 (3rd Cir. 2009), 289, 291–292.

25. Bibby v. Philadelphia Coca Cola Bottling Co., 260 F.3d 257 (3rd Cir. 2001).

26. TerVeer v. Billington, 34 F. Supp. 3d 100 (D.D.C. 2014), 106.

27. Mezey, *Beyond Marriage*, 39.

28. Dave Phillips, "Judge Blocks Transgender Military Ban," *New York Times*, October 31, 2017, A1.

29. Gregory R. Nevins, "Title VII and ENDA Game Plan," Lambda Legal, April 24, 2014, https://www.lambdalegal.org/blog/20140424_of-counsel.

30. Amicus Curiae Brief of Lambda Legal Defense and Education Fund, Inc., *TerVeer v. Billington*, April 23, 2013, 14, 29, https://www.lambdalegal.org/in-court/legal-docs/terveer_dc_20130423_amicus-brief.

31. Braden Campbell, "Decade of Work Pays off in Landmark LGBTQ Rights Ruling," Law360, June 15, 2020, https://www.law360.com/articles/1283136/decade-of-work-pays-off -in-landmark-lgbtq-rights-ruling.

32. Mark Joseph Stern, "Mike Lee Is Sabotaging Trump's EEOC Picks to Feud with the Agency's First Openly Gay Member," Slate, December 19, 2018, https://slate.com/news-and-politics/2018/12/mike-lee-chai-feldblum-eeoc-trump-picks-lgbtq.html.

33. *Baldwin v. Foxx*, EEOC Appeal No. 0120133080, July 15, 2015, 2.

34. *Baldwin*, 15, 7, 14.

35. "Hively v. Ivy Tech Community College," Lambda Legal, https://www.lambdalegal.org/in-court/cases/in_hively-v-ivy-tech.

36. Joe Pinsker, "A Quiet Triumph for Gay Workers," *Atlantic*, July 22, 2015, https://www.theatlantic.com/business/archive/2015/07/a-quietly-triumphant-ruling-in-favor-of -gay-workers-rights/399200/.

37. Ben James, "EEOC Decision No Silver Bullet for Gay Bias Plaintiffs," Law360, July 17, 2015, https://www.law360.com/articles/680583.

38. EEOC v. Scott Medical Health Center, 217 F. Supp. 3d 834 (W.D. Pa. 2016), 841, 842.

39. Doe v. Parx Casino, 381 F. Supp. 3d 425 (E.D. Pa. 2019).

40. Isaacs v. Felder Services, 143 F. Supp. 3d 1190 (M.D. Ala. 2015), 1193.

41. Winstead v. Lafayette County Board of County Commissioners, 197 F. Supp. 3d 1334 (N.D. Fla. 2016), 1346.

42. Roberts v. UPS, 115 F. Supp. 3d 344 (E.D. N.Y. 2015), 358.

43. Boutilier v. Hartford Public Schools, 221 F. Supp. 3d 255 (D. Conn. 2016), 267.

44. Videkis v. Pepperdine University, 150 F. Supp. 3d 1151 (C.D. Cal. 2015).

45. Hinton v. Virginia Union University, 185 F. Supp. 3d 807 (E.D. Va. 2016), 818.

46. *Hively v. Ivy Tech Community College,* 2015 U.S. Dist. LEXIS 25813 (N.D. Ind. 2015).

47. Hively v. Ivy Tech Community College, 830 F.3d 698 (7th Cir. 2016), 699, 717, 718.

48. Anonymous v. Omnicom Group, 852 F.3d 195 (2nd Cir. 2017), 202.

49. Evans v. Georgia Regional Hospital, 850 F.3d 1248 (11th Cir. 2017), 1259–1260.

50. Johnson and Goldmacher, "Trump's Down to 3 in Supreme Court Search."

51. *Evans,* 1262, 1266, 1269.

52. Julie Moreau, "Lesbian's Workplace Discrimination Case May Be Headed to Supreme Court," NBC News, July 10, 2017, https://www.nbcnews.com/feature/nbc-out/lesbian-s-workplace-discrimination-case-may-be-headed-supreme-court-n781416.

53. Evan Gibbs, "What's Happening with Sexual Orientation in the Workplace?" Above the Law, November 14, 2017, https://abovethelaw.com/2017/11/whats-happening-with-sexual-orientation-discrimination-in-the-workplace/; Scott Bomboy, "Supreme Court Gets Next Potential Landmark LGBT Case," *Constitution Daily,* September 7, 2017, https://constitutioncenter.org/blog/supreme-court-gets-next-potential-landmark-lgbt-case.

54. Petition for a Writ of Certiorari, *Evans v. Georgia Regional Hospital,* No. 17-370, 3, https://www.scotusblog.com/wp-content/uploads/2017/10/17-370-petition.pdf; Evans v. Georgia Regional Hospital, 850 F.3d 1248 (11th Cir. 2017), *cert. denied* (Dec. 11, 2017).

6. *BOSTOCK*, STEPHENS, AND *ZARDA* IN THE LOWER FEDERAL COURTS

1. Aimee Ortiz, "Aimee Stephens, Plaintiff in Transgender Case, Dies at 59," *New York Times,* May 12, 2020, https://www.nytimes.com/2020/05/12/us/aimee-stephens-supreme-court-dead.html.

2. Trudy Ring, "Aimee Stephens, Fired for Being Trans, Decided to Live and Fight Back," Advocate, October 1, 2019, https://www.advocate.com/transgender/2019/10/01/aimee-stephens-fired-being-trans-decided-live-and-fight-back.

3. For the Sixth Circuit discussion, see EEOC v. R. G. & G. R. Harris Funeral Homes, 884 F.3d 560 (6th Cir. 2017), 573–574.

4. The findings are described in one of the district court decisions: EEOC v. R. G. & G. R. Harris Funeral Homes, 100 F. Supp. 3d 594 (E.D. Mich. 2015), 596–598.

5. *EEOC v. Harris Funeral Homes* (E.D. Mich. 2015), 604–605. In this decision, Kirkpatrick Law Offices is listed as the funeral homes' legal representation, but according to the ADF, it had represented the business since 2013. Sarah Kramer, "Supreme Court Delivers a Troubling Decision against Harris Funeral Homes," Alliance

Defending Freedom, June 15, 2020, https://www.adflegal.org/blog/supreme-court-de livers-troubling-decision-against-harris-funeral-homes. It is not clear how involved the ADF was in the early stages of the litigation, but it had become more involved by the time the case reached the Sixth Circuit. It was not formally listed as representing the funeral homes during the district court proceedings. According to Melissa Gira Grant, the ADF petitioned to join the case in May 2015. Melissa Gira Grant, "Culture War in the Workplace," *New Republic* 261 (January–February 2020): 20–29.

6. *EEOC v. R. G. & G. R. Harris Funeral Homes*, 2015 U.S. Dist. LEXIS 174621 (E.D. Mich. 2015).

7. EEOC v. R. G. & G. R. Harris Funeral Homes, 201 F. Supp. 3d 837 (E.D. Mich. 2016), 846.

8. Employment Division v. Smith, 494 U.S. 872 (1990).

9. *EEOC v. Harris Funeral Homes* (E.D. Mich. 2016), 842.

10. *EEOC v. Harris Funeral Homes* (E.D. Mich. 2016), 856.

11. *EEOC v. Harris Funeral Homes* (E.D. Mich. 2016), 844.

12. *EEOC v. Harris Funeral Homes* (E.D. Mich. 2016), 847

13. *EEOC v. Harris Funeral Homes* (E.D. Mich. 2016), 863.

14. Oral argument, *EEOC v. RG and GR Harris Funeral Homes*, Sixth Circuit, Case No. 16-2424, October 4, 2017.

15. Daniel Bennett, *Defending Faith: The Politics of the Christian Conservative Legal Movement* (Lawrence: University Press of Kansas, 2017), 20–21.

16. Mark Joseph Stern, "Anti-LGBTQ Firm Tries to Disqualify Judge Because He Won't Let It Misgender Trans Kids," Slate, May 11, 2020, https://slate.com /news-and-politics/2020/05/alliance-defending-freedom-student-athlete-misgender .html.

17. Chris Johnson, "Why Does Website Say Barrett Worked at Anti-LGBTQ Firm Earlier than She Disclosed?" Washington Blade, October 9, 2020, https://www.wash ingtonblade.com/2020/10/09/why-does-website-say-barrett-worked-at-anti-lgbtq -firm-earlier-than -she-disclosed/.

18. Bennett, *Defending Faith*, 21.

19. "Alliance Defending Freedom," Southern Poverty Law Center, https://www .splcenter.org/fighting-hate/extremist-files/group/alliance-defending-freedom.

20. Dave Orrick and Ryan Faircloth, "Doug Wardlow, LGBT Rights and the Gay Man He Allegedly Bullied in School," *Duluth News Tribune*, October 27, 2018, https:// www.duluthnewstribune.com/news/government-and-politics/4520292-doug-ward low-lgbt-rights-and-gay-man-he-allegedly-bullied-high.

21. EEOC v. R. G. & G. R. Harris Funeral Homes, 884 F.3d 560 (6th Cir. 2017), 567.

22. *EEOC v. Harris Funeral Homes* (6th Cir. 2017), 575.

23. *EEOC v. Harris Funeral Homes* (6th Cir. 2017), 577.

24. *EEOC v. Harris Funeral Homes* (6th Cir. 2017), 589.

25. R. G. & G. R. Harris Funeral Homes v. EEOC, 139 S. Ct. 1599 (2019).

26. Gregory Antollino, "Gay Skydiver Don Zarda Is Dead, but His Legal Fight Could Alter History," Advocate, September 23, 2019, https://www.advocate.com

/commentary/2019/9/23/gay-skydiver-don-zarda-dead-his-legal-fight-could-alter-his
tory. Facts are also summarized from the cases cited below.

27. Blue slips are documents submitted by senators that traditionally allow them
to approve or disapprove nominees to the lower federal courts from their own states.

28. Patrick L. Gregory, "Trump Appeals Pick Bianco Set for Confirmation Vote,"
Bloomberg Law, May 16, 2019, https://news.bloomberglaw.com/us-law-week/trump
-judge-pick-bianco-to-get-vote-over-schumer-objection. The summary of district
court activity is from Zarda v. Altitude Express, 883 F.3d 100 (2nd Cir. 2018).

29. Zarda v. Altitude Express, 855 F.3d 76 (2nd Cir. 2017); *Zarda* (2nd Cir. 2018).

30. *Zarda* (2nd Cir. 2018).

31. Oral argument, *Zarda v. Altitude Express*, Second Circuit Court of Appeals,
September 26, 2017, https://www.c-span.org/video/?433984-1/zarda-v-altitude-express
-oral-argument.

32. *Zarda* (2nd Cir. 2018), 119, 128, 115.

33. *Zarda* (2nd Cir. 2018), 134, 136.

34. *Zarda* (2nd Cir. 2018), 141, 137.

35. Gerard E. Lynch, "Complexity, Judgment and Restraint," NYU Law School
James Madison Lecture, November 4, 2019, https://www.youtube.com/watch?v=RQJ
GBEXUyjs.

36. *Bostock v. Clayton County*, 2016 U.S. LEXIS 192898 (N.D. Ga. 2016), 4.

37. Adam Liptak, "Can Someone Be Fired for Being Gay? The Supreme Court Will
Decide," *New York Times*, September 23, 2019, https://www.nytimes.com/2019/09/23
/us/politics/supreme-court-fired-gay.html.

38. *Bostock* (N.D. Ga. 2016), 16.

39. *Bostock v. Clayton County*, 2017 U.S. Dist. LEXIS 217815 (N.D. Ga. 2017).

40. Bostock v. Clayton County, 723 Fed. Appx. 964 (11th Cir. 2018), 964–965.

41. Bostock v. Clayton County, 894 F.3d 1335 (11th Cir. 2018), 1337.

7. THE SUPREME COURT'S SEEMINGLY MINIMALIST
BUT REMARKABLY CONSEQUENTIAL DECISION

1. Ben Penn, "Justice Department Urges Civil Rights Agency to Flip LGBT Stance,"
Bloomberg Law, August 13, 2019, https://news.bloomberglaw.com/daily-labor-re
port/justice-department-urges-civil-rights-agency-to-flip-lgbt-stance; Marcia Coyle,
"EEOC Doesn't Sign Trump DOJ's Supreme Court Brief against Transgender Employees," *National Law Journal*, August 16, 2019, https://www.law.com/national
lawjournal/2019/08/16/eeoc-doesnt-sign-trump-dojs-supreme-court-brief-against
-transgender-employees/.

2. Brief of the United States as Amicus Curiae, *Bostock v. Clayton County*, 15,
https://www.supremecourt.gov/DocketPDF/17/17-1618/113417/20190823143040818_17-1
618bsacUnitedStates.pdf.

3. Bostock v. Clayton County, 140 S. Ct. 1731 (2020), 1774.

4. Brief for the Federal Respondent, *R. G. & G. R. Harris Funeral Homes v. EEOC*, 45, https://www.supremecourt.gov/DocketPDF/18/18-107/112655/20190816163010995_1 8-107bsUnitedStates.pdf.

5. For more on George, natural law theory, and his National Organization for Marriage, see Jason Pierceson, *Same-Sex Marriage in the United States: The Road to the Supreme Court and Beyond* (Lanham, MD: Rowman & Littlefield, 2014).

6. Brief of Ryan T. Anderson as Amicus Curiae in Support of the Employers, *R. G. & G. R. Harris Funeral Homes v. EEOC*, 4, 3, 18, 39, https://www.supremecourt .gov/DocketPDF/18/18-107/113066/20190821130739091_Amicus%20Brief%20of%20 Ryan%20Anderson%20iso%20Employers.pdf.

7. Brief of Amicus Curiae, National Organization for Marriage and Center for Constitutional Jurisprudence, *Bostock v. Clayton County*, 13, 10, https://www.supreme court.gov/DocketPDF/18/18-107/113590/20190826123421822_17-1618%20BSAC%20 NOM%20CCJ.pdf.

8. Brief of Scholars of Philosophy, Theology, Law, Politics, History, Literature, and the Sciences as Amici Curiae in Support of the Petitioner, *R. G. & G. R. Harris Funeral Homes v. EEOC*, 1, https://www.supremecourt.gov/DocketPDF /18/18-107/113249/20190822143850673_18-107%20Amici%20BOM%20Scholars%20et%20al —PDFA.pdf; "Dr. John C. Eastman," Federalist Society, https://fedsoc.org/contri butors/john-eastman.

9. Brief of Anderson, 2, 4.

10. Phillip Picardi, "The Lawyer behind the Biggest LGBTQ+ Legal Victory in History," GQ.com, June 24, 2020, https://www.gq.com/story/chase-strangio-aclu-lgbtq -legal-victory.

11. See Jason Pierceson, "From Kameny to Kennedy: The Road to the Positive Rights Protection of Marriage Equality in *Obergefell v. Hodges*," *Politics, Groups, and Identities* 3, 4 (2005): 703–710.

12. Masha Gessen, "Chase Strangio's Victories for Transgender Rights," *New Yorker*, October 19, 2020, https://www.newyorker.com/magazine/2020/10/19/chase-strangios -victories-for-transgender-rights.

13. Brief for Respondent Aimee Stephens, *R. G. & G. R. Harris Funeral Homes v. EEOC*, 3, 41–42, https://www.supremecourt.gov/DocketPDF/18/18-107/104141/20190626 105814174_No%2018-107%20RG%20and%20GR%20Harris%20Funeral%20 Homes%20v%20EEOC%20and%20Aimee%20Stephens%20Brief%2ofor%20Re spondent%20Aimee%20Stephens.pdf.

14. Brief of William Eskridge Jr. and Andrew M. Koppelman as Amici Curiae in Support of the Employees, *Bostock v. Clayton County*, 4, https://www.supremecourt. gov/DocketPDF/17/17-1618/107102/20190703151152563_Amicus_Eskridge%20and%20 Koppelman.pdf.

15. Brief of Statutory Interpretation and Equality Law Scholars as Amici Curiae, *Bostock v. Clayton County*, 2, 7, https://www.supremecourt.gov/DocketPDF /17/17-1618/105882/20190703091947764_Title%20VII%20Amicus%20Brief%20FINAL.pdf; Brief of Lambda Legal Defense and Education Fund, Inc. as Amicus Curiae in Support

of the Employees, *Bostock v. Clayton County*, 30, https://www.supremecourt.gov/Dock etPDF/17/17-1618/107176/20190703170952032_190704%20for%20E-Filing.pdf; Brief of GLBTQ Advocates & Defenders, National Center for Lesbian Rights, et al. as Amici Curiae in Support of the Employees, *Bostock v. Clayton County*, 8, https://www.su premecourt.gov/DocketPDF/17/17-1618/107669/20190710124523611_REPRINTED%20 -%2017-1618%20-1623%20and%2018-107%20tsacGLBTQLegalAdvocatesAndDefend ersEtAl.pdf.

16. Brief of Eskridge and Koppelman, 15–16, 33.

17. The full list of briefs can be found at SCOTUSblog's archives: https://www .scotusblog.com/case-files/cases/bostock-v-clayton-county-georgia/; https://www.sco tusblog.com/case-files/cases/r-g-g-r-harris-funeral-homes-inc-v-equal-opportunity -employment-commission/.

18. "LGBT," PollingReport.com, http://pollingreport.com/lgbt.htm.

19. Jami K. Taylor, Daniel C. Lewis, Donald P. Haider-Markel, Andrew Flores, Patrick Miller, and Barry Tadlock, "Public Opinion about Transgender People and Policies," in *The Remarkable Rise of Transgender Rights*, ed. Jami K. Taylor, Daniel C. Lewis, and Donald P. Haider-Markel (Ann Arbor: University of Michigan Press, 2018), 81, 85.

20. "Our Attorneys," Alliance Defending Freedom, https://www.adflegal.org /about-us/attorneys; "John K. Bursch," Federalist Society, https://fedsoc.org/contribu tors/john-bursch; "Jeffrey M. Harris," Federalist Society, https://fedsoc.org/contribu tors/jeffrey%20m-harris; Todd Spangler, "Here Are the Lawyers Facing off in Same-Sex Marriage Case," *Detroit Free Press*, April 24, 2015, https://www.freep.com/story/news /local/michigan/2015/04/25/sex-lawyers/26370899/; Marcia Coyle, "How Stanford's Pamela Karlan Got SCOTUS Argument Time in LGBT Cases," Law.com, August 7, 2019, https://www.law.com/nationallawjournal/2019/08/07/how-stanfords-pam-karlan -got-scotus-argument-time-in-lgbt-cases/; Valeria Gonzales, "'I Think It Will Be a Close Vote Either Way': Professor Pamela Karlan on LGBT Discrimination in the Supreme Court," Stanford Politics, November 18, 2019, https://stanfordpolitics.org/2019/11/18 /sexuality-and-the-supreme-court-an-interview-with-professor-pamela-karlan/.

21. Oral argument, *Bostock v. Clayton County*, October 8, 2019, 4–5, https://www .supremecourt.gov/oral_arguments/argument_transcripts/2019/17-1618_7k47.pdf.

22. *Bostock* oral argument, 22.

23. *Bostock* oral argument, 19, 20.

24. *Bostock* oral argument, 21, 23.

25. *Bostock* oral argument, 31.

26. Joan Biskupic, "Anger, Leaks and Tensions at the Supreme Court during the LGBTQ Rights Case," CNN, July 28, 2020, https://www.cnn.com/2020/07/28/politics /neil-gorsuch-supreme-court-lgbtq-civil-rights-act-alito/index.html.

27. *Bostock* oral argument, 45–47.

28. *Bostock* oral argument, 59–60; Biskupic, "Anger, Leaks and Tensions."

29. Oral argument, *R. G. & G. R. Harris Funeral Homes*, October 8, 2019, 11, https:// www.supremecourt.gov/oral_arguments/argument_transcripts/2019/18-107_c18e.pdf.

30. *Harris Funeral Homes* oral argument, 19.

31. *Harris Funeral Homes* oral argument, 25, 22–23.

32. *Harris Funeral Homes* oral argument, 25.

33. *Harris Funeral Homes* oral argument, 33.

34. Aimee Ortiz, "Aimee Stephens, Plaintiff in Transgender Case, Dies at 59," *New York Times*, May 12, 2020, https://www.nytimes.com/2020/05/12/us/aimee-stephens -supreme-court-dead.html.

35. For a summary of this literature, see Robert J. Hume, *Judicial Behavior and Policymaking: An Introduction* (Lanham, MD: Rowman & Littlefield, 2018), 175–180.

36. Biskupic, "Anger, Leaks and Tensions."

37. Biskupic.

38. Robert Barnes, "Neil Gorsuch? The Surprise behind the Supreme Court's Surprising LGBTQ Decision," *Washington Post*, June 16, 2020, https://www.washingtonpost.com/politics/courts_law/neil-gorsuch-gay-transgender-rights-supreme -court/2020/06/16/112f903c-afe3-11ea-8f56-63f38c990077_story.html.

39. *Bostock*, 1743, 1742.

40. *Bostock*, 1741.

41. *Bostock*, 1764.

42. *Bostock*, 1748.

43. *Bostock*, 1747, 1752.

44. *Bostock*, 1750–1752.

45. *Bostock*, 1754.

46. *Bostock*, 1738.

47. *Bostock*, 1739.

48. *Bostock*, 1743.

49. *Bostock*, 1752.

50. *Bostock*, 1747.

51. *Bostock*, 1750.

52. *Bostock*, 1822, 1834, 1824, 1828–1829.

53. *Bostock*, 1774, 1782; Kalvis Golde, "At Federalist Society Convention, Alito Says Religious Liberty, Gun Ownership Are under Attack," SCOTUSblog, November 13, 2020, https://www.scotusblog.com/2020/11/at-federalist-society-convention-alito-says -religious-liberty-gun-ownership-are-under-attack/.

54. *Bostock*, 1755–1756.

55. *Bostock*, 1828.

56. Paul Waldman, "Why the Religious Right Is so Freaked out by the Supreme Court's LGBTQ Ruling," *Washington Post*, June 16, 2020, https://www.washingtonpost.com/opinions/2020/06/16/why-religious-right-is-so-freaked-out-by-supreme -courts-lgbtq-ruling/; David G. Savage, "Gorsuch's Supreme Court Opinion for LGBTQ Rights Sends a Shudder through Conservative Ranks," *Los Angeles Times*, June 17, 2020, https://www.latimes.com/politics/story/2020-06-17/gorsuch-supreme-court -opinion-lgbtq-rights-shakes-conservatives; Robert George, "The Bostock Case and the Rule of Law," *Mirror of Justice* blog, June 15, 2020, https://mirrorofjustice.blogs .com/mirrorofjustice/2020/06/the-bostock-case-and-the-rule-of-law.html.

57. Julie Moreau, "Supreme Court's LGBTQ Ruling Could Have 'Broad Implications,' Legal Experts Say," NBC News, June 23, 2020, https://www.nbcnews.com/feature/nbc-out/supreme-court-s-lgbtq-ruling-could-have-broad-implications-legal-n1231779.

58. *Rouch World v. Michigan Department of Human Rights*, slip opinion, Michigan Court of Claims, Case No. 20-000145-MZ, December 11, 2020; "Christopher Murray," Ballotpedia, https://ballotpedia.org/Christopher_Murray; Gus Burns, "Michigan Court Says Companies Don't Have to Serve Customers Who Are Gay," mlive.com, December 10, 2020, https://www.mlive.com/public-interest/2020/12/michigan-court-says-companies-dont-have-to-serve-customers-who-are-gay.html.

59. Fulton v. City of Philadelphia, 593 U.S. __ (2021).

60. Aaron Belkin, "Supreme Court Poised to Roll Back LGBTQ Rights," Washington Blade, January 12, 2021, https://www.washingtonblade.com/2021/01/12/supreme-court-poised-to-roll-back-lgbtq-rights/.

61. *Gloucester County School Board v. Grimm, cert. denied,* June 26, 2021, https://www.supremecourt.gov/orders/courtorders/062821zor_6j37.pdf.

62. Sadie Burman and Jess Bravin, "Justice Department Seeks to Limit Scope of Landmark LGBT Rights Decision," *Wall Street Journal,* January 19, 2021, https://www.wsj.com/articles/justice-department-seeks-to-curtail-workplace-protections-for-gay-transgender-people-11611091426; Celine Castronuovo, "Biden Official Withdraws Last-Minute Trump LGBT Memo," Hill, January 23, 2021, https://thehill.com/homenews/administration/535536-biden-official-withdraws-last-minute-trump-lgbt-memo.

63. Executive Order on Preventing and Combating Discrimination on the Basis of Gender Identity or Sexual Orientation, January 20, 2021, https://www.whitehouse.gov/briefing-room/presidential-actions/2021/01/20/executive-order-preventing-and-combating-discrimination-on-basis-of-gender-identity-or-sexual-orientation/.

64. Kate Sosin, "A Wave of Anti-Trans Bills Are Hitting Statehouses," 19thnews, February 4, 2021, https://19thnews.org/2021/02/wave-of-anti-trans-bills-are-hitting-statehouses/; Lil Kalish, "Biden Reversed the Military Ban, but the Republican War on Trans Americans Is Just Getting Started," Mother Jones, January 29, 2021, https://www.motherjones.com/politics/2021/01/biden-reversed-the-military-ban-but-the-republican-war-on-trans-americans-is-just-getting-started/.

65. Courtenay W. Daum, *The Politics of Right Sex: Transgressive Bodies, Governmentality, and the Limits of Trans Rights* (Albany: State University of New York Press, 2020), viii.

66. See Dean Spade, *Normal Life: Administrative Violence, Critical Trans Politics, and the Limits of the Law,* rev. ed. (Durham, NC: Duke University Press, 2015).

Index